641.563 Earnest, Barbara.
EAR
        The low-
        chloresterol oat
        plan

        $18.45

DATE			

PLEASANTON

AUG _ 1988

The
Low-Cholesterol
Oat Plan

The Low-Cholesterol Oat Plan

Over 300 delicious and innovative recipes for the new miracle food

Barbara Earnest and
Sarah Schlesinger

Hearst Books
New York

To Sam, whose good heart was our inspiration.

To the many friends, associates, and health professionals whose willingness to share their time and knowledge made this book possible. Special thanks to Dr. James Anderson and Dr. Bruce Roseman, nutritionist Mary Beth Reardon, Grace Schlesinger, Lilyan Alberts, Ruth Reed, Dave Davisson, Blanka Nedela, June Wagerfield, June Harless, Kylie Winkworth, Tim Steinhoff, Joyce Tichenor, and Heather and Gillian Earnest.

Library of Congress Cataloging-in-Publication Data

Earnest, Barbara.
The low-cholesterol oat plan : a cookbook
/ by Barbara Earnest and Sarah Schlesinger.
p.   cm.
Bibliography: p.
Includes index.
ISBN 0-688-07945-8
1. High-fiber diet—Recipes.   2. Cookery (Oats)
3. Hypercholesteremia—Prevention.   4. Hyperglycemia—Prevention.
I. Schlesinger, Sarah.   II. Title.
RM237.6.E17   1988
641.5′63—dc19
88-5898
CIP

Printed in the United States of America

First Edition

1 2 3 4 5 6 7 8 9 10

BOOK DESIGN BY PANDORA SPELIOS

The Low-Cholesterol Oat Plan is a guidebook to the enjoyment of one of nature's most underestimated treasures, the marvelous oat. Now, in addition to its rich history, exceptional nutritional composition, adaptable nature, whole-grain fiber content and delicious flavor, it has become apparent that the oat is also good for your blood chemistry and your heart.

Long a dietary staple of the Scottish, British, Welsh, Scandinavians, and other northern and eastern Europeans, oats are being recognized in America as a miracle food of the eighties.

The Low-Cholesterol Oat Plan is a short course in everything you could ever hope to know about this fibrous wonder, including a simple plan for integrating oats into your daily diet, a glossary of terminology and some helpful cooking hints, and a collection of three hundred recipes, ranging from appetizers to desserts, featuring this amazingly versatile grain.

The Low-Cholesterol Oat Plan is packed full of delectable, nutritious ways to make this natural treasure part of your everyday life. Whether you're fighting a cholesterol or blood sugar problem, striving to control your weight and maintain overall fitness, or looking for new ways to use one of nature's most perfect foods, once you've become better acquainted with this amazing grain, you'll truly begin to "feel your oats."

FOREWORD
James W. Anderson, M.D.

When Barbara Earnest and Sarah Schlesinger invited me to write the foreword for *The Low-Cholesterol Oat Plan*, I greeted their concept of a complete guide to oat cookery with great enthusiasm. Oat bran has had a remarkable effect on my own blood cholesterol and has lowered that of many of my patients as well countless other people who have followed oat bran regimens.

In 1977 I contacted the Quaker Oats Company about obtaining oat bran for research purposes. Prior studies by our metabolic research team at the Lexington Veterans Administration Hospital involving diabetics indicated that high-fiber diets lowered blood cholesterol about 50 milligrams per 100 milliliters, or more than 20 percent. We wanted to test the effect of one potent high-fiber food on lowering blood cholesterol rather than using fifteen or twenty different fiber-rich foods. Earlier studies indicated that oatmeal lowered blood cholesterol, but the participants ate 140 grams, or *five bowls* per day. Our research group did not think that amount was practical, so we approached the Quaker Oats Company about the availability of oat bran.

In 1988 you can buy oat bran in almost any supermarket in America—*if* the grocer has not recently sold out. In 1977, however, the people at the Quaker Oats corporate offices in Chicago had not heard of oat bran and did not know where it could be obtained. When I insisted that surely they should know how to get it, they referred me to their Cedar Rapids oat-milling plant. The millers there informed me that oat bran was a by-product of milling oat flour and was not used in human foods; oat bran was then used in pet foods. They agreed to send me one hundred pounds for human use, and we began testing it. I became the first guinea pig in Lexington to use oat bran in my diet.

From my mother I inherited a high blood cholesterol and had documented my own cholesterol levels of 280 to 300 mg/100 ml over the previous ten years. Since I specialized in the study and treatment of diabetes I had not worried too much about my own cholesterol level up until that time. In the interest of science I began eating 100 grams (about 3 ounces) of oat bran daily—a large bowl for breakfast and three to four muffins later in the day. Over the five-week test period I also cut down on my fat and cholesterol intake and lost some weight. My blood cholesterol dropped from 280 to 175 mg/100 ml; most of the 105-point, or 38 percent, drop was attributable to oat bran intake.

Encouraged by my response, our team began testing oat bran in diabetics. We first incorporated it into the high-carbohydrate and -fiber (HCF) diet that patients on the metabolic research ward were already on (diets that had allowed us to take two thirds of the adults we were treating off insulin. For the first four men who included 100 grams of oat bran in their daily diet, the total blood cholesterol dropped 38 percent. Total cholesterol refers to the combined amount of naturally produced and dietary cholesterol present in the bloodstream. In addition to this remarkable drop, we saw important changes in the types of cholesterol in the blood.

In the bloodstream, cholesterol travels in the form of low-density lipoprotein (LDL) and high-density lipoprotein (HDL). The LDL cholesterols are the "bad guys," depositing cholesterol in the walls of blood vessels and contributing to atherosclerosis, or hardening of the arteries. The HDL cholesterols are the "good guys," which serve a scavenger function by removing cholesterol from blood vessel walls, thereby protecting against atherosclerosis.

In our first careful study of diabetic men, oat bran use decreased the LDL cholesterol by 58 percent, while increasing the HDL cholesterol by 82 percent. As far as we knew, this was the first dietary intervention that selectively lowered the harmful LDL cholesterol while raising the protective HDL cholesterol in this remarkable manner.

Excited about these results, I told other professors at the university about them. Their response was: "These are interesting results in humans, but you need to try oat bran in rats." To maintain my academic credibility, our group did just that. When rats ate oat bran as part of their chow for three weeks, their total cholesterol and LDL cholesterol dropped and their HDL cholesterol increased. When I showed these results to my professional colleagues, they suggested we do carefully controlled tests in humans with high blood cholesterols. Following their advice, our group has conducted extensive studies over the past ten years on what oat bran does and how it works.

Dr. Bob Kirby first recruited eight men with high blood cholesterol whom we studied on our metabolic research ward at the Lexington Veterans Administration Hospital. When these men consumed a typical American diet, plus 100 grams of oat bran daily, their blood cholesterol dropped 13 percent in two weeks. More importantly, the LDL cholesterol fell and the HDL cholesterol did not change significantly. The result was our first scientific report in 1981, entitled "Oat bran intake selectively lowers serum low-density lipoprotein cholesterol concentrations of hypercholesterolemic men." Subsequently, the Quaker Oats Company made oat bran available to the general public through supermarkets.

In further studies, our group documented that the use of 50 to 100 grams of oat bran daily as part of a typical American diet lowered blood cholesterol an average of 19 percent. Since every 1 percent reduction in blood cholesterol reduces the estimated risk for developing a heart attack by 2 percent, the 19 percent reduction in blood cholesterol by oat bran translates into an estimated reduction in the heart attack risk by 38 percent.

Long-Term Effects

If you eat oat bran faithfully and use a prudent diet restricted in fat and cholesterol, what will happen to your blood cholesterol? These are the important questions we next addressed. Most folks can't live their lives on a metabolic research ward. We taught men with high blood cholesterol how to use a low-fat and low-cholesterol diet and asked them to eat about 50 grams of oat bran daily. They could get this amount of oat bran in one bowl of oatmeal and two oat bran muffins daily. Over a two-year period their blood cholesterol dropped 25 percent with this program. Furthermore, the LDL-cholesterol "bad guys" dropped 30 percent while the HDL-cholesterol "good guys" increased 10 percent. Maintaining these important changes in blood cholesterol and its subfractions could reduce their risk for developing a heart attack by more than 50 percent.

How Oat Bran Works

Oat bran works in at least three ways to lower blood cholesterol. First, it increases the loss of bile acids, or cholesterol-containing fat emulsifiers, in the feces. Ordinarily most of the bile acids produced in the liver and released into the intestines to aid in fat digestion are reabsorbed and travel back to the liver. Oat bran, however, causes a twofold increase in the loss of bile acids in the feces. Second, oat bran is fermented by bacteria in the large intestine, becoming small organic acids, like acetic acid present in vinegar. These small acids (technically called short-chain fatty acids) are absorbed from the large intestine, or colon, and travel to the liver, where they slow down the manufacture of cholesterol. Thus, oat bran causes increased loss of cholesterol products and also decreases cholesterol production, giving the liver less cholesterol to release into the bloodstream as blood cholesterol. Third, by mechanisms we do not yet understand, oat bran produces a selective reduction in the LDL cholesterol while raising or not affecting the protective HDL cholesterol.

Fiber Fights the Big Five

Several years ago our group developed the slogan "Fiber fights the big five" to remind us of the broad range of health benefits associated with fiber intake. The big five representing major causes of death in the United States are heart disease, cancer, high blood pressure, diabetes, and obesity. There is persuasive evidence now that oat products and other sources of dietary fiber protect from or delay the onset of these major health hazards and, in addition, offer treatment benefits to individuals with some of these disorders.

Coronary heart disease remains the leading cause of death in Western countries and is closely linked to excessive intake of fat, cholesterol, and calories and to inadequate intake of dietary fiber. Several studies indicate that the use of large amounts of fiber is associated with only one quarter to one third as many heart attacks as is the use of small amounts of fiber. Because of their specific effects in lowering atherogenic LDL cholesterol and raising protective HDL cholesterol, oat products may be especially protective against coronary heart disease.

Certain types of cancer may be linked to a lack of fiber in the diet, although much more research is required to clearly establish these relationships. Available evidence suggests that a generous fiber intake may reduce the risk for developing cancer of the colon.

High blood pressure affects an estimated 40 to 60 million Americans and contributes in a major way to the 1 million deaths annually from cardiovascular disease. High blood pressure, or hypertension, is much less common in countries having high fiber intakes than in typical Western countries having low levels of fiber intake. Furthermore, American vegetarians have lower average blood pressure than nonvegetarians. Preliminary studies suggest that increasing fiber intake lowers blood pressure of mildly hypertensive individuals. Our own studies suggest that incorporating 50 grams of oat bran daily (half the suggested amount for lowering cholesterol) into a prudent diet low in fat and cholesterol will result in a small reduction in blood pressure.

Many individuals with mild hypertension would rather manage the condition with diet, exercise, and relaxation rather than using drugs because of the side effects frequently related to these agents. The dietary approach includes reduced fat, alcohol, and salt intake and increased intake of high-fiber foods such as oat products and other whole grains, vegetables, and fruits. Regular exercise such as walking 12 to 20 miles per week and the use of appropriate stress management techniques round out the nonpharmacologic approach.

Most diabetics are remarkably responsive to diet. Since about 90 percent of them have the adult-onset, or Type II, form of diabetes and since most of them are obese, our studies indicate that three quarters of adult diabetics would benefit substantially by increasing their intake of complex carbohydrate (starchy foods such as potatoes, bread, rice, and beans) and dietary fiber while reducing their fat intake. When we change adult diabetics from traditional high-fat diabetes diets to high-carbohydrate, high-fiber (HCF) diets, we can discontinue insulin therapy in most of these individuals. Increased fiber intake lowers insulin requirements, improves blood glucose control, lowers blood cholesterol and triglycerides, lowers blood pressure, and assists in weight management. I outline this plan for diabetes management in *Diabetes: A Practical New Guide to Healthy Living* published by Warner Books.

Approximately one quarter of American adults are obese, and the percentage is increasing annually. Less physical activity and more fat intake are the primary contributors according to many experts. Increased dietary fiber intake is emerging as one important part of the diet prescription for weight maintenance. High-fiber foods are bulkier and take longer to eat than high-fat foods; they increase the feeling of fullness and decrease hunger between meals. Their fibrous coating decreases the digestion and absorption of starch and thereby results in fewer calories being absorbed than from comparable low-fiber foods. Finally, with high-fiber intake, more calories are lost in elimination.

To Really Feel Your Oats . . .

Like many people, you may have missed some of the fun and health advantages available from the regular use of oatmeal and other oat products because you lacked information about oat cookery and did not have access to a complete collection of oat recipes.

The Low-Cholesterol Oat Plan, which is the first comprehensive low-fat, low-salt, and low-sugar guide to cooking with oats, provides you with more than 300 delicious and practical ways to get your oats in our fast-paced society. I hope that by using the information and recipes provided here, you will experience the full health benefits that oat bran has to offer.

CONTENTS

THE HEALTH STORY

The Fiber Connection

The suggestion that the consumption of soluble fiber in the form of oats can reduce the risk of a heart attack is another dimension of one of the most significant health and nutrition issues of our decade, the link between dietary fiber and disease.

Dietary fiber, which is found in plants such as fruits, vegetables, legumes, cereals, and grains, is composed of husks, stems, seeds, skin, and cell walls that hold the other portions together. Since our digestive enzymes are not capable of breaking down these parts of the plant, most of the components of crude fiber pass straight through our systems.

Dietary fiber can be grouped into two categories, water-soluble and water-insoluble. All plants contain both types of fiber in varying proportions. While the two types of fiber produce different physiological effects, they play equally important roles in maintaining health.

Insoluble fibers, which are derived from plant cell walls, trigger muscular action to increase intestinal regularity. They pass through the gastrointestinal system intact, adding bulk, absorbing water, and decreasing the time it takes foods to move through the digestive process. Insoluble fiber acts as a natural laxative and is useful in preventing constipation. It can be used in treating various forms of diverticulitis such as irritable bowel syndrome. Since the inclusion of insoluble fiber in the diet decreases the amount of time required for food to travel through the body, there is less opportunity for carcinogens and parasitic diseases to come into contact with the gastrointestinal system. Recent research also suggests that through its ability to speed elimination and dilute carcinogens, it may be a possible link to preventing cancer. Good sources of insoluble fiber include unprocessed wheat bran, corn bran, and wheat bran cereals, whole wheat breads, dried peas and beans, nuts, seeds, popcorn, and most fruit and vegetables (best eaten with their skins).

Soluble fibers, in the form of gluey gums and jelly-like pectins, disperse easily in water and form a bulky gel in the intestines during digestion; this slows the rate at which food empties from the stomach. Since soluble fibers lower blood-cholesterol levels and may help control blood pressure, they are useful in treating and preventing diseases of the heart and circulatory system. In addition, they enhance the absorption of sugar and assist in controlling diabetes and hypoglycemia, and they are more palatable than insoluble fibers such as wheat bran.

A significant amount of soluble fiber is found in oat products, barley, chick-peas, black-eyed peas, kidney beans, pinto beans, navy beans, lentils, split peas, sesame seeds, green peas, corn, sweet potatoes, carrots, okra, zucchini, cauliflower, prunes, pears, apples, Concord grapes, and citrus fruits like oranges and grapefruit.

Studies such as those conducted by Dr. James Anderson, as discussed in the Foreword, and others on animals and humans have broadened our understanding of the connection between fiber and disease. One of the earliest studies was conducted by Dr. Dennis Burkitt, a world-renowned cancer specialist, who undertook a comprehensive study of nine African nations in 1970. In the areas he visited, there were no recorded cases of coronary disease, cancer of the colon, diverticulosis, gallstones, hemmorhoids, or appendicitis. Obesity was nonexistent, although the diets of those Africans he studied were heavy in starches and averaged as much as 3,500 calories a day. His subjects ate almost no meat and very little fat; their protein was derived from vegetables, whole grains, nuts, and legumes. The carbohydrates they ate were packed with fiber and never processed or refined.

After comparing their food consumption habits with ours, Dr. Burkitt observed that greater changes had been made in the basic diet eaten in Western countries during the last two hundred years than had taken place over the whole of man's previous existence on earth. As he examined these changes, he concluded that fiber might be the missing element in our diet. We have stopped eating many of the foods our digestive systems are designed to process and replaced them with foods to which our constitutions are not adapted.

Although high fiber consumption used to be a common characteristic of American diets, it has decreased dramatically in our convenience-oriented culture. Our current diet contains only one third to one half as much as that consumed in less industrialized countries. We have tended to overlook the whole-grain breads and cereals, fresh fruits and vegetables that dominated our grandparents' diets in favor of refined foods, fats, and sugars. Since the turn of the century, fiber intake from grains and cereals has dropped 50 percent and 20 percent from fruits and vegatables. And most of the beneficial fiber that occurs naturally has been stripped from our food before it reaches our tables.

Dr. Burkitt theorized that these dietary changes have contributed to the evolution of modern diseases of the digestive and circulatory systems. By removing the fiber and making the carbohydrate portion of our diets too soft and refined, we have severely reduced the efficiency of our gastrointestinal systems. When we don't eat enough fiber, food moves more slowly through the intestines and harmful bacteria flourish. This backup often results in disorders of the circulatory system, small and large intestines, and rectum. Gastrointestinal congestion is believed to contribute to hardening of the arteries, phlebitis, varicose veins, hernias, hemorrhoids, gallstones, and obesity.

During the past eighteen years, evidence has continued to accumulate supporting Dr. Burkitt's theory and clarifying the importance of both types of dietary fiber. And recent studies related to cholesterol reduction have identified oats as the one of the brightest stars in the fiber galaxy.

The Cholesterol Connection

Each year deaths from cardiovascular disease claim over half a million lives in the United States and cost our country over $78 billion. It is the cause of one out of every three deaths and kills one American every minute. Each year a million and a half people suffer heart attacks. Six million Americans are estimated to have coronary artery disease and 40 million more are estimated to have dangerously high cholesterol levels.

Although increasingly sophisticated medical treatment offers more hope to heart attack victims than ever before, our best strategy for fighting this disease is to prevent it from beginning in the first place. Some risk factors such as sex, age and family history are beyond our control, but others, including diet, smoking, blood pressure, weight, physical activity, and blood cholesterol levels are not.

Cholesterol, one of a number of fats, or lipids, found in our bloodstream, is a waxy, tasteless, and odorless substance. Needed by all of our cells for regeneration and rebuilding, cholesterol comes from the foods we eat (one fifth to two fifths) and from our body, which produces it in our liver and intestinal tract. When we use the term cholesterol, we are referring to the total amount of naturally produced and dietary cholesterol present in our bloodstream. These amounts are measured in milligrams per deciliter (mg/dl). The body's only mechanism for disposing of cholesterol is through excretion into the intestine and elimination through the stool.

Cholesterol acts as basic structural material for cell membranes, bile acids, and sex hormones. If we eat too much cholesterol, the body manufactures less; if we eat too little, the body manufactures more. Due to this mechanism of internal balances, it is possible for us to lower the amount of cholesterol in our body through diet modification.

Medical experts estimate that more than 25 percent of adult American men and women exceed currently recommended cholesterol levels and need to initiate immediate cholesterol-lowering diet strategies. Coronary specialists have predicted that 30 to 50 percent of the potential victims of coronary heart disease could be helped by following such a program.

In June 1987, a team of scientists from the University of Southern California School of Medicine reported the first "clear evidence" that a significant reduction in blood cholesterol will slow, and in some cases even reverse, the formation of fatty deposits that clog the arteries and cause heart attacks. Their studies revealed that aggressive cholesterol-lowering treatments had succeeded in shrinking the fatty deposits in 16.2 percent of a small group of patients—the first time such reversal in artery-clogging deposits had ever been demonstrated in humans. While previous studies had shown that lowering cholesterol could reduce the rate of death and sickness from heart disease by preventing the formation of fatty deposits on artery walls, they had been inconclusive as to whether it could slow or reduce preexisting deposits.

At its 1985 meeting, the American Heart Association released a report that indicated we may be at serious risk even if our cholesterol is at a level that might have been called moderate a few years ago. A study of men between the ages of thirty-five and fifty-seven showed that the risk of coronary heart disease increased dramatically as cholesterol levels rose. For example, those with cholesterol levels between 203 and 220 had coronary death rates 73 percent higher than those with levels below 180. The higher the cholesterol level, the greater the risk.

Cholesterol-Lowering Guidelines

In October 1987 a panel of specialists at the National Heart, Lung and Blood Institute (NHLBI), one of the National Institutes of Health, issued a historic report that called on doctors to prescribe strict diets and, in some cases, drug treatment for adult Americans at high risk of heart disease. The panel had been convened by the National Cholesterol Education Program, a cooperative effort that is sponsored by the Institute and twenty-three major medical associations and health organizations, including the American Medical Association, the American Heart Association, and the American College of Cardiology. Their participation in formulating the NHLBI report marked the first time that all of these organizations had joined forces to attack the cholesterol issue.

The panel's guidelines, which seek to identify those adults who need treatment to decrease their cholesterol, created a single set of blood cholesterol goals for all adults, regardless of age or sex. Hopefully, by 1990 cholesterol will be as frequently measured and widely controlled as high blood pressure.

The panel urges all Americans, starting at age twenty, to have their cholesterol levels tested as part of routine medical examinations. According to officials at the National Institutes of Health, increased awareness of the dangers of high cholesterol could save 300,000 lives annually. A recent Institute study revealed that only 46 percent of adults had ever had their cholesterol measured and only 8 percent had been told it was too high. However, according to Federal statistics, one quarter of the American population should be lowering their cholesterol by changing their eating habits and, in extreme cases, by taking drugs.

While establishing new standards and practices related to individual cholesterol testing and treatment plans, the doctors on the NHLBI panel emphasized that dietary treatment should be the foundation of all therapy to reduce blood cholesterol levels. They advised physicians to prescribe drugs only for individuals with genetic forms of high cholesterol who cannot be helped by dietary therapy or for those with severely elevated cholesterol levels.

The panel's treatment regimen begins with a three-month cholesterol-lowering diet that limits saturated fat to 10 percent of total calories and cholesterol to less than 300 milligrams a day. If after that time, cholesterol levels have been sufficiently reduced, long-term monitoring is called for. Blood cholesterol would be tested four times during the first year and twice each year thereafter.

If the first diet is not a success, the patient would be referred to a nutritionist, and a more stringent diet might be prescribed for three additional months. This eating plan, which is more radical, limits saturated fat to 7 percent of total calories and cholesterol to less than 200 milligrams a day.

Only if this intensive diet therapy fails to reduce the cholesterol level are drugs recommended *along with* a cholesterol-lowering diet. Dr. DeWitt Goodman, professor of medicine at Columbia University and chairman of the NHLBI panel, has stated that only 5 to 6 percent of Americans with high blood cholesterol will require drug therapy. In issuing the NIH report, Dr. Goodman stated that "there is little instruction about diet therapy in our medical schools. Busy doctors prefer using drugs, but nutritional treatment should be used for the vast majority of patients, and drug treatment should be used only when all else fails."

What Your Cholesterol Level Means

The NIH panel has established three cholesterol risk categories.

CATEGORY 1   Adults over age twenty with total blood cholesterol of 240 milligrams or more per deciliter of blood have "high blood cholesterol."

CATEGORY 2   Adults over twenty years of age with total cholesterol between 200 and 239 have "borderline high blood cholesterol."

CATEGORY 3   Adults over twenty with total blood cholesterol registering below 200 have "desirable blood cholesterol."

It is important to note that while the 1987 NIH study selected 200 as the cutoff point for safe cholesterol levels, other researchers have suggested a lower "safe" point, and many doctors continue to recommend cholesterol levels between 175 and 200 mg/dl. For example, the Council of Scientific Affairs of the American Medical Association stated in the *AMA Journal* in 1983 that "average plasma cholesterol levels of 180 to 200 mg/dl in adult populations seem to be associated with a low incidence of both cardiovascular and other diseases and probably should be considered optimal."

If you have two risk factors (being male, obesity, cigarette smoking, high blood pressure, or a family history of premature heart disease), you should be sure that your test results determine your "bad" LDL (low-density lipoprotein) and VLDL (very low-density lipoprotein) cholesterol and "good" HDL (high-density lipoprotein) cholesterol counts as well. Since LDL cholesterol appears to be responsible for leaving fat deposits on artery walls and HDL cholesterol is credited with preventing these deposits from adhering to artery walls, ideal test results will indicate low LDLs, high HDLs, and a low ratio between them.

New "desktop" testing methods that are coming on the market will give you an instant total cholesterol report and require only a finger stick. These tests are easy to perform and inexpensive. They do not require fasting and there is no lengthy wait for a laboratory analysis. The simplified tests are administered in doctors' offices and at health fairs in schools, community centers, and shopping malls. If you choose this approach, remember that some of these tests are a preliminary screening device and will not provide information about LDL-HDL levels.

Confronting Your Own Cholesterol Level

We all need to be concerned about maintaining a safe cholesterol level at all stages of our lives. Elevated cholesterol is not a natural part of the aging process. It is never too early to begin taking steps to monitor and control the levels of every member of your family.

If you haven't had a recent cholesterol check, you should arrange to have a standard blood test (following a twelve-hour fast) at a clinic, hospital, or your doctor's office. The NHLBI panel report of October 1987 advises having two tests about a month apart for increased accuracy. The test results will reveal whether your blood cholesterol level is normal, moderate, or high, reported in terms of how many milligrams of cholesterol each deciliter of your blood contains. For example, if your reading is 190, your blood sample contained 190 milligrams of cholesterol per deciliter, or 190 mg/dl.

The Oat Connection

If you need to lower your cholesterol or want to be sure to maintain it at your current level, adding oats to your diet is a simple, safe, and natural way to move toward this goal. As Dr. Anderson points out, the soluble fibers in oat bran can reduce the amount of artery-damaging cholesterol in the blood by increasing the loss of cholesterol products from the body and decreasing cholesterol production in the liver. Oat bran doubles the quantity of cholesterol-containing fat emulsifiers, or bile acids, we eliminate through the feces. The bran is also converted to fatty acids in the large intestine that are sent to the liver to retard the production of cholesterol. During this process, artery-clogging LDL cholesterol is selectively reduced, while helpful HDL cholesterol levels are preserved.

While conducting his studies at the Veterans Administration Hospital in Lexington, Kentucky, Dr. Anderson found that when participants with high blood cholesterol added 50 grams of oat bran a day to a low-fat, low-cholesterol diet, they were able to reduce cholesterol by 25 percent over a two-year period. In addition, his subjects' "bad" LDL cholesterol dropped 30 percent, while the "good" HDL cholesterol increased 10 percent. Dr. Anderson projects that maintaining these new levels of blood cholesterol could reduce the participants' risk of developing a heart attack by more than 50 percent.

A recent study directed by Dr. Linda Van Horn of the Department of Community Health at Northwestern Medical School in Chicago, as reported in the *Journal of the American Dietetic Medical Association* in June 1986, further validates Dr. Anderson's findings.

Implications for Diabetics

Dr. Anderson has also demonstrated that increasing the amount of soluble fiber from sources such as oat bran can prove useful in helping the 5.8 million diabetics in the United States and those suffering from hypoglycemia to prevent wide swings in blood sugar. Diets containing large amounts of soluble fiber assist in controlling the rise in blood sugar after a meal; the fiber appears to slow the absorption of carbohydrates, allowing some of them to pass through the digestive tract unabsorbed.

While diabetics have traditionally been given diets high in protein and fat and low in fiber-rich foods, Dr. Anderson has found that a high-carbohydrate diet that includes large quantities of oat bran can lead to reduced dependence on insulin and other drugs to control blood sugar.

His research has documented a significant drop in insulin requirements by diabetic patients following a high-fiber, high-carbohydrate diet. Patients who require drugs other than insulin have also found such diets helpful; 90 percent of the non–insulin-dependent diabetic patients in Dr. Anderson's studies were able to discontinue drug therapy. Insulin-dependent diabetic individuals experienced fewer insulin reactions on high-fiber, high-carbohydrate diets.

In addition, such a diet lowers cholesterol, thereby reducing a diabetic's risk of heart attack. This is of particular importance, since diabetes accelerates atherosclerosis, and more than half of diabetes-related deaths are caused by heart disease.

More information on Dr. Anderson's diet, used in the successful treatment of more than one thousand patients with adult-onset diabetes, can be obtained from the HCF Diabetes Foundation, P.O. Box 22124, Lexington, Kentucky 40522. Before undertaking any dietary fiber program, diabetics MUST consult with their own physicians because of the changes that will result from the diet.

Weight Control

Weight control is an important factor in lowering your risk of coronary heart disease, high blood pressure, and diabetes, and it plays a significant role in any cholesterol-reducing plan. Obese individuals tend to have low HDL levels, and weight reduction has been reported to assist in decreasing LDL, raising HDL, and improving the LDL-to-HDL ratio.

According to Dr. Anderson (in "Medical Benefits of High Fiber Intakes": *The Fiber Factor*, Quaker Oats Company, Chicago, 1983), adding high-fiber foods to your diet can help with long-term weight control through appetite reduction, calorie control, delayed gastric emptying, and improved regularity.

High-fiber intake depresses your appetite since it lowers the level of blood insulin that stimulates your desire for food. By replacing other higher-calorie and high-fat foods with oats, you can reduce your overall caloric intake. Starch is less easily absorbed from high-fiber foods, resulting in fewer calories being absorbed than from lower-fiber foods of the same caloric value. In addition, fiber in the diet makes our digestive systems work harder and calories are actually used up more quickly.

Since high-fiber foods take longer to eat and make you feel fuller for a longer period of time, they make it easier to stick to reduced-calorie diets. The resulting increased intestinal food mass changes your pattern of intestinal hormonal secretions, leading to slower carbohydrate absorption, which contributes to a feeling of satisfaction. Oat bran actually slows down the rate of "gastric emptying," which controls how fast food travels through your stomach. It also improves regularity, so there is additional calorie loss through faster intestinal elimination.

Beginning Your Own Program of Cholesterol Reduction

Once you have determined your cholesterol level you will be ready to follow a low-fat, high-carbohydrate eating plan and to add oats to your diet. As Bonnie

Liebman, nutritionist for the Center for Science in the Public Interest states, "You can't have your steak and eat it, too. You wouldn't want to eat a lot of fat and hope the oat bran neutralizes it. Eating a lot of fat may increase your risk of other health problems such as cancer and obesity. Oat bran is one more step to protect your heart, not a magic bullet."

Any serious program to reduce your risk of cardiovascular disease should also include a carefully planned program of physical activity. Research indicates that regular physical activity both benefits the heart and helps improve the ratio of LDL-to-HDL cholesterol. While the benefits of heavier aerobic exercises such as jogging and cycling have long been recognized, new attention is being paid to the benefits of more moderate exercise. In the November 1987 issue of the *Journal of the American Medical Association*, Dr. Arthur S. Leon reported that a study recently completed in Minnesota revealed that middle-age men at high risk of heart disease who engage in moderate physical activities can reduce their chances of dying from a heart attack by one third. Dr. Leon's study suggested that 15 to 45 minutes every day of moderate activity such as dancing, gardening, home repairs, swimming, and home exercise were beneficial. Light-duty activities such as walking, bicycling, and bowling also appeared helpful if done for a longer time. In the study, the benefits of exercise seemed to peak at the moderate level, with smaller returns for increased activity after a point. A continuing study of 17,000 Harvard College alumni published last year also indicated that moderate physical exercise in adult life can increase life expectancy. With the assistance of your doctors, you should work out a program of physical activity suited to your own physical condition and goals.

If you are currently smoking, you must also take into consideration the fact that smoking is a major risk factor for coronary disease as well as cancer and emphysema.

Integrating Oats into Your Diet

As you will learn in the next chapter, oats are available in the form of oat bran, oat flour, quick rolled oats, regular rolled oats, steel-cut oats, and oat grains. Each of these varieties has its own special characteristics and ideal uses. Our recipe collection offers you the opportunity to become well acquainted with the whole oat family. We do not include instant oats (the kind that are mixed right in the bowl with boiling water) because they often lose much of their nutritional value from overprocessing and usually contain too much sugar, salt, or artificial flavoring.

Cholesterol-lowering benefits can be gained from eating any of the oat products listed above in either a raw or cooked form. However, pure oat bran seems best for lowering blood sugar.

In general, you will have to eat less oat bran than other oat products to achieve the same results because the bran, which is a fraction of the oat flake, is more concentrated. For example, the benefit gained from consuming 1 ounce of oat bran would be equal to consuming 2 ounces of whole oats. To effectively utilize oats in a cholesterol-lowering program, you should eat the equivalent of 2 to 3 ounces of oat bran a day. One ounce of oat bran is equivalent to ⅓ cup, or 28 grams. Consequently, your daily oat bran intake would be ⅔ to 1 cup, or 56 to 84 grams.

Since it is difficult to consume that quantity of oats at one time, you should plan on having your daily portion of oats spread over two or three meals and snacks. In fact, studies have shown that your oat consumption will be more effective if you distribute it throughout the day. For instance, you might have a bowl of oat bran for breakfast, oat bran muffins as a part of your lunch menu, oat crust pizza for dinner, and a bowl of granola for a midnight snack. In this book, the oat bran content of each serving is indicated in the recipes, so keeping count of your total oat intake will be easy.

On the basis of research results, adding the equivalent of 2 to 3 ounces of oat bran a day to a low-fat diet can result in an initial cholesterol reduction of 6 to 10 mg within thirty days. Maintaining this regimen over a period of twenty-four months should produce a 25 percent reduction. As medical reporter Robert E. Kowalski has stated in his recent best-selling book, *The 8-Week Cholesterol Cure*, "Assuming the same results Dr. Anderson found, some simple arithmetic shows that a person with a 265 mg/dl cholesterol level can anticipate dropping that number down under the 200 mg level."

In addition to the impressive array of potential health benefits outlined above, oats provide a better balance of nutrients and more high-quality protein than any other natural grain. While you are protecting yourself and your family from high cholesterol levels, you will also be getting an excellent high-energy food. One hundred ten calories worth of oat flakes provide twice as much protein as the same quantity of wheat flakes. Whole oats contain 12.4 percent protein, 72.8 percent carbohydrate, and 8.7 percent fat (balanced between saturated and polyunsaturated fatty acids).

Oats are also a source of seven B vitamins, including thiamine (B_1), riboflavin (B_2), niacin, and pyridoxine. They contain vitamin E and nine minerals, including potassium, magnesium, phosphorus, iron, and calcium, and are extremely low in natural sugar and sodium. A 1-ounce serving of oat bran, quick or regular rolled oats has a calorie count of 110.

So whether you choose to make oats part of a carefully planned program of cholesterol reduction or simply introduce them into your diet in a more limited way because of their nutritional benefits, you are about to discover the rewards of striking up an acquaintance with one of nature's most perfect foods.

Oats as Part of
Total Fiber Intake

According to the National Cancer Institute, a sound high-fiber diet should include 25 to 35 grams of total fiber a day. Each of your ⅓ cup servings of oat bran offers 4.2 grams of total fiber, and your recommended daily consumption will supply 8.4 to 12.6 grams of total fiber. Since approximately half of the fiber in the oat groat is soluble, your oat bran serving will be providing approximately 4 to 6 grams of soluble fiber and a bonus 4 to 6 grams of insoluble fiber, which will contribute to digestive efficiency.

To reach your overall fiber goal of 25 to 35 grams, you will want to add a variety of breads, cereals, vegetables, and fruits that are good sources of both soluble and insoluble fiber. To date, there is no scientific evidence that fiber diet aids like pills or wafers offer benefits equivalent to natural high-fiber foods.

By providing your body with ample quantities of each type of fiber from the recommended food sources, you will be stimulating the smooth movement of food through your digestive system, lowering cholesterol levels, and helping to stabilize blood sugar at the same time.

Take a moderate approach to increasing your fiber intake and limit yourself to the suggested 25 to 35 grams of dietary fiber each day. Be sure to eat a well-balanced diet to ensure the proper absorption of minerals such as calcium, iron, magnesium, and zinc into the bloodstream. Introduce fiber into your daily eating plan on a slow, steady basis to avoid the possibility of increased intestinal gas and bloating that can be a temporary by-product of this type of dietary change. Be sure to drink plenty of liquids each day to avoid the possibility of constipation.

How Cholesterol Contributes to Coronary Disease

HOW CHOLESTEROL IS PROCESSED

1. You eat a meal that includes 15 grams of saturated fat and 92 milligrams of cholesterol.
2. The cholesterol and fats are converted to lipoproteins in your intestines and transported through your body by your blood system.
3. Your muscle and fat cells remove the amount of cholesterol and fat required for energy. The remaining cholesterol and fat travel on to your liver.

4. In your liver, the fat and cholesterol are absorbed from your blood. Then your liver sends out body-manufactured fat-cholesterol called VLDL (very low-density lipoproteins). The excess is absorbed again. In the course of this reprocessing, your blood cholesterol levels are stabilized.

HOW THE SYSTEM BREAKS DOWN

1. When you eat too much fat and cholesterol and overtax your liver's processing ability, there is a buildup of a harmful form of lipoprotein in your blood called LDL, or low-density lipoprotein. LDL is responsible for delivering the cholesterol to your cells and appears to be a major contributor to the cholesterol deposited in coronary arteries. When additional LDLs are produced to transport the cholesterol to cells, many of them are attracted to your arteries.
2. HDL, high-density lipoprotein, which is considered protective to the heart, is produced in various parts of your body. This fat-cholesterol packet acts as a cleansing agent, for returning excess cholesterol to the liver for disposal when the cells are through with it. The more "good" HDL you have in your body, the lower your risk of developing coronary heart disease. When the amount of LDL and HDL are in proper balance, cholesterol travels through your arteries with little impact. However, when an improper ratio of LDLs and HDLs occurs, the interior lining of your vessels can become damaged, and the resulting rough spots trap LDLs.
3. Since the LDLs are sticky, they attach to any imperfection or nick in your blood vessel walls. These captive LDLs are joined by other body cells to create blockage points in your circulatory system, which are called plaques.
4. Since your arteries are only one twelfth of an inch in diameter at some points, a very small amount of plaque can narrow and contract arteries. This process of plaque formation is called atherosclerosis.

HOW ATHEROSCLEROSIS PROGRESSES

1. Atherosclerosis is a degenerative disease that restricts arteries throughout your body. Those leading to the heart and brain, called coronary arteries, are arranged in a ring around your heart; as the result of atherosclerosis, your coronary arteries lose their ability to expand and contract and become increasingly narrow.
2. When a coronary artery becomes completely clogged, blood flow decreases and the heart muscle begins to suffocate and angina or a heart

attack often results. While chest pains sometimes signal these blockages, an estimated 40 percent of people with heart disease experience no warnings but suffer instant death from heart attack. Two thirds of the deaths from cardiovascular disease in the United States are due to disorders of these blood vessels that supply blood to the heart.

3. Advancing atherosclerosis can also cause blood pressure to rise when the heart is forced to work harder and harder to send blood through narrow arterial openings. High blood pressure can be a cause and a warning of a possible stroke, heart attack, or other organ disorders that occur when there is a loss of blood supply to the brain.

Oats, Cholesterol, and Triglycerides: The Anderson Studies in Brief

1. In a study reported in 1984, Dr. James Anderson found that when he gave three and a half ounces of oat bran a day to subjects with high blood cholesterol levels (260 mg average) for twenty-one days, serum cholesterol levels fell 21 percent.

2. Dr. Anderson's research also suggests that soluble fiber can reduce the blood levels of triglycerides. Like cholesterol, triglycerides are fatty substances that are related to heart disease when present in the blood at high levels. Although carbohydrate intake has traditionally been associated with increased trigylceride levels, these levels do not appear to rise when carbohydrates are consumed with plant fiber. Dr. Anderson found that serum triglyceride concentrations in nine out of ten of the subjects who entered his study with elevated triglyceride levels were lower after they had been on a diet high in water soluble fiber. Participants who began with normal triglyceride levels were unaffected.

3. In addition to the tests he conducted in a hospital setting, Dr. Anderson studied a group of his subjects at home following their release. These men remained on their high-fiber diets, which included 41 grams of oat bran and less than 200 mg of cholesterol daily. After twenty-four weeks, their cholesterol had fallen 26 percent and their harmful LDL had fallen 22 percent. After ninety-nine weeks, their cholesterol remained reduced by 22 percent and their LDL had fallen 29 percent. By ninety-nine weeks, their helpful HDL level had increased 9 percent above initial values. These results indicate that the longer we include oat bran in our diets, the greater the effects will be.

4. During a study conducted at MIT in 1984, Dr. Anderson observed a group of students in their normal environment while he compared the

effects of oat bran and wheat bran in their diets. He found that when the students ate 1½ ounces of oat bran a day, their cholesterol levels dropped 9 percent. The wheat bran produced no change in cholesterol levels. A 9 percent reduction of cholesterol for a twenty-year-old translates into as much as a 30 percent reduction in the risk of an early heart attack.

KNOW YOUR OATS

While "feeling your oats" traditionally suggested feeling energized and ready for action, the phrase takes on new meaning in light of the oat's emerging significance in our diet. Understanding the development and structure of the oat is an important first step to learning to incorporate it into our daily food regimen.

Like barley and wheat, oats can be planted in the spring or fall. While they are a cool-weather crop that dislikes searing sun, the fall varieties can't stand hard winters if average minimum temperatures are below 10 degrees F. The seed is most often planted in spring and harvested in August or September.

Seventy-five percent of the world's yearly oat crop comes from the United States, USSR, Canada, Poland, Germany, and France. The remaining 25 percent is produced in the United Kingdom, Sweden, Switzerland, Denmark, Czechoslovakia, Australia, and Argentina.

Oat grains resemble a kernel of wheat in structure. An outer covering of bran protects the starchy endosperm and the germ that is located at the bottom of the grain. The bran is the source of fiber, the endosperm is the source of energy, and the germ, or embryo, is the source of B vitamins, vitamin E, and protein. Since oats are not refined, their nutritious bran and germ remain intact after processing.

When oats are harvested, the frond consists of stalks that encase the oat kernel inside two sturdy husks, which are removed before the milling process begins. Prior to milling, the moisture content of the oat kernels is about 16 percent. The grains are graded, cleaned, toasted, hulled, and scoured. After being partially toasted by currents of hot air, they have a reduced moisture content of 6 percent to 7 percent and their flavor and aroma are sealed in.

Following this initial processing, the resulting hulled whole-grain oat, which is called the oat groat, can be turned into pieces, flakes, or flour. Again, most of the nutritional assets will be preserved. Oat products enjoy an unusually long shelf life since they are endowed with a natural preservative. The grain and its derivatives were used for that purpose long before the discovery of chemical preservatives.

As you learn to cook with oats, you will quickly discover that many of the processed forms can be easily interchanged for one another. The following oat products are used in our recipes.

WHOLE (UNHULLED) OATS

Whole oats still have their hulls attached and are only edible when sprouted. Oat sprouts are a fine nutrition-packed addition to salads, pita bread, sandwiches, stir-fried dishes, and soups. They can also be chopped and added to bread dough.

OAT GROATS

Oat groats are natural, complete, whole-grain oats that look like long-grain brown rice. Only the outermost "chaff," or "hull," has been removed, with little change in basic nutritional values. This is done by either heating the oats and running them through hulling stones or using a huller to slam the grains against a surface and crack the hulls, which are then winnowed out. Oat groats have a sweet, nutty flavor and can be used like rice as a side dish or stuffing, as a base for salads, or cooked as a hot cereal. Oats in this form take about forty-five minutes to cook. They can be cooked whole, cut, or ground. (See page 49.)

STEEL-CUT OATS

Steel-cut oats, or Irish or Scottish oats, are natural, unrefined oat groats that have been sliced into two or three small pieces with sharp blades. Since very little heat is applied during the process, they retain most of their B vitamins. They have been popular since Colonial times and are enjoyed for their full flavor and tasty, chewy quality. They make a satisfying cereal and can be used in most recipes calling for oat flakes or oatmeal. Steel-cut oats require thirty minutes of cooking time and are most often used in Scottish-style recipes for oatcakes, griddle cakes, cookies, scones, and porridge. They blend well with other flours for baking.

OLD-FASHIONED ROLLED OATS (OR 5-MINUTE OATS)

Old-fashioned rolled oats, which Americans usually refer to as oatmeal, are large, separate flakes that are produced from the whole oat groat and contain the oat bran. They are first steam-treated to deactivate enzymes and to soften, then rolled and flattened. Old-fashioned rolled oats can be used in a wide range of recipes including cereals, main dishes, and desserts. Their normal cooking time is five minutes.

QUICK ROLLED OATS (OR 1-MINUTE OATS)

Quick rolled oats are rolled oats that have been cut into pieces and pre-processed (heat-treated) for faster cooking. They cook in about one minute.

When either old-fashioned or quick rolled oats can be used in a dish, the recipe will call for rolled oats.

PINHEAD OATS

Pinhead oats are oat groats that are washed and cut into a coarse meal with steel blades instead of being cooked and rolled into a flakelike product. Their texture is somewhat like barley. They are a regional specialty, unique to the area around Cincinnati, Ohio.

INSTANT OATS

Made from partly cooked refined groat pieces and rolled even thinner than quick oats, their preprocessing often results in a lack of nutrients, and they are usually packaged with sugar, salt, additives, and artificial flavorings. Since they are generally less nutritious and more expensive than either quick or rolled oats, we have not included them as a recipe ingredient.

OAT FLOUR

Store-bought oat flour is produced by grinding oat groats to a fine consistency. When it is milled to include the oat bran, it is as nutritious as the whole groats. Oat flour can be blended with other flours for baking and used as a thickening agent for drinks, sauces, soups, and stews. It is a good flour source for infants and people on wheat-restricted diets. Adding it to baked goods helps them remain fresh longer since it has a strong natural antioxidant. *Be sure that the oat flour you buy has been milled to include the oat bran.*

You can make your own oat flour from rolled oats, steel-cut oats, or oat groats. See page 47 for instructions.

OAT BRAN

Oat bran, which has a pleasant, slightly nutty flavor, is a finely ground flour product made from the outer seed casing or bran of the oat groat and three to four tiers of cells called aelurone layers. The protein, thiamine, phosphorus, iron, and other vitamins and minerals that are found naturally in oats are concentrated in the oat bran. It cooks in one to two minutes and can be served as a creamy, hot cereal or used as an ingredient in a wide variety of recipes. Oat bran contains slightly more protein and slightly less carbohydrate than regular rolled oats. It also offers almost twice as much potassium, thiamine, and iron. (Since it is not uniformly processed commercially, it is a good idea to run the bran through a blender or food processor before cooking with it to give it a smoother consistency.)

Buying and Storing Oat Products

Oats have a long history as an item on American shopping lists. In fact, they were the first product in this country that was individually and uniformly packaged in an effort to appeal to the consumer rather than the shopkeeper. Today, rolled oats, quick rolled oats, and oat bran are sold in supermarkets. Look for other oat products in bulk or packaged form in health food stores and in supermarkets with special nutrition centers. The one exception may be whole unhulled oats for sprouting; at this time few outlets besides seed and feed stores carry them. Check the yellow pages for the name of a supplier.

If you find oat products difficult to locate in your area, refer to the list of suppliers and mills on page 333.

When buying prepackaged oat cereals, breads, and other baked goods, be sure to read the labels carefully. You don't want to negate the value of eating oats by loading up on unnecessary saturated fats, sugar, and sodium.

Avoid instant cereal mixes, most of which contain preservatives, added sugar, and salt. Check the labels on crackers for saturated fats such as coconut or palm oil. When buying bread, be sure the first ingredient on the label is oat flour or another whole-grain flour.

Keep grain products stored in tightly covered containers in a cool, dry place. Since insects thrive on grain, be sure that lids are secure. Although the natural preservative in oats gives them a long shelf life, for added protection you can keep oat products in your refrigerator.

Baked goods and granolas made with oat products will also keep fresh longer if well wrapped and stored in the refrigerator.

A Nutritional Profile of Oat Bran
Per 100 grams (1¼ cups)

Calories	381.22	Riboflavin	0.24 mg
Protein	21.1 g	Niacin	1.08 mg
Carbohydrate	58.59 g	Calcium	87.2 mg
Fat	6.94 g	Iron	8.12 mg
Sodium	5.9 mg	Phosphorus	796.0 mg
Vitamin A	0	Potassium	713.0 mg
Vitamin C	0	Magnesium	269.0 mg
Thiamine	1.48 mg		

EATING RIGHT

In keeping with current nutritional thinking, most of our recipes use less meat, eggs, fat, salt, and sugar than you might find in a standard cookbook. In order to gain the maximum benefit from cooking with oats to decrease your cholesterol level, it is important to follow the basic guidelines of the low-fat, high-fiber diets currently recommended by the National Heart, Lung and Blood Institute, the United States Department of Agriculture, the American Heart Association, and the American Cancer Society. If you are already on a special diet related to symptoms of coronary disease, diabetes, high blood pressure, or obesity, you may have to make your own adjustments in the recipes here to conform with the specific requirements of your daily program.

The following cholesterol- and fat-calorie consumption guidelines have been endorsed by the American Heart Association:

• Consume no more than 300 milligrams of cholesterol daily. Cholesterol is found in foods of animal origin such as meat, eggs, and dairy products.
• Consume 50 percent of your calories as carbohydrates.
• Consume 20 percent of your calories as protein.
• Consume 30 percent of your calories as fat with:
    1. Less than 10 percent of fat calories from saturated fat (found in all foods of animal origin and in coconut, palm, and palm kernel oil).
    2. Up to 10 percent of fat calories from polyunsaturated fats (found in fish, canola, safflower, sunflower, corn, soybean, and cottonseed oils; they are liquid at room temperature).
    3. The remaining fat calories come from monounsaturated fat sources (olives, olive oil, peanuts, peanut oil, peanut butter, and avocados).

Following this pattern, if you ate 2,000 calories a day, only 600 of them would come from fat, with saturated fats not exceeding 200 of those calories. (If you have a cholesterol problem that doesn't respond to this level of low fat diet, the American Heart Association recommends no more than 100 milligrams of cholesterol a day and 20 percent fat calories.)

The American Diabetes Association calls for a similar diet; their recommendations are for 55 percent to 60 percent of total calories to come from carbohydrates, 30 percent from fats, and the balance from proteins.

MEAT

• Limit meat, poultry, and fish consumption to no more than 6 ounces daily.
• Choose "choice" or "good" graded beef, including lean, well-trimmed chuck, flank steak, loin, and round. All well-trimmed cuts of veal are acceptable, as are fresh leg, loin, and ribs of pork and leg, loin, rib, shank and shoulder of lamb. Always broil, bake, or roast meat so the fat drips off.
• When purchasing ground beef, choose round steak or chuck with no more than 10 percent fat. Ask to have visible fat removed before grinding. Drain fat before adding other recipe ingredients.

POULTRY

• Chicken and turkey are recommended because they have less saturated fat than red meat. When preparing poultry at home, be certain to remove the skin before cooking. If you are eating chicken in a restaurant, remove the skin before eating. White meat has a lower fat content than dark meat. Ground chicken or turkey can be used in many recipes in place of ground beef.

FISH

• New research results indicate that eating cold-water fish several times a week is particularly beneficial since they are rich sources of Omega-3 oils, which have demonstrated a dramatic ability to decrease cholesterol and triglyceride levels. The highest concentration of Omega-3 is found in deep-sea saltwater fish like salmon and albacore tuna. Sardines, bluefish, mackerel, and herring also have high Omega-3 counts.
• Shrimp, crabs, clams and scallops can be eaten in moderation when prepared without fat. Limit portions to 3 ounces once or twice a week.

COOKING OILS

• Sauté foods in the smallest amount of oil possible. Don't even think about deep-frying. Experiment with using wine, broths, or unsweetened pineapple juice to sauté. Use only nonstick cookware and bakeware such as Silverstone, T-Fal, and Castoflon; keep in good condition and replace when the finish has become ineffective.
• Use polyunsaturated vegetable oil—safflower, canola, sunflower, corn, soybean or sesame—or monounsaturated peanut oil for most cooking. Use extra-virgin olive oil (a monounsaturate) for salads and savory or ethnic recipes. Avoid palm oil and coconut oil, which are saturated fats. In many of our recipes, we have suggested that you use safflower oil (a polyunsaturate or peanut oil (a monounsaturate). Safflower oil is our first choice because it has a high ratio of polyunsaturated to saturated fats and is widely available; but a new product, canola oil, which comes from the seed of the rape plant (a member of the mustard family), is lower in saturated fat than any other vege-

table oil. Canola oil has only 6 percent saturated fat (safflower oil has 10 percent. It also offers the advantage of having 62 percent monounsaturated fat and 10 percent alpha-linolenic acid, an Omega-3 fatty acid that is thought to reduce cholesterol. To date, Procter & Gamble's Puritan Oil, which won the American Health Foundation's product of the year award in 1987, is the only nationally distributed cooking oil made in this country from canola oil.

SPREADS

• Use a polyunsaturated tub margarine that lists *liquid* safflower oil, *liquid* corn oil, or *liquid* sunflower oil as the first ingredient on the label. The phrase *partially hydrogenated* will appear since some hydrogenation is needed to produce spreadable margarines. However, the hydrogenated ingredient should not be listed first. Soft tub margarines are more polyunsaturated than stick margarines; liquid margarines in squeeze bottles even more so, but are not as available. Either soft tub or liquid squeeze margarines are preferable to sticks. Keep total daily consumption within guidelines. *Avoid butter.*

SOUPS AND SAUCES

• Avoid high-fat cream, butter, and cheese sauces that can negate your efforts to reduce your fat intake.
• Chill soups and sauces to rid them of excess fat; if time is short, run an ice cube over the top.

EGGS

• Reduce your total intake of egg yolks to two a week in all foods (including those in prepared foods and recipes you make at home). This is extremely important since a single egg yolk contains 275 milligrams of cholesterol. However, egg whites are cholesterol-free, fat-free, and a good source of protein. While whole eggs have 79 calories each, egg whites have only 16 calories. Experiment with replacing a whole egg by doubling the quantity of egg white or using an egg white and a tablespoon of polyunsaturated vegetable oil. Noncholesterol egg substitutes can also be used. (Try the recipe on page 92.) We call for egg whites only in many of our recipes and suggest whole eggs in those few instances when they are critical to the taste or texture of the dish. An egg separator is very handy.

DRESSINGS

• Create nonfat salad dressings with tomato juice or fresh lemon juice and herbs.
• Since mayonnaise is a fat with 10 milligrams of cholesterol per tablespoon, learn to use it sparingly. Use reduced-calorie mayonnaise or make your own with reduced egg yolk content. Try mixing nonfat yogurt and reduced-calorie mayonnaise for sandwich spreads.

NUTS

- Eat natural fresh-ground peanut butter (ground from fresh peanuts with no salt or sugar added) in moderation. It's a good source of monounsaturated and polyunsaturated fats, although its total fat content is a high 8 grams per tablespoon.
- Restrict your nut intake to limited use in recipes and to unsalted varieties. Walnuts have 4.8 grams of fat per tablespoon but are high in polyunsaturated fat. You can also use small amounts of almonds, pecans, and peanuts. Unsalted raw or dry-roasted pumpkin, sesame, and sunflower seeds are acceptable. Avoid high-fat cashews, macadamias, and pistachios.

CHEESE

- Cheese is a good source of calcium, but many varieties are loaded with saturated fats and cholesterol. You can still enjoy this nutritious food if you buy modified cheeses; you can currently choose between cheese products that are low in fat, low in cholesterol, low in sodium, or low in all three. Reduced-fat or imitation cheeses are also available on your supermarket shelf; select those made from skim milk and safflower, corn, sunflower, or cottonseed oil. Always pick the cheese with the lowest number of fat grams per ounce.
- Use 1% low-fat cottage cheese, which has only 1.6 grams of fat an ounce as compared to creamed cottage cheese with 9.5 grams. Substitute blended 1% cottage cheese for sour cream or ricotta cheese in recipes. If you do use ricotta, be sure to look for the low-fat variety.
- Read yogurt labels carefully. Nonfat plain yogurt has only 0.4 grams of fat per cup, while low-fat plain yogurt has 3.4 grams per cup and regular yogurt has almost 8 grams per cup. Yogurt is a good substitute for sour cream.
- Use skim milk in place of whole milk. While whole milk has 8 grams of fat per cup and 1% milk has 3 grams, the same amount of skim milk contains only 1 gram of fat. Skim milk also had 80 calories a cup compared to whole milk's 150 calories and 1% milk's 100 calories; 2% milk actually contains just slightly less fat than whole milk.
- Other low-fat milk products include buttermilk made from 1% or skim milk, nonfat dry milk, and powdered buttermilk.
- Avoid nondairy creamers. They are free of cholesterol but loaded with saturated fat, sugar, and corn syrup.
- Substitute evaporated skim milk or evaporated 1% milk in recipes calling for cream or evaporated milk. They are full-bodied thanks to the addition of milk solids, and can be partially frozen, slightly whipped, flavored, and used as a dessert topping. Puréed fruits can also be substituted for whipped cream.

BAKING SODA AND BAKING POWDER

- Baking soda and baking powder (baking soda with added cornstarch) both have a high sodium content. Since these ingredients are vital to the success of many recipes, you may want to experiment with producing your own non-sodium baking powder at home by sifting together ½ cup potassium bicarbonate, 1 cup arrowroot flour, and 1 cup cream of tartar. Low-sodium baking powder is available in many health food stores and supermarkets as well.

SWEETENERS

- Relegate sweeteners to the food museum! Try substituting fruit juices. The sugar in these recipes has been dramatically reduced; you may want to adjust the amounts to suit your taste or dietary restrictions, but remember that too much sugar consumption may lead to elevated triglycerides.
- Limit dessert choices to baked goods made at home to conform with low-sugar, low-fat, low-sodium, high-fiber guidelines. Other possibilities include fruit ices, fruit juice–sweetened gelatin desserts, frozen yogurt, ice milk, and sherbet.
- Substitute a small amount of baking cocoa for chocolate, which is high in fat.

SODIUM

- Reduce or eliminate salt in your food either during preparation or at the table; try seasoning food with lemon or herbs instead. Buy canned products that have no added salt. Make your own chicken broth or use salt-free chicken bouillon. Our recipes include a minimal amount of salt, which you may delete for low-sodium diets.

FIBER

- Remember to include as many high-fiber food choices in your daily diet as possible. *Vegetables* include acorn squash, asparagus, broccoli, brussels sprouts, carrots, corn, green beans, onions, green peas, kale, lima beans, potatoes, sauerkraut, spinach, sweet potatoes, and zucchini. *Legumes* include black-eyed peas, navy beans, garbanzos, kidney beans, lentils, and pinto beans. (Don't forget that beans have the same cholesterol-lowering effect as oat bran.) *Fruits* include apples, blackberries, nectarines, pears, prunes, raspberries, and strawberries. (Apples and Concord grapes have pectin, too, which works like oat bran to lower cholesterol.) *Other food choices* with high-fiber counts include All-Bran Cereal with Extra Fiber, almonds, barley, buckwheat, Fiber One Cereal, graham crackers, millet, and pumpernickel bread.
- Eat brown rice instead of white rice for a higher fiber and vitamin count.
- Avoid pasta or noodles made with eggs.
- Eat whole fruits instead of drinking fruit juice whenever possible to take advantage of the added fiber.
- Eat the edible skins and membranes of fruits and vegetables. Eat whole, baked, or boiled potatoes instead of mashed potatoes.
- Eat whole-grain cereals, crackers, and breads.

Cholesterol Counts in Common Foods * †

Food Type	Quantity	Milligrams of Cholesterol
DAIRY PRODUCTS		
Cottage cheese (4% fat)	½ cup	24
Cottage cheese (1% fat)	½ cup	12
American cheese (processed)	1 ounce	27
Cheddar cheese	1 ounce	30
Mozzarella (part-skim)	1 ounce	16
Parmesan	1 tablespoon	4
Heavy cream	1 tablespoon	20
Ice cream (10% fat)	1 cup	59
Whole milk	1 cup	34
1% milk	1 cup	14
Skim milk	1 cup	5
Low-fat yogurt	1 cup	14
MEAT		
Lean beef	3 slices	77
Frankfurters	2 (4 ounces)	112
Boiled ham	2 ounces	51
Lean lamb	3 ounces	85
Lean pork	3 ounces	75
Lean veal	3 ounces	84
Beef liver	3 ounces	372
POULTRY		
Skinned chicken breast	3 ounces	65
Whole eggs	1 large	252
Skinned turkey breast	3 ounces	65

*Foods derived from plant sources, such as peanut butter, vegetable margarines, grains, fruits, and vegetables, do not contain cholesterol.
†(Based on United States Department of Agriculture Statistics)

FISH

Scallops	3 ounces	45
Raw clams	3 ounces	43
Flounder	3 ounces	69
Haddock	3 ounces	42
Canned tuna	3 ounces	55
Canned salmon	3 ounces	30
Canned shrimp	3 ounces	128

BREAD PRODUCTS

Egg noodles	1 cup	50
Cornbread	1 ounce	50
Chocolate cupcake	2½ inch	17
Muffins, plain	3 inch	21

FATS AND OILS

Butter	1 tablespoon	31
Tub margarine	1 tablespoon	0
Mayonnaise	1 tablespoon	8
Corn oil	1 tablespoon	0
Safflower oil	1 tablespoon	0
Olive oil	1 tablespoon	0
Peanut oil	1 tablespoon	0

Traditional Scottish Recipes

You will notice that some familiar Scottish oat recipes are not included in *The Low-Cholesterol Oat Plan*. This is because their ingredients are often high in cholesterol, saturated fat, or sugar. For example, traditional haggis is a sausage that contains organ meats and suet; Atholl Brose, a drink of whiskey, honey, and oats; and Cranachan, a cream crowdie dessert of heavy cream, sugar, and rum.

Happily, however, we have been able to adapt many recipes for more healthful, yet delicious, alternatives. Included are new, easier-on-your-health versions of broonie or gingerbread, cream crowdie, oat sautéed fish, oatmeal cookies, and many, many more.

GETTING STARTED

The Healthful Pantry

You will want to find a convenient, economical source of oat bran, old-fashioned (5-minute) rolled oats, and quick (1-minute) rolled oats. You can create oat flour in your blender or food processor from rolled oats, or you can purchase commercially milled whole oat flour. Keep your shelves stocked with oat groats, whole oats, and steel-cut oats as well, to provide more variety in your menu choices.

To maintain your low-fat diet, be sure to have the following ingredients on hand:

- Skim milk or 1% milk
- Low-fat dry milk
- Evaporated skim milk
- Polyunsaturated tub margarine or liquid margarine
- Cold-pressed polyunsaturated vegetable oils (e.g., canola, safflower, corn, or sunflower oil)
- Extra-virgin olive oil
- Peanut oil
- Low-fat 1% cottage cheese
- Imitation or reduced-fat cheddar, Swiss, and/or Icelandic cheese
- Imitation or reduced-fat Parmesan or Romano cheese
- Eggs (remember you'll be using mostly egg whites) **or** cholesterol-free egg substitutes
- Reduced-calorie mayonnaise
- Low-fat or nonfat plain yogurt

In addition, start to acquire a supply of:

- Pure fruit preserves (sweetened only with fruit juice)
- Fresh and dried herbs (including parsley, chives, basil, dill, oregano, and thyme)
- Nonhydrogenated natural peanut butter (no sugar or salt added)
- Dry-roasted unsalted peanuts, walnuts, and almonds
- Dry-roasted unsalted pumpkin, sunflower, and sesame seeds
- Low-sodium baking powder (for a restricted-sodium diet)
- Unbleached all-purpose flour

- Whole wheat pastry flour
- Whole wheat flour
- Wheat germ
- Low-sodium (or no-salt-added) staples such as canned tomatoes and tomato paste
- Raisins and dried fruits
- Canned unsweetened fruits
- A variety of beans

To reduce the amount of fats used in cooking, use nonstick baking sheets, baking pans, muffin cups, and skillets.

Oils and Margarines

When selecting oils and margarines, it is helpful to know their ratio of saturated, monounsaturated, and polyunsaturated fat contents. The most desirable margarines are those that are in a softer, more liquid state such as tub or squeeze-bottle types.

Product labels often include a P/S ratio figure: the ratio of polyunsaturated to saturated fats. The P/S ratio on the fats you buy should always be at least 2 to 1. If you don't see a P/S ratio on a product, you can compute your own by dividing the amount of polyunsaturates by the amount of saturates. The first ingredient on a margarine that is appropriate for a low-fat diet will always be a liquid vegetable oil. If the first listed ingredient is a hardened oil, look for another product.

The following figures will help guide you through this fat selection process.

Fat Type	Quantity	Total Fat Grams	Saturated	Mono-unsaturated	Poly-unsaturated	P/S Ratio
Tub margarine (made with liquid corn oil)	1 tablespoon	11.4	2.0	4.5	4.4	2.2
Stick margarine (partially hydrogenated)	1 tablespoon	11.4	2.3	4.9	3.7	1.7
Mayonnaise	1 tablespoon	11.0	2.0	2.4	5.6	2.8
Safflower oil	1 tablespoon	14.0	1.3	1.6	10.0	7.7
Corn oil	1 tablespoon	14.0	1.7	3.3	7.8	4.6
Olive oil	1 tablespoon	14.0	1.9	9.7	1.1	0.6
Peanut oil	1 tablespoon	14.0	2.3	6.2	4.2	1.8
Coconut oil	1 tablespoon	14.0	12.1	0.8	0.3	0.02

Sources: American Heart Association

Understanding RDOBs

It's a good idea to plan some daily menus in advance to be sure you are consuming your daily quota of oat bran. For most effective cholesterol reduction, the goal is ⅔ to 1 cup each day. We call this the RDOB—the "recommended daily oat bran." The maximum RDOB is one cup of oat bran; in other words, 1 cup = 100% RDOB. (Whole and rolled oats are only half oat bran, so for them 1 cup = 50% RDOB.)

If your schedule and life-style demands make it difficult to consume that much bran each day, you should eat as much of the recommended amount as possible. Any quantity will have a positive impact on your cholesterol level.

These recipes include a wide variety of oat products that incorporate oat bran. To make life simpler for you, we have indicated the amount of oat bran in each serving as a percentage of the maximum recommended daily total that it represents—your "RDOB."

For example:

Creamy Oat Bran Cereal

YIELD: 1 serving

PREPARATION TIME: 12 minutes

RDOB: 25%

In other words, when you eat one serving of creamy oat bran cereal, you will be getting 25 percent of your recommended daily oat bran.

Sample Oat Bran Consumption Guides

The following plans, based on recipes you will find in *The Low-Cholesterol Oat Plan*, demonstrate how to work oat dishes into your diet and how to use RDOBs to compute your daily intake. Plan to add oat dishes to your meals throughout the day. Remember, they are only part of a low-fat, high-fiber diet that should include plenty of fresh fruits and vegetables.

By following these suggested menus, you can easily reach your recommended daily oat bran (RDOB) intake of 67% to 100% a day.

DAY 1	TOTAL RDOB: 89%

Breakfast

Blueberries
LEMON PANCAKES
Herbal tea
RDOB: 44%

Lunch

Chicken rice soup
Spinach salad
PEANUT BUTTER CRACKERS
RDOB: 11%

Dinner

EGGPLANT CREOLE
Whole wheat French bread
Tomatoes vinaigrette
RDOB: 25%

Snack

APPLE SAUCE SHAKE
RDOB: 9%

DAY 2	TOTAL RDOB: 71%

Breakfast

Sliced Bananas
CRUNCHY OAT BRAN
Decaffeinated coffee
RDOB: 25%

Lunch

CHICKEN CURRY SOUP
Tuna salad sandwich
Grapes
RDOB: 17%

Dinner

DILLED BAKED CHICKEN
NO-KNEAD CHEESE BREAD
Green beans and cauliflower
RDOB: 13%
RDOB: 10%

Snack

PEACH-PEANUT COOKIES
RDOB: 6%

Breakfast

Orange juice
BAKED OIL-FREE GRANOLA
Decaffeinated coffee
RDOB: 33%

Lunch

Fish chowder
SESAME CRISP CRACKERS
Tangerine
RDOB: 8%

Dinner

PORK CHOPS WITH WHOLE OATS
VEGETABLE CRISP
Fresh mushroom salad
RDOB: 31%
RDOB: 17%

Snack

Skim milk

Breakfast

Sliced peaches
ALL-SPICE OAT CEREAL
Skim milk
RDOB: 31%

Lunch

CORN CHOWDER
APPLESAUCE BARS
RDOB: 13%
RDOB: 15%

Dinner

CREPES WITH FLORENTINE FILLI
Green salad
Mandarin oranges
RDOB: 15%

Snack

CRISPY CARAWAY CRACKERS
RDOB: 10%

| DAY 5 | TOTAL RDOB: 69% |

Breakfast

Apple juice
CREAMY MAPLE OAT BRAN
Herb tea
RDOB: 25%

Lunch

Breast of turkey sandwich
Apricots

Dinner

SCALLOPS AND OAT SAUTÉ
Baked potato
Asparagus
RDOB: 25%

Snack

WHEAT GERM OATMEAL COOKIES
RDOB: 19%

| DAY 6 | TOTAL RDOB: 67% |

Breakfast

Tangerine
OAT PANCAKES
Skim milk
RDOB: 25%

Lunch

Chili
VEGETABLE CORN BREAD
RDOB: 10%

Dinner

BAKED FLOUNDER PARMIGIANA
Steamed broccoli
Brown rice
RDOB: 19%

Snack

FRUIT SALAD
RDOB: 13%

Breakfast

Strawberries
PEAR PORRIDGE
RDOB: 25%

Dinner

CHICKEN CREOLE AND WHOLE
OATS
Romaine and orange salad
RDOB: 25%

Lunch

Seafood chowder
Mixed vegetable salad

Snack

GRANOLA BAKED APPLES
RDOB: 16%

About the Recipes

- As you start cooking with oat products, remember that they tend to absorb liquid, especially after sitting. You may find it necessary to add liquid to compensate for this characteristic. Variations in the milling of oat bran, from fine to coarse, may also make more liquids necessary.

- A note on sifting: Take special care to mix dry ingredients well, especially the baking powder and baking soda to be sure it is evenly distributed. With the exception of cakes, recipes do not call for sifting. If you do sift, make sure that any bran that doesn't pass through the sifter gets incorporated in the recipe anyway.

- You will find that while oats last longer on the shelf than other grains, baked goods and cereals made with oats keep even longer if refrigerated.

BASIC PREPARATIONS

OAT SPROUTS

Oat sprouts are crisp and crunchy, rich in proteins and vitamins (particularly vitamin C, which is not present in ungerminated oats), and good to eat! Fresh oat sprouts can be tossed in a salad, added to soups or hot vegetable dishes like stir-fries, or used in sandwiches in place of lettuce.

You'll need to find a supply of whole oats with their hulls intact; look for them at a health food store or feed supplier. Although you may be told that packaged oat groats and whole oats are the "same thing," you won't be able to sprout a groat with its hull removed. Always buy *untreated whole oats*.

METHOD FOR ONE CUP OF SPROUTS

Place ½ cup of whole oats in a jar of warm water to soak overnight. Drain the oats in the morning and place them in a large glass jar. Fill the jar with warm water and cover with a piece of cheesecloth or nylon net. Place a rubber band or canning jar ring around the fabric to seal tightly. Shake the jar energetically, then drain the water off quickly; too much soaking will make the sprouts sour. Put the jar on its side in a dark place like a kitchen cabinet. Ideal sprouting temperature is between 68 and 80 degrees.

Rinse sprouts twice a day. With each rinsing, fill the jar with water, shake energetically, and drain. Return the jar to the cabinet. (It should take the oats two to four days to sprout.) The sprouts are ready to eat when the shoot is as long as the original oat. Cut off any remaining hulls before eating. Sprouts can be eaten as long as they are crispy. Store in the refrigerator.

OAT FLOUR

You can make your own oat flour at home from either rolled oats, steel-cut oats, or oat groats if you have an electric blender or food processor. You can substitute either oat flour or oat bran for up to one third of the all-purpose flour called for in recipes for baked goods. Oat flour is also useful for thickening, breading, baking, dredging, and browning. Ground oat flour can be stored in airtight containers in cool and dry locations for as long as six months. Don't sift oat flour or you will lose the vital bran content. Your oat flour will have a sweet scent and a nutlike taste.

METHOD A: Oat Flour from Rolled Oats

To make 1 cup of oat flour, place 1¼ cups of rolled oats in your blender or food processor. Blend or process for one minute using the highest speed or "grind" setting, stopping occasionally to stir the oats to make sure they are ground evenly.

METHOD B: Oat Flour from Steel-Cut Oats or Oat Groats

To make 1 cup of oat flour, place 1¼ cups of oat groats in your blender or processor container. Blend for 1½ minutes using the highest speed or "grind" setting. When the blender is turned off, stir the oats as needed to make sure they are ground evenly.

GROUND OAT BRAN

If you want your baked goods to have a more cakelike texture, you may want to blend or process your oat bran to a finer consistency. Set the blender or processor on "grind" or use the highest speed. Blend or process for one minute or as long as it takes you to achieve a more flourlike texture. Stir the oats when the blender or processor is turned off to make sure they are ground evenly.

OAT THICKENERS

Use oat bran, flour, or rolled oats to thicken soup, gravy, sauce, stew, or pudding. Use the same amount of oat products as you would regular flour. Oats are equally effective at thickening hot or cold liquids; they will thicken recipes like muesli cereals or puddings while they chill for a few hours or overnight.

TOASTED OATS

Try toasted rolled oats, steel-cut oats, or oat groats as a substitute for nuts, wheat germ, wheat bran, or bread crumbs. They also make excellent snacks by themselves. Toasted oats have a crunchy nutlike taste. They make an economical, nutritious addition to baked goods, meat dishes, commercial cereals, and salads.

METHOD A: Toasted rolled oats

Place 2 cups on an unoiled cookie sheet and bake at 350°F. for about fifteen minutes or until lightly browned. Stir several times while baking.

METHOD B: Toasted oat groats or steel-cut oats

Place 1 cup in a dry skillet. Toast over medium heat for five minutes, stirring frequently.

Refrigerate toasted oats or groats in a tightly covered container. They should keep for three or four months.

TOASTED CHEESE AND OAT TOPPING

To make 1½ cups of cheese-flavored oat topping, combine 1 cup old fashioned (5-minute) oats, ¼ cup melted tub margarine, 2 tablespoons grated Parmesan or Romano cheese, ½ teaspoon dried oregano, and ¼ teaspoon dried basil leaves. Bake in a 15 × 10-inch pan at 350 degrees F. for 15 minutes. This topping can be refrigerated in a tightly covered container and kept for several months. It's a zesty addition to tossed salads, casseroles, vegetable dishes, and soups.

OAT GROATS

Like most other whole grains, oat groats are cooked in liquid until they are swollen and tender. You should allow ½ cup cooked grain per person for a side dish and 1 cup cooked grain for a main dish.

To prepare groats, rinse under tap water and drain. This removes surface dirt and begins the swelling process. Heat the correct amount of broth, juice, or water in a pot large enough to hold the groats, which will double in size when cooked. The ratio of oat groat to cooking liquid is 1 to 2. When the liquid comes to a boil, add groats and stir once. Let liquid return to boiling point, then turn heat down to lowest setting. Cover and cook groats slowly until they are tender and the cooking liquid has been absorbed, about forty-five minutes. If the groats are not done when the liquid has been absorbed, add more liquid and continue cooking.

If you use a pressure cooker, you can cut cooking time in half. To enhance flavor and decrease cooking time, you can toast the groats in a dry medium-hot skillet with a heavy bottom before cooking. They can also be coarsely ground in the blender before cooking if you want a finer-textured dish.

If cooking facilities are limited, you can place groats in a wide-mouth quart thermos and add boiling water to within several inches of the top. Use a long wooden spoon handle to stir. Close thermos and let sit for at least four hours.

TARRAGON-OAT CRISPY COATING

This is a basic coating for browning poultry, fish, meat, or vegetables for pan or oven "frying." Either put in a bag and shake or put in a shallow dish and dredge the food being prepared in it. Increase the recipe for larger proportions of cooking. Make ahead and keep some stored in the refrigerator for quick, tasty meals.

For ¼ cup coating, mix ¼ cup oat bran, ½ teaspoon dried tarragon, ½ teaspoon dried basil, ⅛ teaspoon pepper, and salt to taste (optional). For poultry and some meats, add ⅛ teaspoon paprika. Coat food with oat bran mixture and follow recipe to bake or sauté.

For a double coating: Dip in oat bran mixture, then in skim milk or a beaten egg white, and then again in oat bran mixture.

CRUNCHY SAVORY TOPPING

This topping will keep well in the refrigerator, in an airtight container, for several weeks. It is excellent sprinkled on soups, salads, vegetables, and casseroles. Makes 3 cups.

Preheat the oven to 350°F. Combine 2 cups rolled oats; ⅓ cup olive oil, peanut, or safflower oil; ⅓ cup wheat bran or wheat germ; ½ teaspoon dried thyme; and ⅓ cup grated Parmesan or Romano cheese or ½ teaspoon onion or garlic salt. Bake on a 10 × 15-inch unoiled baking sheet for 15 minutes. Remove from oven, stir, and return to oven for 5 more minutes or until lightly browned. Cool before serving.

SWEET TOPPING FOR DESSERTS

To make 1 cup of dessert topping, combine ½ cup oats with 1½ tablespoons brown sugar, 2 tablespoons safflower oil, 2 tablespoons chopped walnuts, and ¼ teaspoon cinnamon or cloves. Stir-fry in a skillet over medium heat for five minutes. Cool and store in closely covered container. This topping will keep in the refrigerator for about three months. It's an excellent addition to low-fat or nonfat yogurt, fruit, pudding, or frozen desserts.

WHIPPED DESSERT TOPPING

Place half the contents of a can of evaporated skim milk in the freezer for two hours. Refrigerate the beaters and bowl you're going to use to whip the topping. Toast 4 tablespoons oats in a skillet for about five minutes, stirring frequently. Remove milk from freezer and in a bowl combine with 1 egg white and 1 teaspoon maple syrup or brown sugar. Whip this mixture until it reaches the consistency of whipped cream. Stir in toasted oats and serve at once.

For Whipped Dessert Topping with Toasted Oats: Toast 4 tablespoons oats in a skillet for about 5 minutes. After whipping mixture, stir in toasted oats and serve at once.

SPICED YOGURT "CREAM"

This is a creamy low-fat, no-sugar substitute for whipped cream. The flavor can be varied by changing the spice and fruit juice used. It can be stored in refrigerator for 1 to 2 weeks. Makes 1 cup.

Mix the following ingredients in blender for 30 seconds: ½ cup low-fat or nonfat plain yogurt, ½ cup 1% cottage cheese, ¼ teaspoon vanilla, or maple, or almond extract, 2 teaspoons fruit juice (such as orange, apple, or grape), ⅛ teaspoon cinnamon, cardamon, allspice, or nutmeg.

VANILLA WHIPPED TOPPING

Combine ⅓ cup ice water, 1¼ tablespoons lemon juice, and ½ teaspoon vanilla extract in a mixing bowl. Stir in ⅓ cup nonfat dry milk powder. Beat for 5 to 10 minutes to stiffen. Add 2 tablespoons sugar. Beat for 2 minutes longer. If the mixture separates before serving, beat again.

NONFAT BUTTERMILK

If you have difficulty finding low-fat or nonfat buttermilk, you can create your own by bringing 1 cup of skim milk to room temperature and adding 1 teaspoon of lemon juice. Allow to stand for 5 minutes, then beat to combine.

EGG SUBSTITUTE (FOR 1 EGG)

Combine 1 egg white, 2 teaspoons safflower oil, and 2¼ teaspoons nonfat dry milk powder in a blender container and process until smooth. Store in the refrigerator (for up to 1 week) or freeze. Or use 2 egg whites in place of 1 whole egg.

Quick Tips for Using Oats in Your Kitchen

- Keep a box of oat bran on the stove next to your salt and pepper shakers. Use it as a filler or replacement in any kind of recipe.
- Substitute oat bran for all-purpose flour to thicken soups, stews, or sauces; allow 1 tablespoon for every 2 cups of liquid.
- If substituting oat bran or ground oat flour for another flour in a recipe for muffins, pastry, breads, cookies, or cakes, substitute only up to one third the total amount specified to maintain an airy consistency. Since oat bran and oat flour contain no gluten, you need to use some gluten-containing flour in your recipe or your baked goods won't rise. Oat flour produces breads that are denser, sweeter, smoother, and moister; it may seem to make other baked goods more tender, crumbly, and slightly darker in color.
- If substituting regular rolled oats for whole wheat flour, use 1½ cups of rolled oats for each cup of whole wheat.
- You can substitute 1½ cups regular rolled oats for 1¼ cup quick rolled oats.
- Use oat products instead of bread crumbs as a meat extender or in stuffings and fillings. To extend ground meats, add up to ½ cup of oats or oat bran per 1 pound of meat. Then add 2 tablespoons more liquid (tomato sauce or whatever you are using) to the recipe.
- Make up a batch of oat bran cracker crumbs to have ready as needed. Mix ¾ cups oat bran, ¾ cup oat crackers, and 2 teaspoons of dried herbs. Store in an airtight container and use as needed.
- Coat skinned chicken in oat bran before baking, broiling, or sautéing to seal in juices.

- Toss a handful of oat groats into a bubbling pot of soup and cook for 45 minutes.
- Replace chopped nuts with rolled oats in a recipe by reducing the amount of flour by half the volume of the added toasted or raw oats.
- Create a casserole topping from a mixture of oat bran, crushed shredded wheat, grated cheese, and pepper.
- Use oat bran instead of heavy cream to thicken vegetable purées. Use ¾ cup of oat bran and ¼ cup of skim milk for each 4 cups of vegetables. Blend in a food processor or blender adding seasoning to taste.
- Use a teaspoon of oat bran or rolled oats to thicken salad dressings. Allow to stand for several hours before using.

Quick Ways to Add Oats to Your Diet

At breakfast:

- Add a handful of oat bran to your scrambled eggs or cold cereal.
- Sprinkle toasted oat bran over sliced bananas or applesauce.
- Make up a batch of Refrigerator Make-Ahead Muffin batter (page 95) and spoon out as much as you need daily, then bake in a flash.
- Make up a big batch of oat bran muffins and freeze. Either remove one from the freezer the night before you plan to eat it or defrost it in the morning in the microwave or toaster oven.
- Eat a bowl of one of the commercially produced oat bran cereals (read the label first).

At lunchtime:

- Make sandwiches on oatmeal bread and pack a cookie, muffin, or piece of quickbread made with oat ingredients.
- Sprinkle a handful of a commercial oat bran crunch cereal on a serving of yogurt and strawberries or a bowl of low-fat or nonfat plain yogurt, pears, and maple syrup.
- Add oat sprouts to almost any tossed salad or sandwich.
- Sprinkle oat bran over cottage cheese, peanut butter, chowders or soups, coleslaw, pasta sauce, or potato salad.

At snacktime:

- Keep toasted oat cereal O's on your shelf for a bowl of cereal or for snacking right from the bag.
- Toast one or two cups of oat groats in a dry skillet over low heat for five minutes, stirring frequently. Eat for a snack as you would sunflower seeds or nuts.
- Make one of our quickbread recipes and slice the loaf when cool. Wrap individual slices in freezer wrap and freeze. For a convenient treat, remove single frozen slice and toast. Spread with 1 percent cottage cheese, natural peanut butter, or polyunsaturated tub margarine.

APPETIZERS, SNACKS, AND CRACKERS

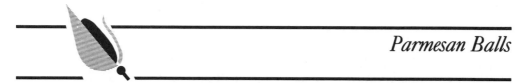

Parmesan Balls

These spicy appetizers are convenient to serve to guests since they can be made ahead and stored in an airtight container in the refrigerator for several days.

YIELD: 60 balls

PREPARATION TIME: 25 minutes

COOKING TIME: 15 to 20 minutes

RDOB FOR 6 BALLS: 5%

1 cup quick rolled oats
2 tablespoons peanut or safflower oil
1/2 cup tub margarine
1 cup freshly grated Parmesan cheese

1/2 cup 1% or skim milk
1 cup whole wheat flour
1/2 teaspoon chili powder

1. Heat oil in a skillet. Add oats and lightly toast until uniformly browned. Transfer to a large bowl.
2. Melt margarine.
3. Preheat oven to 350° F. Oil a baking sheet.
4. Add margarine, cheese, milk, flour, and chili powder to oats and stir until well mixed.
5. Roll the mixture into balls approximately 1/2 inch in diameter and arrange on prepared baking sheet.
6. Bake for 15 to 20 minutes until the bottoms are lightly browned.

VARIATION: Use 1/2 cup oat bran and 1/2 cup quick rolled oats for an 8% RDOB.

These unusual and delicious triangular potato puffs are best if cooked right before serving. A bowl of unsweetened applesauce makes an excellent dip.

YIELD: 24 triangles

PREPARATION TIME: 10 minutes

COOKING TIME: 15 minutes

RDOB 6 TRIANGLES: 6%

2 large baking potatoes, peeled and boiled
3/4 cup oat flour (page 47)
2 tablespoons skim milk

1 small onion, finely grated
1/4 cup peanut or safflower oil
1/8 teaspoon nutmeg
1/4 teaspoon cayenne pepper

1. Mash potatoes in a mixing bowl. Stir in flour, milk, onions, oil, nutmeg, and cayenne to form a dough.

2. Working with about one quarter of the dough at a time, place a section on a floured board and press with your hands (or roll out) until dough is about 1/4 inch thick. (Add a tablespoon of water if it is too crumbly to handle.)

3. Cut into 3-inch strips, then cut the strips into small triangles.

4. With a spatula, place the triangles on a lightly oiled, heated griddle or large skillet. Cook over medium heat until the first side is lightly browned and the triangle begins to appear dry. Brown the second side. Serve hot.

Korean Zucchini Beef Rounds

Zucchini rounds are spread with a spicy beef mixture, dipped in a bran batter, and sautéed. This is an adaptation of a traditional Korean recipe.

YIELD: 4 servings

PREPARATION TIME: 20 minutes

COOKING TIME: 10 minutes

RDOB PER SERVING: 13%

ROUNDS:

- 1 medium-size zucchini
- 1/2 cup lean ground beef
- 1/2 tablespoon low-sodium soy sauce
- 1 teaspoon vinegar
- 1 teaspoon sesame oil
- 1 clove garlic, minced
- 1/2 cup oat bran
- 2 egg whites, beaten
- 1/4 cup peanut, olive, or safflower oil

DIP:

- 1/2 cup vinegar
- 1/2 cup low-sodium soy sauce

1. Slice zucchini 1/4 inch thick. Pat with paper towels to remove excess liquid.

2. Mix together beef, soy sauce, vinegar, sesame oil, and garlic in a bowl.

3. Spread each zucchini slice thinly with beef mixture.

4. Place oat bran and egg whites in two separate shallow bowls. Dip each slice in oat bran, then egg, then oat bran again.

5. Heat peanut oil in skillet over medium-high heat until hot. Brown zucchini gently for 5 minutes on each side until cooked.

6. To make dip, mix vinegar and soy sauce. Serve with zucchini.

Chicken Nuggets

These crunchy nuggets are a quick and healthful alternative to the popular commercially prepared variety. Serve with brown mustard or yogurt sauce for dipping.

YIELD: 4 servings

PREPARATION TIME: 15 minutes

COOKING TIME: 8 to 10 minutes

RDOB PER SERVING: 25%

NUGGETS:

1 cup oat bran
1/2 teaspoon black pepper
2 egg whites, lightly beaten
2 cups skinned and boned chicken breast cut into 1-inch pieces

1/4 cup peanut or safflower oil

SAUCE:

1/3 cup low-fat or nonfat plain yogurt
1 tablespoon honey

1. Mix oat bran and pepper in a shallow bowl. Place egg whites in a second bowl.
2. Dip chicken cubes first in bran, then in egg, then in bran again.
3. Heat oil in skillet over medium-high heat until hot. Stir-fry chicken nuggets until tender and crisp.
4. Mix yogurt and honey in a small bowl and serve as a dip.

Cheese and Carrot Balls

These lovely appetizers can be made ahead and kept in the refrigerator for guests to enjoy as a double-fiber oat bran and carrot crunch treat.

YIELD: 16 balls

PREPARATION TIME: 25 minutes, plus 1-1/2 hours chilling time

RDOB FOR 4 BALLS: 19%

1 tablespoon tub margarine
3/4 cup oat bran
1 medium carrot
1/2 cup reduced-fat sharp cheddar cheese
1 package (3 ounces) reduced-fat cream cheese, at room temperature

3 tablespoons minced fresh parsley
Dash hot red pepper sauce
1/4 teaspoon Worcestershire sauce

1. Melt margarine in a heavy skillet and toast oat bran over medium heat for 3 to 4 minutes, until lightly browned; stir to prevent burning. Transfer to a bowl and set aside.

2. Peel carrot and shred in food processor. Transfer to a medium-size bowl and set aside.

3. Shred cheddar cheese in food processor. Add softened cream cheese and mix well.

4. Add carrot, parsley, 1/2 cup toasted oat bran, hot sauce, and Worcestershire sauce to the cheese mixture in processor and blend until well mixed.

5. Cover and chill for 1 hour.

6. Form chilled cheese mixture into balls about 1 inch in diameter. Roll each ball in remaining 1/4 cup toasted oat bran.

7. Chill for at least 30 minutes before serving.

Peanut Crunch Spread

Serve with a basket of oat crackers, celery and carrot sticks, or sliced fruit, or use on sandwiches. Store in the refrigerator in a covered container.

YIELD: 6 quarter-cup servings

PREPARATION TIME: 10 to 20 minutes

RDOB PER SERVING: 6%

2/3 cup rolled oats
1 1/4 cups unhydrogenated peanut
     butter

1/4 cup honey

1. Toast oats in a dry heavy-bottomed skillet for 5 minutes over medium heat, or bake on a baking sheet at 350°F. for 15 minutes.
2. Combine oats, peanut butter, and honey in a bowl and mix well.
3. Chill, covered, until ready to serve.

Garlic Dip

Garlic lovers will enjoy the nip of this otherwise cool dip.

YIELD: 8 servings

PREPARATION TIME: 10 minutes, plus 1 hour
     chilling time

RDOB PER SERVING: 4%

1 1/2 cups low-fat or nonfat plain
     yogurt
1/3 cup oat bran
2 cloves garlic, minced

1 tablespoon olive oil
1 tablespoon water
1/2 teaspoon sugar (optional)

1. Mix all ingredients together in a medium-size serving bowl.
2. Cover and chill for 1 hour.
3. When ready to serve add a little water, a teaspoon at a time, if dip is thicker than desired.

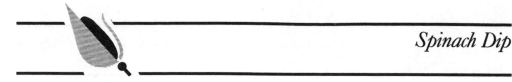

The spinach gives this low-fat dip a rich texture and taste that holds up to any cracker, oat or otherwise.

YIELD: 8 servings

PREPARATION TIME: 15 minutes, plus 1 hour chilling time

RDOB PER SERVING: 4%

1 cup 1% cottage cheese

1 package (10 ounces) chopped spinach, thawed, or 1 pound fresh spinach, washed and chopped

1/2 cup low-fat or nonfat plain yogurt

1/3 cup oat bran

2 scallions, thinly sliced

1 tablespoon water

1/8 teaspoon nutmeg

1/8 teaspoon cayenne pepper

1. In a saucepan, place spinach in a steamer basket over 1 inch of boiling water. Cover tightly and steam for 3 minutes until wilted. Cool.

2. Mix all ingredients in a medium-size serving bowl.

3. Cover and chill for 1 hour.

4. When ready to serve, add a little water, a teaspoon at a time, if dip is thicker than desired.

Tuna Dip with Scallions and Pepper

Toasted oats and yogurt are combined with a zesty tuna dip. Serve with raw carrot sticks, celery, cherry tomatoes, broccoli, and cauliflower.

YIELD: 4 servings

PREPARATION TIME: 10 to 20 minutes, plus 1 hour chilling time

RDOB PER SERVING 6%

1/2 cup rolled oats

1 can (7 ounces) water-pack tuna

1/2 cup finely chopped green pepper

1 cup low-fat or nonfat plain yogurt

1/2 cup skim milk

3 tablespoons thinly sliced scallions

1. Toast oats in a heavy-bottomed dry skillet for 5 minutes, stirring frequently, or bake on a baking sheet at 350°F. for 15 minutes.

2. Combine oats, tuna, green pepper, yogurt, milk, and scallions in a large bowl and mix well.

3. Transfer to a small serving dish, cover, and chill for 1 hour.

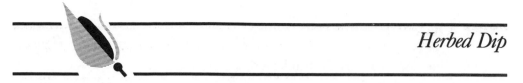

This low-fat alternative mixes nippy herbs and scallions. It keeps well in the refrigerator for up to two weeks.

YIELD: 8 servings

PREPARATION TIME: 10 minutes, plus 1 hour chilling time

RDOB PER SERVING: 4%

1 1/2 cup 1% cottage cheese

1/3 cup oat bran

5 tablespoons low-fat or nonfat plain yogurt

1/3 cup minced fresh parsley or 2 teaspoons dried parsley

1/4 cup minced fresh dill or 1 teaspoon dried dill

2 scallions, thinly sliced

1 tablespoon water

1. Place all ingredients in food processor or blender and process at medium speed for 1 minute. Use a rubber spatula to help stir ingredients while blender is on.

2. Transfer to a small serving bowl, cover, and chill for 1 hour.

3. When ready to serve, add a little water, a teaspoon at a time, if the dip is thicker than desired.

CRACKERS

Although you probably don't think about commercially made crackers as a source of fat calories, the fact is they are loaded with saturated fats and coconut, palm, and cottonseed oils—plus salt. Crackers are simple to make and can provide an excellent source of oat bran. Here is a variety that you can bake at home and keep on hand. Store them in airtight containers in the refrigerator for maximum freshness. Omit salt from dough and sprinkle a little on top to give the taste of salt without the quantity.

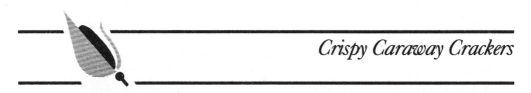

Crispy Caraway Crackers

These deliciously thin crackers are perfect as an appetizer spread with sardines, tuna, or reduced-fat cheese.

YIELD: 90 crackers

PREPARATION TIME: 15 minutes

COOKING TIME: 30 minutes

RDOB PER SERVING
(6 CRACKERS): 10%

1 1/2 cups oat bran	1/4 teaspoon salt
1 cup whole wheat flour	1/3 cup peanut or safflower oil
1/2 cup wheat germ	1/2 cup water
1/4 cup caraway or toasted sesame seeds	Salt (optional)

1. Lightly oil 2 10 × 15-inch baking sheets. Preheat oven to 300°F.
2. Mix together oat bran, flour, wheat germ, seeds, and salt in a bowl.
3. Add oil, then slowly add water, stirring, to form a fairly stiff dough.
4. Once dough holds together as a ball, place half on a prepared baking sheet. Cover with waxed paper and roll out as thin as possible. Repeat with second half of dough.
5. Cut in 1 × 1 1/2-inch rectangles and sprinkle lightly with salt if desired. Bake for 30 minutes until tops are lightly browned. Separate crackers on sheet. Serve hot, or cool on wire racks.

Crackerlike flatbreads are a tradition in many ethnic cuisines. This sweet version contains raisins, walnuts, and seeds and can be eaten as a snack.

YIELD: 24 pieces

PREPARATION TIME: 20 minutes

COOKING TIME: 20 minutes

RDOB FOR 2 PIECES: 8%

3/4 cup whole wheat flour

3/4 cup rye flour

1 cup oat bran

1/4 cup ground unsalted raw sunflower seeds

1/2 cup finely chopped walnuts

1/3 cup raisins

1 cup low-fat or nonfat plain yogurt

1/4 teaspoon salt

1/2 teaspoon baking soda

1. Preheat oven to 400°F. Lightly oil baking sheet.
2. Combine all ingredients in a bowl and mix to form a dough.
3. Divide dough in 2 and roll each half out on the baking sheet as far as it will stretch.
4. Bake for 10 minutes on each side until crisp. Cool and serve.

DILL FLATBREAD   Omit the seeds, walnuts, and raisins and add 1 tablespoon minced fresh dill or 1/2 teaspoon dried dill.

Rye, wheat, and oat crackers are flavored with apple juice and topped with sesame seeds.

YIELD: 70 crackers

PREPARATION TIME: 20 minutes

COOKING TIME: 20 to 25 minutes

RDOB FOR 7 CRACKERS: 15%

1 1/2 cups oat bran

1 cup whole wheat flour

1 cup rye flour

1/4 cup wheat bran

1/4 teaspoon salt

2/3 cup peanut or safflower oil

2/3 cup apple juice

4 teaspoons sesame seeds for cracker tops

Salt (optional)

1. Preheat over to 300°F.
2. Combine oat bran, whole wheat flour, rye flour, wheat bran, and salt in a mixing bowl.
3. Add oil and apple juice. Mix well to form a fairly stiff dough. Divide dough in half.
4. Roll out as thin as possible on 2 unoiled 10×15 baking sheets.
5. Sprinkle top with seeds. Pass a rolling pin over surface of dough several times to make sure seeds will stick. If desired, sprinkle lightly with salt.
6. Cut into 70 2-inch squares. Bake for 20 to 25 minutes until tops are crisp and brown. Cool on sheet before serving.

Three-Cheese Wafers

The dough for these nippy wafers is easy to prepare and can be made in advance and frozen. When ready to serve, defrost, slice, and bake. They can be stored in a covered container in the refrigerator for several days.

YIELD: 72 wafers

PREPARATION TIME: 20 minutes, plus 5 hours chilling time

COOKING TIME: 15 minutes

RDOB FOR 4 WAFERS: 10%

10 tablespoons tub margarine

3 cups grated imitation or reduced-fat cheddar cheese, loosely packed

1 cup grated reduced-fat Swiss or Icelandic cheese

1/2 cup grated Parmesan cheese

1 tablespoon Dijon-style mustard

3 tablespoons beer or nonalcoholic malt beverage

1 3/4 cups oat bran, ground to a fine consistency in blender or food processor

1/2 cup unbleached all-purpose flour

1 teaspoon baking powder

1/4 teaspoon cayenne pepper

1/2 cup chopped walnuts

Salt (optional)

1. Using an electric mixer set at medium speed, combine margarine with cheddar, Swiss, and Parmesan cheeses until completely blended. Add mustard and beer and mix again.

2. Mix oat bran, flour, baking powder, and cayenne in a separate bowl. Add to cheese mixture in electric mixer and blend at low speed until dough is just combined.

3. Remove mixer blades and stir in walnuts with a spoon.

4. Divide dough into 3 sections. Roll out each to an elongated shape and wrap in a piece of plastic wrap. Continue to roll out until 9 inches long and 1 1/2 inches thick. Twist the ends of the plastic wrap.

5. Chill overnight or at least 5 hours.

6. When ready to bake, preheat oven to 350°F. Slice dough into rounds about 3/8 inch thick. Place on unoiled baking sheets or sheets of heavy foil. If desired, sprinkle lightly with salt.

7. Bake for 15 minutes until lightly browned. Serve warm or at room temperature.

Sesame Crisp Crackers

The dough for these nutty, crunchy crackers is made with milk and chilled to make it easier to roll out. After baking, they can be refrigerated for up to four weeks.

YIELD: 70 crackers

PREPARATION TIME: 1/2 hour, plus 30 minutes to 1 hour chilling

BAKING TIME: 20 minutes

RDOB FOR 7 CRACKERS: 8%

1 3/4 cups whole wheat flour

3/4 cup oat bran, plus 1/4 cup for the pans

1 tablespoon sesame seeds

1 teaspoon baking powder

1/4 cup peanut or safflower oil

3/4 cup plus 2 tablespoons buttermilk or skim milk

Salt (optional)

1. Combine flour, 3/4 cup oat bran, seeds, and baking powder in a mixing bowl.
2. Add oil and buttermilk and mix well to form a ball. (Add more milk by the tablespoon if dough is too stiff or crumbly.)
3. Divide ball in half. Roll out each section into a patty 6 to 7 inches in diameter. Cover and refrigerate for about 1 hour until firm, or put in the freezer for 30 minutes.
4. When dough is cold, preheat oven to 325°F. Lightly oil a 10 × 15-inch baking sheet and sprinkle with half the reserved 1/4 cup oat bran.
5. Roll out dough on a floured surface to form a rectangle approximately the same size as the pan. Fold in half as you would for a pie crust. Place in the prepared pan, open, and spread to fill the whole sheet so it will be thin enough for crispy crackers. Trim rough edges and press them back into the dough to fill any holes.
6. Prick with a fork and cut into 2-inch squares with a knife or pizza cutter. If desired, sprinkle lightly with salt.
7. Bake for 20 minutes or until lightly browned.
8. Cool on wire racks.

Ground peanuts give these whole wheat crackers an added crunch.

YIELD: 40 crackers

PREPARATION TIME: 30 minutes

COOKING TIME: 8 to 10 minutes

RDOB FOR 4 CRACKERS: 11%

1/2 cup whole wheat flour	1/2 cup peanuts, ground in blender into small pieces
1/4 cup wheat germ	1/3 cup tub margarine, melted
3/4 cup old-fashioned rolled oats	1/3 cup plus 2 tablespoons water
3/4 cup oat bran	Salt (optional)

1. Preheat oven to 375°F.
2. Mix together flour, wheat germ, oats, oat bran, and peanuts in a large bowl.
3. Combine margarine and water and add to flour mixture in a slow stream, stirring until dough reaches a consistency that can be rolled out. (Slowly add more water if necessary.)
4. Divide dough in half and roll out one section to a thickness of 1/8 inch on a floured work surface. Cut into 2-inch squares. Transfer to an unoiled baking sheet. If desired sprinkly lightly with salt.
5. Repeat process with remaining dough.
6. Bake for 10 minutes, or until browned to taste.
7. Serve warm, or cool on wire racks.

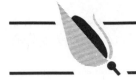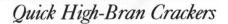

These solid crackers have a distinctly nutty flavor.

YIELD: 30 crackers

PREPARATION TIME: 20 minutes, plus 1 hour chilling time

COOKING TIME: 20 minutes

RDOB FOR 2 CRACKERS: 17%

1 tablespoon honey
1/2 cup peanut or safflower oil
1 cup water

1 cup oat bran
3 cups quick rolled oats
Salt (optional)

1. Preheat oven to 350°F.
2. Combine honey, oil, and water in a medium-size bowl.
3. Add oat bran and oats, stirring constantly until it forms stiff dough.
4. Cover bowl and refrigerate for 1 hour.
5. Roll dough out to 1/8 to 1/4 inch thick (the thinner, the better). Cut into 2 1/2-inch squares.
6. With a spatula, lift squares onto a nonstick baking sheet. If desired, sprinkle lightly with salt. Bake for 20 minutes. Cool on wire racks.

Scottish Oatcakes

Oatcakes are standard Scottish fare but are unlike anything that Americans are used to. These are a denser oat version of the rice cakes that have become popular here, and they go well with soups, salads, fish, and all-fruit jam for breakfast. A big, crunchy, and satisfying treat that can fit in well with all three of the day's meals, they pack well for carrying as a snack or for lunches. Store them in the refrigerator.

YIELD: 32 wafers

PREPARATION TIME: 20 minutes

COOKING TIME: 20 to 25 minutes

RDOB PER WAFER: 5%

3 cups steel-cut oats (or "Midlothian" Scottish oats)
1 cup all-purpose flour
1/4 teaspoon salt

1 teaspoon baking soda
1 teaspoon sugar
4 tablespoons tub margarine
1 cup hot water

1. Preheat oven to 375°F. Lightly oil 2 10×15-inch baking sheets.
2. Mix oats, flour, salt, baking soda, and sugar in a bowl.
3. Melt margarine in the hot water and add gradually to the dry mixture. Mix well to form a dough.
4. Roll out to 1/4 inch thick. Cut into 3-inch circles with a cookie cutter or glass. Use all the dough by rerolling the scraps.
5. Place on baking sheets and bake for 20 to 25 minutes until lightly browned.
6. Cool on wire racks.

SOUPS

Soups can be served sprinkled with Crunchy Savory Topping for added crunch and a higher oat bran count per meal.

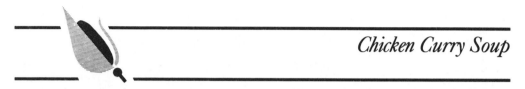

Chicken Curry Soup

This pungent soup has the aroma and taste of a Scottish Mulligatawny. It's best when you eat it immediately after cooking; if you let it stand, you may need to add more liquid.

YIELD: 3 servings

PREPARATION TIME: 5 minutes

COOKING TIME: 35 minutes

RDOB PER SERVING: 17%

1/2 cup oat bran
2 cups water
1 cup chicken broth
1 tablespoon tub margarine (optional)

1/2 cup diced cooked chicken
1/8 teaspoon black pepper
1/4 teaspoon curry powder

1. Combine oat bran and water in a medium-size saucepan. Stir well and bring to a boil. Simmer 30 minutes.
2. Add broth, margarine (if desired), chicken, pepper, and curry powder. Stir to blend flavors and simmer 5 minutes more.

CHICKEN VEGETABLE CURRY SOUP   Add a peeled chopped apple and 1/2 cup of chopped onion, green pepper, carrots, or tomatoes with the chicken. Stir in an additional 1/2 cup of chicken broth and increase simmering time by 5 minutes.

A good, hearty soup with crisp vegetables added during the last ten minutes of cooking. It reheats well; add a little water if the consistency is too thick.

YIELD: 6

PREPARATION TIME: 30 minutes; add 10 minutes if chicken is uncooked

COOKING TIME: 25 minutes; add 25 minutes if chicken is uncooked

RDOB PER SERVING: 8%

1 1/2 cups chicken broth, canned or homemade

1 1/2 cups chopped cooked chicken (2 whole breasts or equivalent) (see Note)

2 cups water

2 cups carrots, peeled and sliced diagonally (about 4 medium carrots)

1 stalk celery, sliced diagonally

2 cups chopped broccoli or one 10-ounce frozen package

1/2 cup finely chopped onion

1 teaspoon dried tarragon or 1 tablespoon minced fresh tarragon

1/2 teaspoon salt (optional)

1/4 teaspoon black pepper

1/2 cup oat bran

2 cups skim or 1% milk

Crunchy Savory Topping (page 50)

1. Strain broth into 4- to 6-quart soup pot. Add chopped chicken, 2 cups of water, carrots, celery, broccoli, onion, tarragon, salt (if desired), and pepper.

2. Stir with a wooden spoon and bring to a quick boil. Reduce heat and simmer, covered, for 10 minutes.

3. Slowly stir in oat bran. Add milk and mix well. Simmer gently for 10 minutes, stirring once or twice.

4. Serve with Crunchy Savory Topping.

CLEAR CHICKEN VEGETABLE SOUP   Increase broth by 2 cups and omit milk.

NOTE: Use leftover chicken or prepare uncooked chicken by removing skin and simmering in 1 1/2 cups water and half of the tarragon for 25 minutes. Cool in broth while preparing the vegetables. Remove chicken from broth and pick meat from bones. Chop.

Toasted Oats, Tomato, and Onion Soup

A hearty, fresh soup made with an unexpectedly delicious combination of ingredients. It's one of our favorites.

YIELD: 4 servings

PREPARATION TIME: 20 minutes

COOKING TIME: 6 minutes

RDOB PER SERVING: 9%

3/4 cup old-fashioned rolled oats
3 tablespoons tub margarine
1 medium onion, finely chopped
1 large clove garlic, minced

1 can (8 ounces) tomatoes, broken up, or 1 large ripe tomato, chopped
3 cups chicken broth

1. Melt 1 tablespoon margarine in a large heavy-bottomed skillet. Add oats and toast over medium heat, stirring and shaking frequently, for 5 minutes until lightly browned. Transfer to a bowl and set aside.

2. Melt remaining 2 tablespoons margarine in the skillet. Sauté onions and garlic for 5 minutes to soften.

3. Add tomatoes and stir. Stir in broth and toasted oats and gently boil for 6 minutes over medium heat, stirring 2 or 3 times. Serve immediately.

Tomato Minestrone

This adaptation of an Italian favorite offers two sources of water-soluble fiber in the form of oat groats and beans. You can vary the vegetables according to what's in season.

YIELD: 12 servings

PREPARATION TIME: 30 minutes

COOKING TIME: 1 hour 15 minutes

RDOB PER SERVING: 6%

1 cup whole oat groats, rinsed and drained

1/2 teaspoon salt (optional)

3 cups water

2 tablespoons olive oil

1 clove garlic, minced

1/4 cup chopped fresh parsley

1/2 small head cabbage, chopped

3 stalks celery, chopped

1 medium onion, chopped

2 carrots, peeled and chopped

4 cups canned tomatoes

1/4 cup oat bran

1 teaspoon each dried oregano, thyme, and basil

1 cup fresh or frozen lima beans

1 cup fresh or frozen corn

1 cup fresh or frozen cut green beans

1 cup cooked pinto or kidney beans

5 to 6 cups water

Grated Parmesan cheese for garnish

1. In a saucepan, combine oat groats, salt (if desired), and 3 cups water and simmer, covered, for 40 minutes.

2. Meanwhile, heat oil in a large soup pot and sauté garlic and parsley for 1 minute.

3. Add cabbage, celery, onions, and carrots. Sauté 1 to 2 minutes.

4. Stir in tomatoes, oat bran, and herbs. Simmer, covered, until vegetables are tender, about 20 minutes.

5. Add lima beans, corn, green beans, pinto beans, cooked oat groats, and 5 to 6 cups water.

6. Simmer until beans and corn are tender. Sprinkle with Parmesan cheese and serve at once. To reheat, add water to reach desired consistency.

Vegetable and Whole Oat Soup

The vegetables are crisp and fresh in this rich broth. Serve with toasted oats sprinkled on top for extra oat bran.

YIELD: 4 servings

PREPARATION TIME: 15 minutes

COOKING TIME: 45 minutes

RDOB PER SERVING: 6%

3 cups water

1/2 cup oat groats, rinsed and drained

1/2 teaspoon salt (optional)

2 stalks celery, sliced diagonally into 1/2-inch slices

1 carrot, peeled and sliced diagonally into thin slices

2 stalks broccoli, peeled and sliced diagonally into thin slices (save florets for other use)

1 (11 to 13 ounces) can beef broth or 1 1/2 cups vegetable broth

1 teaspoon dried parsley or 3 tablespoons minced fresh parsley

1 teaspoon dried thyme

1 clove garlic, minced

1. Combine water, oat groats, and salt (if desired) in a 3-quart saucepan. Stir, then cover and simmer gently over low heat for 40 minutes.

2. Add remaining ingredients, stir, and simmer for 5 more minutes to lightly cook the vegetables. Serve hot.

Celery, turkey, and herbs combine to make this simple, delicious soup. Make turkey broth from the carcass of your holiday turkey for a frugal stock without the extra salt found in canned broths.

YIELD: 4 servings

PREPARATION TIME: 15 minutes

COOKING TIME: 20 minutes

RDOB PER SERVING: 6%

1 medium onion, chopped

3 stalks celery, thinly sliced

1 tablespoon peanut or safflower oil

1 cup cubed cooked turkey

2 1/2 cups turkey or chicken broth

1/4 cup oat bran

1 teaspoon dried tarragon

1/2 teaspoon dried thyme

Salt and pepper to taste

1/4 cup minced fresh parsley

Crunchy Savory Topping (page 50)

1. Sauté onion and celery in oil in a 2-quart saucepan for 5 minutes.

2. Add turkey, broth, oat bran, tarragon, thyme, salt and pepper, and half of the parsley. Simmer for 10 minutes.

3. Add remaining parsley and serve with Crunchy Savory Topping.

Chicken Soup with Meat Dumplings

This clear broth with little meatball dumplings is similar to some Chinese soups, but it's actually a variation of a classic Czech recipe.

YIELD: 4 servings (12 dumplings)

PREPARATION TIME: 15 minutes

COOKING TIME: 5 minutes

RDOB PER SERVING: 13%

1/2 cup oat bran
1/4 cup fine bread crumbs
1/4 pound very lean chopped beef or veal
1 egg white, beaten
3 tablespoons plus 4 cups chicken broth
2 cloves garlic, minced

1/4 teaspoon dried marjoram
1/4 teaspoon dried herbes de Provence, or basil and tarragon
1/4 teaspoon salt (optional)
1/8 teaspoon black pepper
1/4 cup minced fresh parsley for garnish

1. With a large wooden spoon, mix oat bran, bread crumbs, beef, egg white, 3 tablespoons chicken broth, garlic, herbs, salt, and pepper in a large bowl.
2. Form 12 small balls. (Add a little chicken broth if too dry to roll.)
3. Bring 4 cups chicken broth to a rapid boil in a large soup pot and drop in all the dumplings. Boil for about 5 minutes, until they rise to the top.
4. Garnish each bowl of soup with 1 tablespoon parsley.

Cream of Broccoli Soup

Scallions, thyme, and parsley accent this full-flavored puréed soup.

YIELD: 3 servings

PREPARATION TIME: 20 minutes

COOKING TIME: 35 minutes

RDOB PER SERVING: 11%

1 onion, finely chopped

1 tablespoon tub margarine

1/3 cup oat bran

1/8 teaspoon black pepper

2 cups chicken broth

2 cups thinly sliced broccoli

1/2 medium green pepper, chopped

1 1/2 cups skim milk

1 tablespoon minced fresh parsley

1/8 teaspoon white pepper

1/8 teaspoon dried thyme

2 scallions, chopped, for garnish

1. Melt margarine in a medium-size saucepan and sauté onions until soft. Stir in oat bran and black pepper.

2. Add chicken broth slowly, stirring constantly. Bring to a boil, lower heat, cover with a tight-fitting lid, and simmer for 30 minutes.

3. In a separate saucepan, steam broccoli and green peppers, or cook with a little water and then drain, for 5 minutes, until tender but still green.

4. Place vegetables and milk in blender or food processor and purée until smooth. Return to saucepan.

5. Let oat/broth mixture cool slightly, then pour into blender or food processor and blend for 1 minute.

6. Add to milk/broccoli purée. Reheat to desired temperature and season with parsley, white pepper, and thyme. (Add more milk if soup is too thick.) Garnish with scallions.

Toasted oats accent the tomatoes, onions, garlic, and basil in this hearty "creamed" soup.

YIELD: 6 servings

PREPARATION TIME: 10 minutes

COOKING TIME: 20 minutes

RDOB PER SERVING: 8%

1 cup rolled oats

4 tablespoons peanut, olive, or safflower oil

1 large onion, chopped

3 cloves garlic, minced

3 large tomatoes, chopped

5 cups chicken or vegetable broth

1/2 teaspoon dried basil

1/4 teaspoon black pepper

1 cup skim milk

2 tablespoons minced parsley for garnish

1. Toast oats in a dry heavy soup pot over medium heat, stirring frequently to avoid burning, for about 5 minutes or until lightly browned. Transfer to a bowl and set aside.

2. Sauté onion and garlic in oil in the soup pot for 3 to 5 minutes, until onion has softened.

3. Stir in tomatoes, chicken broth, basil, pepper, and toasted oats. Bring to a boil.

4. Lower heat and simmer gently for 6 to 7 minutes.

5. Stir in milk and heat. Garnish with parsley.

CLEAR TOMATO OAT SOUP   Omit skim milk and add 1 more cup of broth.

Corn Chowder

Dijon-style mustard, cheese, onion, and white pepper are supporting players in this piquant chowder.

YIELD: 4 servings

PREPARATION TIME: 15 minutes

COOKING TIME: 15 minutes

RDOB PER SERVING: 13%

1/2 cup chopped onion

1/2 cup chopped green pepper

3 tablespoons tub margarine

1/2 cup oat bran

3 1/2 cups skim milk

1 1/2 cups cooked fresh or canned corn, drained

1 tablespoon Dijon-style mustard

1/2 cup grated reduced-fat or imitation cheddar cheese

3/4 cup diced canned tomatoes

1/4 teaspoon white pepper

1. Sauté onion and green pepper in margarine in a large heavy-bottomed saucepan for 5 minutes until tender.

2. Add oat bran and continue cooking while stirring for 1 minute.

3. Slowly pour in milk. Stir in corn and mustard and heat gently until chowder is hot but not boiling.

4. Add cheese, tomatoes, and white pepper and heat 1 or 2 minutes. (Add more milk if soup is too thick for your taste.) Serve immediately.

Quick "Vichyssoise"

The classic cold soup gets a new twist with oat bran and is easy to prepare in the blender.

YIELD: 2 servings

PREPARATION TIME: 30 minutes

RDOB PER SERVING: 9%

1 medium onion or 2 well-washed leeks, chopped

1 medium potato, peeled and cubed

3/4 cup chilled chicken or vegetable broth

3/4 cup skim milk

1/4 teaspoon dried chives or 1 teaspoon minced fresh chives

1/8 teaspoon white pepper

3 tablespoons oat bran

1. Place onions and potatoes in a small saucepan and cover with water. Cook over medium heat for 15 minutes, until tender.

2. Drain and cool. Combine with broth, milk, chives, pepper, and bran in blender container and blend on medium speed for 2 minutes or until free of lumps. Serve immediately.

NOTE: Use the liquid from the potatoes and onions as the broth for the soup.

BREADS AND MUFFINS

Yogurt Biscuits

Yogurt and evaporated skim milk give these quick-to-prepare, low-fat biscuits a rich texture.

YIELD: 12 biscuits

PREPARATION TIME: 5 minutes

COOKING TIME: 15 minutes

RDOB PER BISCUIT: 8%

2 cups finely ground oat flour (page 47)

1 tablespoon baking powder

1/4 teaspoon salt (optional)

1 cup evaporated skim milk

4 teaspoons low-fat or nonfat plain yogurt

1. Lightly oil a baking sheet. Preheat oven to 425°F.
2. Combine oat flour, baking powder and salt (if desired) in a mixing bowl. Add milk and yogurt. Mix until just blended.
3. Drop batter by heaping spoonfuls onto prepared baking sheet. Bake for 12 to 15 minutes or until lightly browned. Serve warm.

These biscuits are made with cottage cheese and still taste good when split and toasted the day after you've baked them.

YIELD: 18 biscuits

PREPARATION TIME: 30 minutes

COOKING TIME: 10 to 13 minutes

RDOB FOR 2 BISCUITS: 11%

1 cup oat bran

2 cups unbleached all-purpose flour

1/2 teaspoon sugar

4 teaspoons baking powder

1/4 cup tub margarine, cold

4 egg whites, beaten

1 1/2 cups 1% cottage cheese

1/4 cup cornmeal

1. Mix oat bran, flour, sugar, and baking powder in a bowl. Cut in margarine with a pastry blender or 2 forks.

2. Add egg whites and cottage cheese and mix well to form a dough.

3. Transfer to a floured surface and knead with your hands for several minutes until dough has a smooth texture.

4. Preheat oven to 400°F. Dust 2 baking sheets with cornmeal.

5. Divide dough in half. Roll out one section until 1/2 inch thick. Using a 2 1/2-inch biscuit cutter, cut out 9 biscuits. Repeat with remaining dough.

6. Place biscuits on baking sheets about 1 1/2 inches apart. Bake for 10 to 13 minutes until lightly browned. Serve warm.

Apple-Raisin Biscuits

This excellent tea or breakfast cake was adapted from a traditional Scottish recipe.

YIELD: 12 biscuits

PREPARATION TIME: 10 minutes, plus 30 minutes soaking time

COOKING TIME: 20 to 25 minutes

RDOB PER BISCUIT: 8%

2/3 cup quick rolled oats
1/2 cup skim milk
2/3 cup oat bran
2 cups whole wheat pastry flour
1 tablespoon peanut or safflower oil

1/4 cup honey
1 cup raisins
1 large apple, peeled, cored, and grated

1. Lightly oil a 7 × 11-inch baking pan. Preheat oven to 350°F.
2. In a mixing bowl, soak oats in milk for 30 minutes.
3. Combine oat bran and flour in a large bowl. Stir in oat/milk mixture, oil, honey, raisins, and apple. (Stir in additional milk, a tablespoon at a time, if batter seems dry.)
4. Spread batter in baking pan and level the surface with a knife. Bake at 350° for 20 to 25 minutes until lightly browned.
5. Cut into 12 pieces and cool slightly in the pan.

Crisp Mini Biscuits

These small, crisp dropped biscuits are satisfying, full of good oat bran, and fine with any meal. Leftovers can be refrigerated or frozen and reheated.

YIELD: 18 biscuits

PREPARATION TIME: 10 minutes

COOKING TIME: 30 minutes

RDOB FOR 3 BISCUITS: 13%

1/2 cup rolled oats

1/2 cup oat bran

1 cup unbleached all-purpose flour

2 teaspoons baking powder

1/4 teaspoon salt (optional)

2 tablespoons peanut or safflower oil

1 cup water

1. Lightly oil 2 baking sheets. Preheat oven to 375°F.
2. Combine oats, oat bran, flour, baking powder, and salt (if desired) in a mixing bowl.
3. Add oil and water and mix until combined.
4. Drop batter by heaping teaspoonfuls onto prepared baking sheets. Bake for 30 minutes until lightly browned on the bottom. Serve hot.

Whole wheat biscuits, full of melted cheese, taste best if eaten warm.

YIELD: 10 biscuits

PREPARATION TIME: 15 minutes

COOKING TIME: 12 to 15 minutes

RDOB PER BISCUIT: 10%

1 cup whole wheat pastry flour
1/4 teaspoon salt (optional)
1 tablespoon baking powder
1/4 cup tub margarine

1 cup oat bran
3/4 cup grated imitation or reduced-fat cheddar cheese
1 cup evaporated skim milk

1. Lightly oil a baking sheet. Preheat oven to 400°F.

2. Combine flour, salt (if desired), and baking powder in a large bowl. With a pastry blender or 2 forks, work in margarine until dough resembles coarse crumbs.

3. Add oat bran and cheese. Stir to combine thoroughly. Add milk and mix to create a workable dough.

4. Knead 12 times on a well-floured surface. Roll out to a uniform thickness of 1/2 inch. Use a 2-inch biscuit cutter or a glass to cut 10 biscuits.

5. Place on prepared baking sheet and bake for 12 to 15 minutes. Serve warm.

These yeast-risen cloverleaf rolls are an excellent choice for a special dinner. The dough can also be shaped into round or braided rolls.

YIELD: 12 rolls

PREPARATION TIME: 25 minutes

RISING TIME: 35 to 40 minutes

COOKING TIME: 25 to 35 minutes

RDOB PER ROLL: 13%

2 cups plus 2 tablespoons warm water

1 cup oat bran

1 cup rolled oats

1 1/2 tablespoons quick-acting yeast

1/2 cup honey

3 1/2 tablespoons peanut or safflower oil

1/4 teaspoon salt

5 1/2 to 6 cups whole wheat pastry flour

2/3 cups sesame seeds

2 tablespoons tub margarine, melted

1. Mix together water, oat bran, oats, yeast, and honey in a large bowl. Allow ingredients to sit for 5 minutes.

2. Add oil and salt, slowly stir in flour, and mix until well combined. Stir in seeds.

3. Transfer dough to a large oiled bowl. Turn dough to oil all surfaces. Let sit in a warm place for 35 to 40 minutes until doubled in bulk.

4. Punch dough down and divide into 12 parts.

5. Preheat oven to 350°F.

6. For cloverleaf dinner rolls, make 1-inch dough balls and roll them in margarine. Group the balls in threes in lightly oiled muffin cups. For a pan of rolls, make 1-inch dough balls and roll them in margarine. Place them on an unoiled baking sheet, about 1 inch apart. (They will expand until they touch as they bake and can be pulled apart to serve.)

7. Bake for 25 to 35 minutes. Serve hot.

Honey-Bran Rolls

A quick roll, made with finely ground oat bran and self-rising flour.

YIELD: 10 rolls

PREPARATION TIME: 15 minutes

COOKING TIME: 10 minutes

RDOB PER ROLL: 8%

3/4 cup oat bran
1/2 cup self-rising flour
1/4 cup skim milk

2 tablespoons honey
3 tablespoons peanut or safflower oil

1. Lightly oil a nonstick baking sheet. Preheat oven to 375°F.
2. Put oat bran in blender or food processor and grind to consistency of flour.
3. Mix oat bran with self-rising flour.
4. In a second mixing bowl, beat milk, honey, and oil together with a wire whisk until well combined.
5. Add oat bran/flour mixture to milk mixture and beat well with a spoon.
6. Drop batter by heaping tablespoonfuls onto prepared baking sheet. Bake for 8 to 10 minutes until lightly browned. Serve hot.

These traditional Scottish scones are delicious eaten with breakfast, lunch, or dinner.

YIELD: 12 scones

PREPARATION TIME: 15 minutes

COOKING TIME: 12 to 15 minutes, plus 20 minutes if oats are toasted

RDOB PER SCONE: 4%

1 cup steel-cut oats	1/2 cup oat flour (page 47)
3/4 cup buttermilk, warmed	1 teaspoon baking soda
1 1/4 cups whole wheat pastry flour	1/4 cup margarine, cold

1. If a toastier scone is desired, toast steel-cut oats on a baking sheet at 350°F. for 20 minutes. Stir once or twice while baking for even browning; be careful not to burn them. Let cool.

2. Preheat oven to 400°F.

3. Mix together oats and buttermilk in a small bowl. Let stand for 10 minutes.

4. Mix together whole wheat flour, oat flour, and baking soda in a large bowl.

5. Cut margarine into flours with a pastry blender, 2 forks, or a food processor until crumbly.

6. Add oat/buttermilk mixture and mix well to form a dough.

7. Divide dough in half. Dust with oat flour, place on a lightly oiled baking sheet, and press into 2 patties about 1/2 inch thick each. Score each patty, cutting only partially into the dough, to form 6 wedges.

8. Bake for 12 to 15 minutes until lightly browned. Cut the pieces all the way through and serve hot.

These smaller scones cook more quickly and are less crumbly than the cut wedges of more traditional scones.

YIELD: 6 scones

PREPARATION TIME: 10 minutes

COOKING TIME: 10 to 12 minutes

RDOB PER SCONE: 6%

2/3 cup oat flour (page 47)

1/3 cup unbleached all-purpose flour

2 teaspoons baking powder

1/4 teaspoon salt (optional)

1/8 teaspoon cream of tartar (optional)

1 tablespoon maple syrup

3 tablespoons low-fat or nonfat plain yogurt

2 tablespoons tub margarine, melted

2 egg whites, beaten until stiff

1. Oil a baking sheet. Preheat oven to 400°F.

2. Mix flours, baking powder, salt, and cream of tartar (if desired) in a large bowl.

3. Mix together syrup, yogurt, and margarine in a separate small bowl. Add to the dry ingredients and mix.

4. Fold in egg whites.

5. Drop batter by the spoonful onto prepared baking sheet. Bake for about 12 minutes until lightly browned. Serve hot.

Scones made on top of the stove are especially crunchy and toasty brown.

YIELD: 12 scones

PREPARATION TIME: 15 minutes

COOKING TIME: 20 minutes

RDOB PER SCONE: 5%

1 1/4 cups oat flour (page 47)
1/2 cup whole wheat pastry flour
1/4 teaspoon baking soda
1/4 teaspoon salt (optional)

1 egg, beaten, or 2 egg whites, beaten
1 tablespoon tub margarine, melted
1/2 cup water

1. Combine flours, baking soda, and salt (if desired) in a large mixing bowl.

2. Combine egg, margarine, and water in a separate bowl. Add to the dry ingredients and mix to form a dough. (If crumbly, add a little water.)

3. Dust a board with a little oat flour and roll out dough until 1/4 inch thick. Cut into 3-inch circles or squares.

4. Fry cakes in a well-oiled griddle until brown, about 10 minutes a side. Be sure they are cooked all the way through. Serve hot.

MUFFINS

As you work to increase your daily oat consumption, you'll discover that muffins can be an exceptionally convenient and delicious part of your diet. They're great at breakfast, lunch, or dinner, and they make excellent in-between-meal or evening snacks. You can bake them immediately before serving, or try freezing them in single or double batches for later use.

Muffins are a particularly attractive alternative on busy days, since they don't require much preparation or cooking time. You can even make the batter the night before and bake fresh muffins in a flash in the morning (add a little extra liquid just before baking if the batter has thickened overnight).

For muffins that are consistently light and tender, follow these general guidelines:

- Follow preheating suggestions and temperature specifications carefully. Be sure oven is really hot.
- Stir wet ingredients into dry ingredients, just enough to moisten the batter, using as few strokes as possible. Overmixing results in tough muffins.
- Ingredients are best at room temperature, not ice cold. Heat the liquid and oil to lukewarm if you're in a hurry.
- Since the oats make a denser batter than wheat flour batter, folding in stiffly beaten egg whites *at the end* will help the muffins rise. Cups can be filled almost to *near* the top because they don't rise very much.
- Yields are for medium-size muffins with a 2-inch base unless stated otherwise.
- Most muffins can be made in paper or aluminum baking cups; but since some tend to stick to the liners, use them only if they're mentioned in the recipe.

Dr. Anderson's Basic Oat Muffins

This recipe was developed by Dr. James Anderson and his staff as part of his pioneering research on oat bran. It has a high RDOB, and the low sugar and oil content make it an attractive choice for calorie counters.

YIELD: 10 muffins

PREPARATION TIME: 10 minutes

COOKING TIME: 17 minutes

RDOB PER MUFFIN: 25%

2 1/2 cups oat bran
  2 teaspoons brown sugar or
    sugar substitute
1/2 cup raisins
  1 tablespoon baking powder

1/2 teaspoon salt
  1 cup skim milk
  4 ounces egg substitute or 3
    egg whites
  1 tablespoon safflower oil

1. Oil bottoms only of 10 medium-size muffin cups or line with baking cups. Preheat oven to 425°F.

2. Combine oat bran, sugar, raisins, baking powder, and salt in a mixing bowl.

3. Add milk, eggs, and oil and mix just until dry ingredients are moistened.

4. Fill muffin cups with batter. Bake for 17 minutes or until lightly browned.

5. Turn out onto wire racks to cool.

Fruit-Nut Bran Muffins

These low-fat cinnamon and honey-flavored muffins are enhanced by your favorite nuts and dried or fresh fruit.

YIELD: 12 muffins

PREPARATION TIME: 15 minutes

COOKING TIME: 25 minutes

RDOB PER MUFFIN: 13%

1 cup rolled oats
1 cup oat bran
1/2 cup whole wheat pastry flour
1 tablespoon baking soda
1/4 teaspoon cinnamon
1/2 teaspoon salt
1 cup skim milk

1/3 cup peanut or safflower oil
1 egg, separated, plus 2 egg whites
1 tablespoon honey
1/2 cup chopped walnuts, peanuts, or pecans
1/2 cup raisins, blueberries, or chopped dates

1. Lightly oil 12 muffin cups and dust with a little oat bran. Preheat oven to 400°F.
2. Put oats and oat bran in large mixing bowl.
3. Combine flour, baking soda, cinnamon, and salt in a sifter and sift into oats. Add milk, oil, egg yolk, and honey and mix well with a wooden spoon. Stir in nuts and fruit.
4. In a small bowl, beat 3 egg whites with an electric mixer at high speed until stiff. Fold gently into batter.
5. Fill muffin cups with batter.
6. Turn out onto wire racks to cool.

Oil-Free Raisin-Buttermilk Muffins

Sweetened with honey and raisins, these muffins are made without oil and have a high oat bran content.

YIELD: 12 muffins

PREPARATION TIME: 10 minutes

COOKING TIME: 35 minutes

RDOB PER MUFFIN: 17%

2 cups oat bran
2 cups whole wheat pastry flour
3/4 cup raisins or currants
1 1/3 teaspoons baking powder
1/3 cup honey
2 cups buttermilk or skim milk

1. Lightly oil 12 muffin cups and dust with a little oat bran. Preheat oven to 350°F.

2. Combine oat bran, flour, raisins, and baking powder in a small bowl and mix well.

3. Put honey and milk in a large bowl and beat well with a wire whisk until combined.

4. Add bran mixture to the honey/milk mixture. Stir until dry ingredients are moist and all large lumps have disappeared.

5. Fill muffin cups with batter. Bake for 30 to 35 minutes until lightly browned and slightly pulled away from the sides of the cups.

6. Turn out onto wire racks to cool.

Refrigerator Make-Ahead Muffin Mix

You can bake a portion of this mix now and save some for later; the batter will keep for several weeks in the refrigerator in covered jars if eggs are not added until you are ready to bake. Having the batter already mixed will allow you to bake fresh muffins quickly each morning.

YIELD: 48 muffins

PREPARATION TIME: 20 minutes

COOKING TIME: 15 to 20 minutes (20 to 25 minutes if batter has been refrigerated)

RDOB FOR 2 MUFFINS: 13%

1 cup boiling water
1 cup wheat bran
1/2 cup peanut or safflower oil
1/2 cup brown sugar
2 cups skim milk
1 whole egg
2 egg whites

2 cups old-fashioned rolled oats
2 cups oat bran
2 1/2 cups unbleached all-purpose flour
1/2 teaspoon salt
2 1/2 teaspoons baking soda
Raisins and/or nuts (optional)

1. When ready to bake, oil muffin cups and dust with a little oat bran or line with baking cups. Preheat oven to 375°F.

2. Pour boiling water over wheat bran in a large bowl and let stand.

3. Combine oil, sugar, milk, whole egg, and egg whites in a small bowl and mix well. In a large bowl mix oats, oat bran, flour, salt, and baking soda. Add milk/egg mixture and soaked wheat bran and mix lightly.

4. If you are going to cook a portion of the batter immediately, you can stir in a handful of raisins and/or nuts to the muffin mixture you are about to cook. Fill muffin cups and bake for 15 to 20 minutes until lightly browned.

5. To store a portion of the batter, place it in tightly closed glass jars and keep in the refrigerator until ready to use. When using batter straight from the refrigerator, add extra water if it has thickened. Add raisins and nuts if desired. Bake for 20 to 25 minutes until lightly browned.

6. Turn out onto wire racks to cool.

Toasted Oat–Nut Muffins

Toasting the oats in this recipe before adding them to the other dry ingredients provides a crunchy texture that blends well with the chopped walnuts and nutmeg.

YIELD: 18 small muffins

PREPARATION TIME: 25 minutes

COOKING TIME: 20 to 25 minutes

RDOB PER MUFFIN: 5%

3/4 cup old-fashioned rolled oats

3/4 cup chopped walnuts or pecans

1/2 cup oat bran

1 1/4 cup unbleached all-purpose flour

1 1/2 teaspoons baking powder

1/2 teaspoon baking soda

1/4 teaspoon salt (optional)

1/4 teaspoon nutmeg

1 cup buttermilk or skim milk

3 tablespoons tub margarine, melted

3 tablespoons brown sugar

1/2 teaspoon vanilla extract

2 egg whites, stiffly beaten

1. Lightly oil 18 1 1/2-inch muffin cups and dust with a little oat bran. Preheat oven to 350°F.

2. Toast the rolled oats and nuts in a dry heavy skillet over medium heat for 5 minutes until browned, stirring frequently.

3. Mix oat bran, flour, baking powder, baking soda, salt (if desired), and nutmeg in a large bowl until combined. Stir in toasted oat mixture.

4. With a wooden spoon, beat milk, margarine, brown sugar, and vanilla together in a separate bowl. Add to the oat/flour mixture and mix lightly to blend.

5. Fold in beaten egg whites.

6. Fill muffin cups with batter. Bake for 20 to 25 minutes until lightly browned and slightly pulled away from the sides of the cups. Serve warm, or turn out onto wire racks to cool.

This classic takes on a whole new personality when the blueberries are combined with oat bran, rolled oats, and cinnamon. Serve them hot from the oven for Sunday breakfast!

YIELD: 12 muffins

PREPARATION TIME: 20 to 25 minutes

COOKING TIME: 25 minutes

RDOB PER MUFFIN: 6%

1 1/3 cups unbleached all-purpose
    flour
1/2 cup old-fashioned rolled oats
1/2 cup oat bran
1/3 cup brown sugar
  1 tablespoon baking powder

1/2 teaspoon cinnamon
  2 egg whites
  3 tablespoons safflower oil
  1 cup skim milk
  1 cup blueberries, rinsed and
    drained

1. Lightly oil 12 muffin cups and dust with a little oat bran or line with baking cups. Preheat oven to 425°F.

2. Combine flour, oats, oat bran, sugar, baking powder, and cinnamon in a large bowl.

3. With a wooden spoon, beat together egg whites, oil, and milk in a separate bowl. Add to dry ingredients; stir only until blended.

4. Fold in blueberries.

5. Fill muffin cups with batter. Bake for 20 to 25 minutes or until lightly browned.

Maple-Spice Gems

These tasty muffins are laced with maple syrup and prepared in tiny gem muffin cups. Their miniature size makes them ideal for carrying with you on days when you need to get your RDOB on the run.

YIELD: 18 bite-size muffins

PREPARATION TIME: 10 minutes

COOKING TIME: 8 to 10 minutes

RDOB FOR 3 MUFFINS: 13%

3/4 cup whole wheat pastry flour
3/4 cup oat bran
1 1/2 teaspoons baking powder
1/2 teaspoon cinnamon
3 tablespoons peanut or
safflower oil

3 tablespoons maple syrup
3/4 cup skim milk
1/2 cup raisins
1/3 cup chopped pecans

1. Oil small gem or mini muffin tins or line with baking cups. Preheat oven to 375°F.
2. Mix flour, oat bran, baking powder, and cinnamon in a large bowl.
3. Combine oil, maple syrup, and milk in a second bowl. Add to flour mixture and mix.
4. Fold in raisins and pecans.
5. Fill with batter and bake for 8 to 10 minutes or until lightly browned.
6. Turn out onto wire racks to cool.

Fresh, whole cranberries join with maple syrup and orange juice in a tangy muffin that will be equally at home at Thanksgiving dinner or as a midnight snack.

YIELD: 8 muffins

PREPARATION TIME: 10 minutes

COOKING TIME: 25 minutes

RDOB PER MUFFIN: 13%

1/2 cup uncooked fresh cranberries, rinsed and drained

1/4 cup maple syrup or honey

2 tablespoons peanut or safflower oil

3/4 cup skim milk

1 teaspoon grated orange peel

1 cup oat bran

1 cup whole wheat pastry flour

1 tablespoon baking powder

1. Lightly oil 8 cups and dust with a little oat bran or line with baking cups. Preheat oven to 400°F.
2. Place cranberries, syrup, oil, milk, and orange peel in an electric blender and blend at medium speed for 30 seconds.
3. Add oat bran, flour, and baking powder and beat until just mixed.
4. Fill muffin cups with batter. Bake for 25 minutes or until lightly browned.
5. Turn out onto wire racks to cool.

The walnuts and orange rind give wonderful flavor and texture to this recipe.

YIELD: 12 muffins

PREPARATION TIME: 15 minutes

COOKING TIME: 20 minutes

RDOB PER MUFFIN: 21%

2 1/2 cups oat bran	1/2 cup orange juice
1/2 cup chopped walnuts	1/4 cup peanut or safflower oil
1 tablespoon baking powder	3 egg whites
1 teaspoon grated orange peel	2 tablespoons brown sugar

1. Lightly oil 12 muffin cups and dust with a little oat bran. Preheat oven to 375°F.

2. Combine oat bran, walnuts, baking powder, and orange peel in a large bowl. Add orange juice and oil. Mix until combined.

3. Beat egg whites until soft peaks begin to appear. Stir sugar into egg whites and continue beating until whites form stiff peaks. Fold into batter.

4. Fill muffin cups with batter. Bake for 20 minutes until lightly browned.

5. Turn out onto wire racks to cool.

These muffins offer a high RDOB combined with a pleasant medley of tastes from vanilla to bananas and chopped apples. Try serving them hot from the oven.

YIELD: 12 muffins

PREPARATION TIME: 20 minutes

COOKING TIME: 25 minutes

RDOB PER MUFFIN: 21%

1 large ripe banana, mashed	1/4 cup raisins or currants
1 2/3 cups skim milk	2 1/2 cups oat bran
1 teaspoon peanut or safflower oil	1 tablespoon baking powder
1 teaspoon vanilla extract	3/4 teaspoon baking soda
1/2 cup chopped apples	1 teaspoon cinnamon

1. Lightly oil 12 muffin cups and dust with a little oat bran. Preheat oven to 400°F.
2. Mix together banana, milk, oil, vanilla, apples, and raisins in a large bowl.
3. Combine remaining ingredients in a separate bowl. Add banana mixture and mix lightly.
4. Fill muffin cups with batter. Bake for 25 minutes until lightly browned and slightly pulled away from the sides of the cups.
5. Cool 5 minutes. Serve hot, or turn out onto wire racks to cool.

Sugar-Free Cinnamon-Apple Muffins

You'll never miss the sugar in these spicy muffins thanks to the sweet taste of apples and raisins.

YIELD: 9 muffins

PREPARATION TIME: 15 minutes

COOKING TIME: 30 minutes

RDOB PER MUFFIN: 13%

1 cup oat flour (page 47)
2/3 cup oat bran
1 tablespoon baking powder
1 teaspoon cinnamon
1/4 teaspoon nutmeg
3/4 cup skim milk

3/4 cup finely chopped peeled apple (about 1 large apple) or unsweetened applesauce
2/3 cup raisins
2 egg whites, stiffly beaten

1. Oil 9 muffin cups and dust with a little oat bran. Preheat oven to 350°F.
2. Combine ingredients:

FOOD PROCESSOR OR BLENDER METHOD:

Mix all ingredients except raisins and egg whites in food processor with mixing blades or in blender at medium speed for 30 seconds. Fold in raisins and egg whites.

BOWL METHOD:

Mix dry ingredients with a wooden spoon. Add milk and apple and mix, leaving batter a little lumpy. Fold in raisins, then egg whites.
3. Fill muffin cups with batter. Bake for 25 minutes or until lightly browned.
4. Turn out onto wire racks to cool.

The walnuts in these spiced muffins provide a wonderful contrast to the smooth, moist applesauce batter.

YIELD: 12 muffins

PREPARATION TIME: 15 minutes

COOKING TIME: 20 minutes

RDOB PER MUFFIN: 8%

1/3 cup tub margarine	1 teaspoon cinnamon
1/3 cup brown sugar	1 teaspoon baking powder
2 egg whites	1/4 teaspoon nutmeg
3/4 cup unsweetened applesauce	1 cup oat bran
1 1/2 cups unbleached all-purpose flour	1/2 cup skim milk
	1/4 cup chopped walnuts

1. Lightly oil 12 muffin cups and dust with a little oat bran. Preheat oven to 375°F.

2. In a large bowl, combine margarine and sugar with an electric mixer or wire whisk. Add egg whites and mix well. Remove blades and stir in applesauce.

3. Sift together flour, cinnamon, baking powder, and nutmeg in a separate bowl. Stir in oat bran.

4. Add half the flour mixture and 1/4 cup milk to the margarine mixture. Mix until just combined. Repeat with remaining flour mixture and milk.

5. Fold in walnuts.

6. Fill muffin cups with batter. Bake for 20 minutes until lightly browned.

7. Turn out onto wire racks to cool.

Pears and allspice give this tangy muffin a taste reminiscent of holiday fruitcake.

YIELD: 12 muffins

PREPARATION TIME: 20 minutes

COOKING TIME: 20 minutes

RDOB PER MUFFIN: 13%

1 1/2 cups oat bran
1/2 cup unbleached all-purpose flour
1/4 teaspoon cinnamon
1/2 teaspoon allspice
2 teaspoons baking powder
2 tablespoons brown sugar
1/2 cup skim milk
Grated rind of 1 orange

2 tablespoons peanut or safflower oil
1/2 teaspoon vanilla extract
1 medium-size apple, cored and chopped
1 medium-size pear, cored and chopped
2 egg whites, stiffly beaten

1. Oil 12 muffin cups and dust with a little oat bran or line with baking cups. Preheat oven to 450°F.
2. Mix together oat bran, flour, cinnamon, allspice, baking powder, and sugar in a large bowl.
3. Mix together milk, orange rind, oil, and vanilla in a separate bowl.
4. Add milk mixture to oat bran mixture, stirring only long enough to moisten the dry ingredients. Fold in the fruit, then egg whites.
5. Fill muffin cups with batter. Bake for 20 minutes or until lightly browned.
6. Turn out onto wire racks to cool.

Carrot-Orange Muffins

Shredded carrots and orange rind blend with buttermilk and vanilla in a rich-tasting snack. The unique combination of flavors and textures also goes well with salad.

YIELD: 12 muffins

PREPARATION TIME: 30 minutes

COOKING TIME: 20 to 25 minutes

RDOB PER MUFFIN: 8%

1 cup buttermilk or skim milk
1 cup oat bran
2 tablespoons brown sugar
1/3 cup peanut or safflower oil
1 cup shredded carrots
1 teaspoon vanilla

Grated rind of 1 orange
1 cup whole wheat pastry flour
1 teaspoon baking powder
1 teaspoon baking soda
1/2 cup raisins or currants
2 egg whites, stiffly beaten

1. Oil 12 muffin cups and dust with a little oat bran. Preheat oven to 375°F.

2. In a large bowl, pour milk over oat bran. Add sugar, oil, carrots, vanilla, and orange rind and mix.

3. Mix together flour, baking powder, baking soda, and salt in a separate bowl. Add to oat mixture, stirring to moisten.

4. Fold in raisins, then egg whites.

5. Fill muffin cups with batter. Bake for 20 to 25 minutes until lightly browned and slightly pulled away from the sides of the cups.

6. Cool in cups for 5 minutes, then turn out gently onto wire racks. Serve warm for an especially rich taste from the carrot-oat combination.

These rich-textured muffins offer a high RDOB plus the extra nutritional advantages of sweet potatoes.

YIELD: 12 muffins

PREPARATION TIME: 20 minutes

COOKING TIME: 30 to 35 minutes

RDOB PER MUFFIN: 13%

1 1/2 cups oat bran

1/2 cup unbleached all-purpose flour

1 tablespoon baking powder

1 teaspoon cinnamon

1/4 teaspoon allspice

1/4 teaspoon salt

2 1/2 cups (1 pound) grated peeled sweet potatoes or yams

1 cup water

2 tablespoons tub margarine, melted

1 egg, separated, plus 3 egg whites

1. Oil 12 muffin cups and dust lightly with a little oat bran. Preheat oven to 350°F.

2. Mix together oat bran, flour, baking powder, cinnamon, allspice, and salt in a large bowl until well combined.

3. Add sweet potatoes, water, margarine, and egg yolk and mix well.

4. In a separate bowl, beat the 4 egg whites with an electric mixer at high speed until stiff. Fold gently into the sweet potato mixture.

5. Fill muffin cups with batter. Bake for 30 to 35 minutes until lightly browned.

6. Serve hot, or turn out onto wire racks to cool.

The unexpected presence of onions, dill, and yogurt in these savory muffins makes them an ideal accompaniment for fish, salad, or vegetable soups.

YIELD: 12 muffins

PREPARATION TIME: 30 minutes

COOKING TIME: 25 to 30 minutes

RDOB PER MUFFIN: 13%

1 tablespoon finely chopped onion

2 tablespoons olive, peanut, or safflower oil

1 1/2 cups low-fat or nonfat yogurt

1 teaspoon minced fresh dill or 1/2 teaspoon dried dill

1/2 cup grated reduced-fat Swiss cheese

1/2 cup whole wheat pastry flour

1/4 teaspoon salt (optional)

2 teaspoons baking powder

1 cup quick rolled oats

1 cup oat bran

2 egg whites

1. Lightly oil 12 muffin cups and dust with a little oat bran. Preheat oven to 375°F.

2. Sauté onions in oil in a medium-size skillet for 5 minutes until softened.

3. Add yogurt and dill to onions and mix well. Add cheese and mix again.

4. Combine flour, salt, baking powder, oats, and oat bran in a large bowl until well mixed.

5. Add yogurt mixture to the flour mixture and stir. Beat egg whites until stiff, then fold into batter.

6. Fill muffin cups with half of the batter. Bake for 25 minutes until lightly browned.

7. Turn out onto wire racks to cool. (Reheat muffins if you prefer them warm; they're a little doughy right out of the oven.)

CHEDDAR-MUSTARD MUFFINS   Substitute cheddar cheese for the Swiss and mustard for the dill.

Parmesan topping provides a zesty accent for these moist, colorful muffins.

YIELD: 18 muffins

PREPARATION TIME: 20 minutes

COOKING TIME: 20 to 25 minutes

RDOB FOR 2 MUFFINS: 8%

1 cup sifted unbleached all-purpose flour

3/4 cup oat bran

1 tablespoon baking powder

2 egg whites, beaten

3/4 cup skim milk

1/4 cup peanut or safflower oil

3 tablespoons minced fresh dill, or 1 teaspoon dried dill

1 cup grated zucchini

Grated Parmesan cheese for garnish

1. Oil bottoms only of 18 muffin cups or line with baking cups. Preheat oven to 400°F.

2. Combine flour, oat bran, and baking powder in a large bowl.

3. Mix egg whites, milk, oil, dill, and zucchini in a separate bowl.

4. Add zucchini mixture to flour mixture. Stir only until dry ingredients are moist; leave batter a little lumpy.

5. Fill muffin cups with batter and sprinkle with Parmesan cheese. Bake for 20 to 25 minutes until lightly browned.

6. Serve hot, or turn out onto wire racks to cool.

QUICK BREADS

Quick breads offer many different possibilities for adding oat bran to meals throughout the day. Sweet quick breads are good at breakfast time and also make satisfying, light desserts. Savory quick breads finish off ethnic meals and casserole dinners in style. A slice of wrapped quick bread slips easily into your pocket or purse for a convenient snacktime serving of RDOB!

Banana-Pecan Bread

Old-fashioned banana bread is even richer with oat bran, and its full flavor comes out the day after it's baked—well worth the wait!

YIELD: 1 loaf (12 slices)

PREPARATION TIME: 15 minutes

COOKING TIME: 50 minutes

RDOB PER SLICE: 8%

1/2 cup tub margarine

2 egg whites

1/2 cup honey

2 very ripe bananas, mashed

1/2 cup skim milk

1 cup oat bran

1 cup whole wheat pastry flour or unbleached all-purpose flour

2 teaspoons baking powder

1/2 teaspoon cinnamon

1/2 cup chopped pecans

1. Lightly oil a 9 × 5-inch loaf pan and dust with a little oat bran. Preheat oven to 375°F.

2. In a large bowl, cream margarine in an electric mixer or by hand. Gradually add egg whites and honey while mixing. Add mashed bananas and milk and beat well.

3. Combine oat bran, flour, baking powder, and cinnamon in a separate bowl. Add to banana mixture. Fold in pecans.

4. Transfer batter to loaf pan. Bake for 50 minutes or until done.

5. Cool in pan for 10 minutes. Turn out onto a wire rack to finish cooling. Wrap and refrigerate overnight before serving.

Maple-Walnut Bread

Try this bread as a substitute for English muffins at breakfast or as dessert with applesauce.

YIELD: 1 loaf (12 slices)

PREPARATION TIME: 30 minutes

COOKING TIME: 45 minutes

RDOB PER SLICE: 13%

1 cup buttermilk

1 whole egg, separated, plus 2 egg whites

1/3 cup maple syrup

1/4 cup tub margarine, melted

2 tablespoons lemon juice

1/2 teaspoon vanilla extract

1 cup unbleached all-purpose flour

1/2 cup whole wheat pastry flour

1 1/2 teaspoons baking soda

1/2 teaspoon baking powder

1/2 teaspoon allspice

1/4 teaspoon salt

1 cup oat bran

1 cup quick rolled oats

1/2 cup chopped walnuts

1. Lightly oil a 9 × 5-inch loaf pan and dust with a little oat bran. Preheat oven to 350°F.

2. Pour buttermilk into a large bowl and add eggs, maple syrup, margarine, lemon juice, and vanilla. Mix well with a wooden spoon.

3. Sift flours, baking soda, baking powder, allspice, and salt into the bowl on top of the liquid ingredients. Add oat bran, oats, and nuts and mix all ingredients quickly but well.

4. Pour into loaf pan. Bake for 45 to 55 minutes until lightly browned and pulled away from the sides of the pan.

5. Cool in pan for 10 minutes. Serve warm, or turn out onto a wire rack to cool.

Tart apricots give this bread a tantalizing taste. Refrigerate overnight before slicing.

YIELD: 1 loaf (12 slices)

PREPARATION TIME: 25 minutes

COOKING TIME: 50 minutes

RDOB PER SLICE: 8%

1 1/2 cups chopped dried apricots

2/3 cup orange juice

2 tablespoons tub margarine

1/2 cup brown sugar, tightly packed

1 3/4 cups unbleached all-purpose flour

1 cup oat bran

1/2 cup chopped peanuts

1 3/4 tablespoons baking powder

2 egg whites, or 1 whole egg, beaten

1 cup (approximately) buttermilk or skim milk

1. Place chopped apricots and orange juice in a small saucepan and simmer for 5 to 6 minutes. Stir in margarine and sugar while still hot.

2. Oil a 9 × 5-inch loaf pan and dust with a little oat bran. Preheat oven to 350°F.

3. Mix flour, oat bran, peanuts, and baking powder in a separate bowl.

4. Add apricot mixture to the flour mixture. Add the beaten egg white and enough of the milk to form a soft dough.

5. Place batter in loaf pan. Bake for 50 minutes or until top is golden brown.

6. Cool in pan for 10 minutes. Turn out onto a wire rack to finish cooling. Wrap and refrigerate overnight before serving.

Crushed pineapple gives a tropical accent to this crunchy orange-flavored loaf.

YIELD: 14 slices

PREPARATION TIME: 15 minutes

COOKING TIME: 50 to 60 minutes

RDOB PER SLICE: 11%

2 cups unbleached all-purpose flour

1 1/2 cups oat bran

1/4 cup brown sugar

1/4 teaspoon salt

2 tablespoons baking powder

1/2 teaspoon baking soda

2 egg whites, beaten

1/2 cup orange juice

1 tablespoon peanut or safflower oil

1 cup unsweetened crushed pineapple, drained (reserve 1/2 cup of the juice)

1/4 cup walnuts

1. Lightly oil a 9 × 5-inch loaf pan and dust with a little oat bran. Preheat oven to 350°F.

2. Mix flour, oat bran, sugar, salt, baking powder, and baking soda in a large bowl.

3. In a separate bowl, with a wooden spoon beat together egg whites, orange juice, oil, and pineapple plus 1/2 cup pineapple juice.

4. Add to oat bran mixture and mix only until dry ingredients are moist. Fold in walnuts.

5. Pour into loaf pan. Bake for 50 to 60 minutes until lightly browned and pulled away from the sides of the pan. Turn out onto a wire rack to cool completely.

Double Bran Brown Bread

A brown bread recipe that is baked in the oven in round loaves, it includes a generous portion of wheat bran.

YIELD: 2 loaves (20 slices)

PREPARATION TIME: 20 minutes

COOKING TIME: 40 to 50 minutes

RDOB PER SLICE: 10%

3 1/4 cups whole wheat pastry flour, sifted once before measuring

2 teaspoons baking soda

1/2 teaspoon salt (optional)

2 cups oat bran

1 cup wheat bran

2 tablespoons tub margarine, cold

2 cups buttermilk

1. Lightly oil a baking sheet. Preheat oven to 400°F.
2. Sift measured whole wheat flour, baking soda, and salt (if desired) into a large bowl. Stir in oat bran and wheat bran.
3. Stir well with a large spoon or use hands to work air into the mixture.
4. Cut in margarine with a pastry blender or 2 forks. Pour in buttermilk and stir quickly with a wooden spoon until the dough holds together.
5. Transfer dough to a work surface dusted with a little oat bran and shape into 2 round loaves. Do not knead. Dust lightly with oat bran and position on the baking sheet. Cut a cross to a depth of 3/4 inch on the top of each loaf. Bake for 40 to 50 minutes.
6. Cool for 10 minutes. Serve warm, or cool completely on the baking sheet.

This easy-to-make bread "bakes" on top of the stove in coffee cans instead of in the oven. When you serve it with New England–style baked beans, you'll be getting water-soluble fiber from both dishes.

YIELD: 2 loaves (16 slices)

PREPARATION TIME: 15 minutes

COOKING TIME: 3 hours

RDOB FOR 2 SLICES: 16%

1 1/4 cups oat bran

1 cup cornmeal

1 cup unbleached all-purpose flour

1/2 teaspoon salt (optional)

2 teaspoons baking powder

1 cup raisins

2 cups buttermilk

1 cup molasses

1. Lightly oil the insides of two 1-pound coffee cans and dust with a little oat bran.

2. Mix together oat bran, cornmeal, flour, salt (if desired), and baking powder in a large bowl. Stir in raisins.

3. Combine buttermilk and molasses in a small bowl. Stir into the dry ingredients.

4. Pour batter into the coffee cans, filling each two thirds full. Cover with lightly oiled plastic lids. (You may want to tape the lids to the cans to prevent the rising bread from breaking the seal.)

5. Place cans in a large soup pot. Fill pot with enough water to reach halfway up the sides of the cans when simmering. Cover and simmer over low heat for 3 hours. Watch water and replace it with additional boiling water if necessary.

6. Turn off heat and carefully remove cans from water. Remove plastic lids and turn cans upside down on plates. If breads do not slide easily from cans, slide a knife around their perimeters to release. Allow to cool before slicing. (Try cutting the bread with a piece of thin tough string, using a sawing motion to keep it from crumbling.)

Gingerbread

This classic gingerbread has been adapted from a traditional Scottish recipe called "broonie." It should be allowed to sit overnight before cutting.

YIELD: 1 cake (16 pieces)

PREPARATION TIME: 20 minutes

COOKING TIME: 50 to 55 minutes

RDOB PER SLICE: 7%

3/4 cup oat bran
3/4 cup rolled oats
1 1/2 cup unbleached all-purpose flour
1/4 cup sugar

1 teaspoon ground ginger
1 teaspoon baking powder
2 tablespoons molasses
2 tablespoons tub margarine
1 cup buttermilk or skim milk
2 egg whites, beaten

1. Lightly oil an 8-inch square baking pan. Preheat oven to 350°F.
2. Mix oat bran, oats, and flour in a large mixing bowl.
3. Stir in sugar, ginger, and baking powder.
4. Heat molasses and margarine in a saucepan until warm. Stir in 1/2 cup milk and then egg whites. Mix well.
5. Stir the molasses mixture into the oat/flour mixture. Add the rest of the milk gradually and beat well.
6. Pour batter into baking pan. Bake for 50 minutes or until center of cake tests clean with a toothpick. Cool in pan for 15 minutes, then remove and finish cooling on a wire rack. Wrap and refrigerate before serving.

This version of Mexican corn bread is made with green pepper, onions, butter-milk, and oats. Served warm, it has a crumbly texture and is a perfect complement to a bowl of chili. You'll get a double serving of water-soluble fiber from the oat bran in your corn bread and the beans in your chili.

YIELD: 1 loaf (10 slices)

PREPARATION TIME: 15 minutes

COOKING TIME: 30 minutes

RDOB PER SLICE: 10%

6 tablespoons tub margarine	1/4 teaspoon salt (optional)
1 3/4 cups unbleached all-purpose flour	2 cups buttermilk or skim milk
1 cup cornmeal	1 whole egg, plus 2 egg whites
1 cup oat bran	1/4 cup finely chopped green pepper
2 tablespoons sugar	1/4 cup finely chopped onion
2 teaspoons baking powder	
1 1/2 teaspoons baking soda	

1. Preheat oven to 375°F. In the oven melt 2 tablespoons margarine in a 7 × 10-inch baking pan. Tilt to coat evenly.

2. Mix together flour, cornmeal, oat bran, sugar, baking powder, baking soda, and salt (if desired) in a large bowl. Stir in remaining 4 tablespoons margarine, milk, eggs, green pepper, and onions.

3. Pour in hot baking pan and bake for 30 minutes until top is lightly browned.

4. Serve warm.

A simple whole-grain loaf pungent with herbs and onions that goes well with soup and salad.

YIELD: 1 loaf (18 slices)

PREPARATION TIME: 20 minutes

COOKING TIME: 35 to 40 minutes

RDOB PER SLICE: 8%

1 1/2 cups oat bran

2 1/2 cups whole wheat pastry flour

1/8 teaspoon black pepper

1 1/2 teaspoons baking soda

2 tablespoons tub margarine

1 large onion, grated

1 clove garlic, minced

1/4 teaspoon dried basil

1/4 teaspoon dried marjoram

1/4 teaspoon dried oregano

1/4 teaspoon dried dill

1 teaspoon dried parsley or 1 tablespoon chopped fresh parsley

1 to 1 1/4 cups skim milk

2 teaspoons lemon juice

1/4 cup grated Parmesan cheese or reduced-fat cheddar cheese

1. Dust a baking sheet with a little oat bran. Preheat oven to 400°F.

2. Combine oat bran, flour, pepper, and baking soda in a large bowl. With a pastry blender or 2 forks, cut in margarine until mixture has the texture of coarse crumbs.

3. Mix onion, garlic, basil, marjoram, oregano, dill, and parsley into the bran mixture.

4. In a small bowl, combine 1 cup skim milk and lemon juice. Add to the bran mixture. (If the dough seems too dry and crumbly, add the remaining milk.) Transfer to a floured surface and knead gently with hands until dough is smooth.

5. Shape into a 9-inch round and place in the center of the baking sheet. Score the top six or seven times, brush with skim milk, and top with Parmesan cheese. Bake for 35 minutes or until the loaf has risen moderately and is nicely browned. Serve warm.

YEAST BREADS

Although many of us don't have time in our busy lives to practice the culinary arts of the past, one of the most worthwhile ways to invest time spent in the kitchen is by baking yeast-risen breads.

Baking your own bread requires a mixing bowl, a kneading surface, a baking pan, an oven and the willingness to spend a few extra minutes creating a finished product that will be well worth the extra effort. We know a busy executive who relaxes every weekend by baking bread, and a harried nursing supervisor who takes out her frustrations by kneading dough after particularly difficult days.

Few kitchen activities afford as much satisfaction as baking bread; and bread made with oat products is among the most delicious. Oats afford bread doughs a distinctive nutty flavor and texture as they enrich their nutritional content and increase your RDOB.

We've begun this section with five breads that don't require kneading to get you started; they're followed by some of our favorite kneaded breads.

Bread freezes well, so it makes good sense to bake a number of loaves when you've got the time and inclination. To freeze freshly baked bread, allow the loaves to reach room temperature, then wrap them tightly in freezer wrap or foil and store. Be sure your packing is airtight. You can keep frozen bread for ten to twelve weeks before moisture and flavor are lost. If you slice it before freezing it, you can defrost the slices in the toaster. When defrosting whole loaves, leave the bread in its wrapping and thaw at room temperature for three hours or place in a 375-degree F. oven for twenty minutes.

When working with yeast, follow package instructions regarding liquid temperatures since yeast can be killed with excess heat. Allow adequate rising time and follow preheating suggestions and temperature specifications carefully. Be sure your oven is really hot before you start baking.

NO-KNEAD BREADS

Although this bread goes through two rising periods, no kneading is necessary. The finished result is a hearty loaf of wheat, oat, and rye flours accented by walnuts.

YIELD: 2 loaves (36 slices)

PREPARATION TIME: 30 minutes, plus 1 hour 15 minutes rising time

COOKING TIME: 30 to 35 minutes

RDOB FOR 2 SLICES: 14%

1 1/2 cups boiling water	2 cups rye flour
1/2 cup tub margarine	2 cups whole wheat flour
1/3 cup honey	2 cups oat bran
2 packages (1/4 ounce) quick-rising yeast	1 whole egg plus 2 egg whites, lightly beaten
1 cup warm water	1 cup finely chopped walnuts
1 cup rolled oats	1/2 teaspoon salt (optional)

1. Combine boiling water, margarine, and honey in a large bowl. Stir until margarine melts. Cool to room temperature.

2. Dissolve yeast in warm water in a small bowl.

3. Combine oats, rye flour, and whole wheat flour in a third bowl.

4. Stir yeast mixture, 2 cups of the oat/flour mixture, oat bran, eggs, nuts, and salt (if desired) into the margarine/honey mixture. Mix well. Add remaining flour to form a stiff dough. (It will be slightly sticky.)

5. Spoon dough into a large oiled bowl and cover with a damp towel. Let rise in a warm place until doubled in size, approximately 45 minutes.

6. Oil two 9 × 5-inch loaf pans. Divide dough in half and spoon into pans. Let rise, uncovered, in a warm place until once again doubled in size, about 30 minutes.

7. Preheat oven to 375°F.

8. Bake for 30 to 35 minutes until golden brown.

9. Turn out onto a wire rack to cool completely before slicing.

No-Knead Apple-Raisin Bread

An aromatic, full-bodied loaf that will fill your kitchen with the scent of spices and apples.

YIELD: 1 large loaf (20 slices)

PREPARATION TIME: 30 minutes, plus 1 1/2 hours rising time

COOKING TIME: 50 to 60 minutes

RDOB FOR 2 SLICES: 10%

1 1/4 cups skim milk
3/4 cup oat bran
1/2 cup old-fashioned rolled oats
1/4 cup tub margarine
1 tablespoon active dry yeast
1/4 cup warm water
1/4 cup maple syrup
2 egg whites, beaten

1/4 cup wheat germ
1/2 teaspoon cinnamon
2 1/2 cups whole wheat flour, or 1 cup all-purpose flour plus 1 1/2 cups whole wheat flour
1/2 cup raisins or currants
1/2 cup diced peeled apple
2 tablespoons oat groats

1. Bring skim milk to a boil over medium heat in a heavy-bottomed saucepan. Remove from heat and stir in oat bran, 1/4 cup oats, and margarine. Allow to cool to room temperature.

2. Dissolve yeast in warm water in electric mixer bowl or in a separate large bowl if you are using a hand mixer. Add 1 teaspoon maple syrup and allow mixture to stand until yeast is bubbling. Add oat mixture, remaining maple syrup, egg whites, wheat germ, cinnamon, and 1 cup flour.

3. Beat by hand or with electric mixer at medium speed for 3 minutes. Remove mixing blades.

4. Using a wooden spoon, stir in raisins and apples. Gradually mix in remaining flour to form a smooth, elastic dough. (It will become quite stiff, and you'll have to work rather hard to add all the flour.)

5. Smooth the top of the dough, cover with a damp towel, and let rise in a warm place until doubled in size, about 40 minutes.

6. Toast oat groats in a dry skillet for 5 minutes.

7. Oil a 1 1/2-quart baking dish or loaf pan and sprinkle with remaining 1/4 cup oats.

8. Punch down batter and transfer to the baking dish. Sprinkle top with

toasted oat groats. Let rise in a warm place for 30 to 45 minutes.

9. Preheat oven to 350°F. Bake for 50 to 60 minutes, until lightly browned and slightly pulled away from the sides of the pan.

10. Cool in pan for 10 minutes. Turn out and serve warm, or cool on a wire rack.

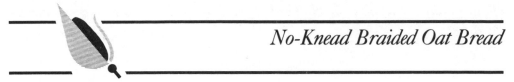

No-Knead Braided Oat Bread

A good choice for a special brunch. The slightly sweet dough, which is full of fruit and nuts, is braided before baking.

YIELD: 1 loaf (18 slices)

PREPARATION TIME: 15 minutes, plus 45 minutes rising time

COOKING TIME: 30 minutes

RDOB FOR 2 SLICES: 11%

1 cup skim milk

1 package (1/4 ounce) active dry yeast

1/3 cup sugar

1 cup unbleached all-purpose flour

1 cup oat bran

1 egg white

1/4 cup tub margarine, melted

1 teaspoon vanilla extract

3 tablespoons raisins or currants

3 tablespoons chopped walnuts or pecans

1. Heat 1/3 cup milk to lukewarm in a saucepan. Mix in yeast and 1 tablespoon sugar. Cover and let sit for about 5 minutes.

2. In the meantime mix together flour, oat bran, remaining milk and sugar, egg white, margarine, and vanilla in a large bowl.

3. When yeast mixture is foamy, add to the flour mixture and mix well with a wooden spoon.

4. Fold in raisins and nuts.

5. Cover and let rise in a warm spot for 45 minutes until doubled in size.

6. Preheat oven to 350°F.

7. On a surface dusted with a little oat bran, divide dough into 3 parts. Roll out each into a long, cigar-shaped piece. Braid the 3 pieces together.

8. Place on an unoiled baking sheet and bake for 30 minutes, until lightly browned.

9. Cool for 10 minutes. Serve warm, or turn out onto a wire rack to finish cooling.

No-Knead Cheese Bread

Here's another easy no-knead bread that requires only one rising period and is mixed in an electric mixer bowl. The finished product is a superb, crusty, cheese-laced loaf.

YIELD: 1 loaf (20 slices)

PREPARATION TIME: 20 minutes, plus 45 minutes rising time

COOKING TIME: 45 to 55 minutes

RDOB FOR 2 SLICES: 10%

4 1/2 cups unbleached all-purpose flour

1 package (1/4 ounce) active dry yeast)

2 tablespoons sugar

2 teaspoons salt

2 tablespoons tub margarine

1 1/2 cups skim milk

2 egg whites

1 cup shredded reduced-fat or imitation cheddar cheese

1 cup oat bran

1. Put 2 cups of the flour with yeast, sugar, and salt in a large bowl and combine with electric mixer at medium speed.

2. Heat margarine and milk together in a saucepan until margarine is melted. Add to flour mixture and mix 2 minutes longer.

3. Add egg whites, cheese, and 1/2 cup oat bran and mix at a higher speed for 2 more minutes.

4. Remove mixer blades. Stir in remaining flour and oat bran to form a stiff dough. Continue beating until all ingredients are thoroughly mixed.

5. Cover and let rise in a warm place for 45 minutes.

6. Lightly oil a 3-quart casserole dish. Preheat oven to 325°F.

7. Punch dough down, stir it with a wooden spoon with gusto for about 30 seconds, and transfer it to the casserole dish. Bake for 45 to 55 minutes until slightly pulled away from the sides of the dish.

8. Cool for 10 minutes, turn out, and serve warm.

No-Knead Dill Bread

The unique texture is provided by creamy cottage cheese, and the flavor punch is delivered by dill, onion, and sesame seeds.

YIELD: 1 loaf (16 slices)

PREPARATION TIME: 20 minutes, plus 1 hour rising time

COOKING TIME: 35 to 40 minutes

RDOB FOR 2 SLICES: 13%

DOUGH:

2 cups unbleached all-purpose flour

1 cup oat bran

1 tablespoon sugar

1/2 small onion, chopped

1 tablespoon fresh dill or 1 teaspoon dried dill

1/2 teaspoon salt

1/4 teaspoon baking soda

1 package (1/4 ounce) active dry yeast

1 cup 1% cottage cheese

1/4 cup water

1 tablespoon tub margarine

2 egg whites

TOPPING:

1/4 cup tub margarine

2 tablespoons toasted sesame seeds

1. To make the dough, combine flour and oat bran in a large bowl. Transfer 1 cup to a separate bowl, add sugar, onions, dill, salt, baking soda, and yeast, and mix well.

2. Heat cottage cheese, water, and margarine in a saucepan until margarine melts.

3. Add the cottage cheese mixture to the flour/bran/sugar mixture and stir. Add egg whites and beat with an electric mixer at medium speed for 3 minutes.

4. Stir in remaining flour/bran mixture by hand to form a very stiff dough. Cover and let rise in a warm place for about 30 minutes.

5. Punch down dough and transfer to a well-oiled 1 1/2- or 2-quart casserole dish. Let rise again for about 30 minutes.

6. Preheat oven to 350°F. Bake for 35 to 40 minutes until lightly browned.

7. To make the topping, combine 1/4 cup margarine and sesame seeds in a mixing bowl. Brush on hot baked bread.

8. Cool 10 minutes. Serve warm, or turn out onto a wire rack to finish cooling.

KNEADED BREADS

When adding oat bran to kneaded bread recipes, blend or process it to a very fine consistency to achieve the finest and lightest breads.

While many cooks develop their own unique kneading techniques, you might want to follow some basic guidelines if you're venturing into kneading for the first time:

- Dust your working surface and hands with flour before turning out the dough. If the dough seems sticky, sprinkle it with flour.
- Press the dough into a ball and flatten it. Using both hands, fold the upper side of the dough toward you. Push the dough away from you with the heels of your hands. Turn the dough half a turn and repeat. After five minutes, turn the bread over and continue for five additional minutes. Be aggressive; the dough will respond positively. If it doesn't seem elastic enough after ten minutes, add more force!

This basic loaf, made with unbleached white flour, is ideal for sandwiches.

YIELD: 2 loaves (36 slices)

PREPARATION TIME: 45 minutes, plus 2 hours rising time

COOKING TIME: 45 minutes

RDOB FOR 2 SLICES: 11%

1 package (1/4 ounce) active dry yeast

1/4 cup warm water

2 cups scalded skim milk

1/4 cup tub margarine

2 tablespoons brown sugar

1 teaspoon salt

2 cups oat bran

4 cups sifted unbleached all-purpose flour

1. Process oat bran in a blender or food processor until it reaches a smooth, flourlike consistency. Set aside.

2. In a small bowl, sprinkle yeast into water and stir to dissolve. Set aside.

3. Combine margarine, sugar, and salt in a large bowl. Add hot milk and mix. Cool to a lukewarm temperature.

4. Stir in yeast, add 1 cup oat bran and 1 cup all-purpose flour. Mix well with a wooden spoon. Gradually add remaining bran and flour as you mix the dough.

5. Transfer to a floured work surface. Knead for 10 to 12 minutes or until smooth.

6. Wash and lightly oil the mixing bowl. Swirl dough around in bowl to oil surface. Cover and let rise until doubled in size, about 1-1/2 hours.

7. Punch dough down and let rise for 30 minutes more.

8. Lightly oil two 9 × 5-inch loaf pans. Mold dough into 2 loaves and place in pans. Let rise again until doubled in size, about 45 minutes.

9. About 10 minutes before rising time is finished, preheat oven to 400°F. Bake loaves for 35 minutes or until lightly browned.

10. Cool in pans for 10 minutes. Serve hot, or turn out onto wire racks to finish cooling.

Steel-Cut Oat Bread

The nutty texture of steel-cut oats is at the heart of this robust loaf. Keep this one refrigerated after cooling to room temperature. It makes great toast!

YIELD: 1 large or 2 small loaves
(18 slices)

PREPARATION TIME: 1 1/2 hours, plus 45 minutes rising time

COOKING TIME: 40 minutes (large loaf); 20 minutes (small loaves)

RDOB FOR 2 SLICES: 7%

3/4 cup steel-cut oats

1/2 cup rolled oats

1/4 cup dark molasses

1 tablespoon tub margarine

1/2 teaspoon salt

2 cups boiling water

1 package (1/4 ounce) quick-rising yeast

1 teaspoon sugar

1/4 cup warm water

1/4 cup finely chopped unsalted raw sunflower seeds

1 cup whole wheat flour

1 1/4 to 1 3/4 cups unbleached all-purpose flour

1. Combine steel-cut oats, rolled oats, molasses, margarine, and salt in a large bowl. Add boiling water and mix. Let mixture stand until it reaches room temperature.

2. In a small bowl, dissolve yeast and sugar in warm water.

3. When yeast is bubbly and oat mixture has cooled, combine them in a large bowl.

4. Stir in sunflower seeds, whole wheat flour, and 1 1/4 cups all-purpose flour. Add remaining flour slowly until dough has reached an easily handled consistency. (You may not need to add all of it.)

5. Turn dough out onto a floured kneading surface and form into a ball. Cover with a damp cloth and let rest for 15 minutes.

6. Uncover and knead 10 to 12 minutes until very elastic.

7. Place in an oiled bowl and cover with a damp towel. Let rise in a warm place until doubled in size, about 45 minutes.

8. Oil a 9×5-inch loaf pan or two 6×3 1/2-inch loaf pans and dust with oat bran.

9. Punch dough down, shape into 1 large loaf or 2 smaller loaves, and place in pan(s). Cover with damp towel. Let stand in a warm place until doubled in bulk, about 20 minutes.

10. Preheat oven to 375°F. Bake until lightly browned, approximately 40 minutes for 1 large loaf, 20 minutes for 2 smaller loaves.

11. Cool 10 minutes in pan(s). Serve warm, or turn out onto a wire rack to finish cooling.

Wheat and Bran Bread

A simple whole wheat loaf is enriched with dry milk and sweetened with honey.

YIELD: 1 loaf (18 slices)

PREPARATION TIME: 35 minutes, plus 1 hour 20 minutes rising time

COOKING TIME: 60 minutes

RDOB PER SLICE: 7%

1 package (1/4 ounce) active dry yeast
1 1/2 cups warm water
3 tablespoons honey
1/2 cup nonfat dry milk

2 1/2 cups whole wheat flour
1 cup unbleached all-purpose flour
1/4 cup peanut or safflower oil
1 1/4 cups oat bran

1. In a large bowl, dissolve yeast in water. Add honey and milk. Stir in 1 cup whole wheat flour and 1 cup all-purpose flour. Let rest for 10 minutes.

2. Stir in oil, oat bran, and remaining whole wheat flour and mix until it forms a dough. Transfer to a floured working surface and knead for 10 to 12 minutes until smooth.

3. Wash and oil the bowl. Turn dough around in bowl to oil surface. Cover and let rise in a warm place until doubled in size, 45 to 50 minutes.

4. Lightly oil a 9×5-inch loaf pan. Punch dough down, shape into a loaf, and place in pan. Allow to rise again in a warm place for 35 minutes.

5. Preheat oven to 350°F. Bake for 1 hour until lightly browned.

6. Cool in pan for 10 minutes. Serve warm, or turn out onto a wire rack to finish cooling.

The vegetables—cabbage, carrots, celery, and parsley—add both texture and moistness to this delectable bread, which can be served with soups, salads, and casseroles.

YIELD: 2 loaves (36 slices)

PREPARATION TIME: 25 minutes, plus 1 hour 45 minutes rising time

COOKING TIME: 30 minutes

RDOB FOR 2 SLICES: 6%

1 package (1/4 ounce) active dry yeast
1/3 cup warm water
1/2 cup plus 1 tablespoon skim milk
1/4 cup peanut or safflower oil
2 egg whites
1/2 cup chopped cabbage
2 carrots, chopped

1/2 cup chopped celery
1/4 cup chopped parsley
2 tablespoons honey
1/2 teaspoon salt
1 cup oat bran
2 cups whole wheat flour
1 1/4 cup unbleached all-purpose flour

1. Dissolve yeast in warm water in a large bowl.

2. Place milk, oil, egg whites, cabbage, carrots, celery, parsley, honey, and salt in blender container and blend until puréed. Add to dissolved yeast.

3. Combine oat bran, whole wheat flour, and all-purpose flour in a separate bowl. Gradually add to the vegetable purée, stirring vigorously, until the mixture will not absorb any additional flour.

4. Dust a kneading surface with flour and knead dough for 6 to 7 minutes, working in any of the remaining flour if possible. Finished dough should be pliable and free of lumps. Form into a ball.

5. Oil a large bowl. Turn dough into bowl and cover. Allow to rise in a warm spot for 60 to 90 minutes, until doubled in size.

6. Punch dough down and separate into equal halves. Allow to rest, covered, for 10 minutes.

7. Oil a baking sheet. Form dough into 2 round loaves and place on sheet. Cover and let rise for 30 minutes, until doubled in size.

8. Preheat oven to 350°F. Bake in top part of oven for 30 minutes or until lightly browned.

9. Turn out onto a wire rack to cool.

CEREALS AND PANCAKES

GRANOLAS

Granola, made from old-fashioned oats, grains, brans, and dried fruits, is a nutritious and healthful staple cereal that can be served with yogurt or skim milk and fresh fruit. It's also handy as an ingredient in other recipes such as stuffings and crusts. Make it and bake it in big batches. Because of the oils and fruits used in granolas, they taste fresher if kept in the refrigerator, though they can be stored on the shelf for two to three weeks.

We've suggested a number of ways to dress up granola with ingredients such as exotic dried fruits, nuts, nut butters, spices, wheat germ, and seeds. Feel free to experiment with new combinations and to expand on your favorites.

Use large 15 × 10-inch nonstick baking pans with edges for best results.

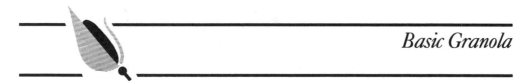

Basic Granola

A pure and wholesome staple for breakfasts or snacks that can be served with yogurt or milk and dressed up with fruit. Bake a big batch; it keeps well and is handy as an ingredient for stuffings, crisps, and pie crusts, too.

YIELD: 10 cups

PREPARATION TIME: 10 minutes

COOKING TIME: 40 to 60 minutes

RDOB PER CUP: 65%

1/2 cup honey

1/2 cup peanut or safflower oil

7 cups old-fashioned rolled oats

3 cups oat bran

1. Lightly oil two 15 × 10-inch baking pans. Preheat oven to 250°F.
2. Heat honey and oil in a saucepan over medium heat, stirring to blend.

3. Mix oats and oat bran in a large bowl. Drizzle honey mixture over them and mix until well coated.

4. Spread on baking sheets to a depth of 1/2 inch. (Bake any remaining granola in a second batch.)

5. Bake, stirring 2 or 3 times, for 40 to 60 minutes until the granola is lightly browned. Cool on the pans.

6. Keep refrigerated in airtight containers.

Baked Oil-Free Granola

Designed for calorie-conscious eaters, this granola contains no oil, but is very rich and flavorful.

YIELD: 6 cups

PREPARATION/COOKING TIME: 10 minutes

COOKING TIME: 30 to 40 minutes

RDOB PER CUP: 33%

2 cups old-fashioned rolled oats	1/2 cup sesame seeds
1 cup oat bran	1/2 cup chopped walnuts
1/2 cup honey	1/2 cup toasted wheat germ
1/2 cup brown sugar	1/2 cup raisins
1 teaspoon vanilla extract	

1. Preheat oven to 350°F.

2. Sprinkle oats and oat bran in a lightly oiled 9 × 13-inch baking pan and bake in oven for 10 minutes. Remove pan but leave oven on.

3. Mix honey, brown sugar, and vanilla in a bowl. Add to oat mixture and mix.

4. Stir in seeds and walnuts and toss lightly to mix.

5. Return pan to oven and bake for 20 to 30 minutes, stirring once or twice.

6. Remove from oven and cool. Stir in wheat germ and raisins.

7. Keep refrigerated in airtight containers.

Big-Batch Double-Bran Granola

If your cooking time is limited, this recipe, made with wheat bran as well as oat bran, will provide you with enough cold cereal to last for several weeks.

YIELD: 16 cups

PREPARATION TIME: 10 minutes

COOKING TIME: 40 minutes

RDOB PER CUP: 25%

5 cups old-fashioned rolled oats
1 1/2 cups oat bran
1 1/2 cups wheat bran
3 cups wheat germ

3 cups unsalted raw sunflower seeds
1 cup honey
1 tablespoon vanilla extract
1 cup peanut or safflower oil

1. Preheat oven to 300°F.

2. Mix oats, oat bran, wheat bran, wheat germ, and sunflower seeds in a large bowl. Combine honey, vanilla, and oil in a separate bowl. Pour over dry ingredients.

3. Spread half of mixture on two 15 × 10-inch baking pans to a depth of 1/2 inch or less. Bake, stirring once or twice, for 20 minutes or until evenly and lightly browned; be careful not to overcook. Bake second batch.

4. Can be stored in the refrigerator in airtight containers for up to 8 weeks.

Seed and Almond Granola

YIELD: 8 cups

PREPARATION TIME: 15 minutes

COOKING TIME: 1 hour 45 minutes

RDOB PER CUP: 25%

2 cups old-fashioned rolled oats
1 cup oat bran
1/2 cup wheat germ
1 cup raw unsalted sunflower
    seeds
1/4 cup sesame seeds

1/2 cup honey
1/4 cup peanut or safflower oil
1/2 cup cold water
1 cup chopped almonds
1/2 cup raisins

1. Lightly oil a large baking pan or 2 baking pans. Preheat oven to 225°F.

2. Combine oats, oat bran, wheat germ, sunflower seeds, and sesame seeds in a large bowl. Mix well.

3. Mix honey and oil in a second bowl. Pour over oat mixture and combine well. Slowly add water and stir until texture is crumbly.

4. Transfer mixture to two 15 × 10-inch baking pans and spread to edges. Bake in middle of oven for 1 hour 15 minutes, stirring 3 times.

5. Stir in almonds and bake for 30 minutes longer or until granola is crispy.

6. Turn off heat and cool granola in oven. Stir in raisins.

7. Keep refrigerated in an airtight container.

YIELD: 6 cups

PREPARATION TIME: 15 minutes

COOKING TIME: 35 minutes

RDOB PER CUP: 25%

1 cup old-fashioned rolled oats	1/3 cup brown sugar
1 cup oat bran	1/2 cup peanut or safflower oil
1/2 cup wheat germ	1/2 cup water
1/2 cup cornmeal	1 cup raisins
1/2 cup ground unsalted raw sunflower seeds	1 cup diced dried pineapple

1. Preheat oven to 300°F.
2. Combine oats, oat bran, wheat germ, cornmeal, sunflower seeds, sugar, oil, and water in a large bowl. Mix well.
3. Spread mixture 1/2 inch thick in two 15 × 10-inch baking pans. Bake, stirring once or twice, for 35 minutes or until lightly browned.
4. Allow granola to cool, then stir in raisins and pineapple.
5. Keep refrigerated in airtight containers.

Maple-Walnut Granola

YIELD: 5 cups

PREPARATION TIME: 10 minutes

COOKING TIME: 40 minutes

RDOB PER CUP: 30%

1 cup old-fashioned rolled oats
1 cup oat bran
1 cup chopped walnuts
1/3 cup peanut or safflower oil

1/4 cup maple syrup
1/2 teaspoon vanilla extract
1 cup raisins or other dried fruit

1. Preheat oven to 300°F.
2. Mix oats, oat bran, walnuts, oil, maple syrup, and vanilla in a large bowl.
3. Spread mixture in two 15 × 10-inch baking pans and bake for 40 minutes. Stir twice to allow granola to brown evenly.
4. Cool. Add raisins and mix well.
5. Keep refrigerated in an airtight container.

Raisin-Peanut-Sunflower Granola

YIELD: 6 cups

PREPARATION TIME: 15 minutes

COOKING TIME: 35 minutes, plus 5 minutes
to toast oats

RDOB PER CUP: 38%

2 1/2 cups old-fashioned rolled oats
1 cup oat bran
1 cup raisins
1/2 cup chopped peanuts
1/2 cup sunflower seeds

2/3 cup tub margarine, melted
1/3 cup honey
2 egg whites
1/2 teaspoon vanilla extract

1. Toast oats in a heavy-bottomed dry skillet for 5 minutes, stirring to prevent burning.

2. Preheat oven to 300°F.

3. Combine toasted oats, oat bran, raisins, peanuts, seeds, margarine, and honey in a large bowl. Beat egg whites and vanilla together in a second bowl and stir into oat mixture. Combine well.

4. Spread mixture 1/2 inch thick on two 15 × 10-inch baking pans. Bake for 35 minutes.

5. Keep refrigerated in airtight containers.

Nut Butter-Cinnamon-Raisin Granola

YIELD: 8 cups

PREPARATION TIME: 15 minutes

COOKING TIME: 35 to 40 minutes, plus 1 1/2 hours standing time

RDOB PER CUP: 31%

2/3 cup unhydrogenated peanut butter or almond butter

2/3 cup honey

1/2 teaspoon cinnamon

1 teaspoon vanilla extract

3 cups old-fashioned rolled oats

1 cup oat bran

1 cup raisins

1 cup unsalted peanuts

1. Preheat oven to 300°F.

2. Combine peanut butter, honey, and cinnamon in a saucepan and stir until they are all liquefied. Stir in vanilla.

3. Spread oats and oat bran in two 15 × 10-inch baking pans. Drizzle with peanut/honey mixture and stir to coat uniformly.

4. Bake for 35 to 40 minutes. Remove from oven and turn off heat, keeping door closed.

5. Add raisins and peanuts to mixture in baking pan. Stir well. Put pan back in turned-off oven for 1 1/2 hours.

6. Keep refrigerated in an airtight container.

Stove-Top Oil-Free Granola

This oil-free mixture features toasted oats, peanuts, wheat germ, and sunflower seeds.

YIELD: 3 cups

PREPARATION TIME: 10 minutes

COOKING TIME: 20 minutes

RDOB PER CUP: 17%

1 cup old-fashioned rolled oats
1/3 cup chopped unsalted peanuts
1/3 cup wheat germ
1/3 cup unsalted raw sunflower seeds
1 tablespoon brown sugar
1/2 cup raisins

1. Put oats and peanuts in a large dry skillet and toast, stirring, over medium heat for 5 minutes.
2. Add wheat germ and sunflower seeds and continue stirring over medium heat for 10 more minutes.
3. Add brown sugar. Cook, stirring, for 5 more minutes.
4. Remove from heat and add raisins. Cool.
5. Keep refrigerated in an airtight container.

FAMILIAS AND MUESLI

Oat bran and rolled oats can also be used in preparing other kinds of cold cereals, including uncooked familias and mueslis. Familia is quite similar to granola but is made from uncooked oats and eaten raw. Muesli is mixed with liquids, soaked, and chilled in the refrigerator before serving.

Try alternating these recipes with granola or hot cereal for a variety of breakfast and snack taste treats.

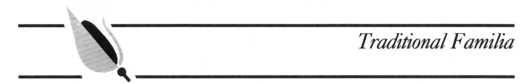

Traditional Familia

The added wheat germ in this recipe is a good source of insoluble fiber.

YIELD: 10 cups

PREPARATION TIME: 10 minutes

RDOB PER CUP: 20%

1 cup oat bran
2 cups rolled oats
1 1/2 cups toasted wheat germ
1 cup chopped dried apricots
1 cup chopped almonds, peanuts, or walnuts

3 cups wheat bran or wheat flakes
2 cups raisins
1/2 cup brown sugar (optional)

1. Mix all ingredients together in a bowl.
2. Keep refrigerated in airtight containers.

Processed Cold Cereal Mix

This mix is processed in a food processor or blender and is more finely textured than the other cold cereals. Try it with skim milk.

YIELD: 11 cups

PREPARATION TIME: 10 minutes

RDOB PER CUP: 27%

2 cups rolled oats

1 cup wheat flakes

2 cups oat bran

2 cups wheat germ

1 cup chopped pitted prunes

1/2 cup chopped pecans

1/2 cup chopped dates

1/2 cup unsalted raw sunflower seeds

1 teaspoon cinnamon

1. Stir all ingredients together in a large bowl.
2. Chop with the steel blade of a food processor or in batches in a blender at medium setting for 1 minute, stirring once or twice while motor is off.
3. Keep refrigerated in airtight containers.

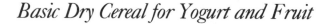

Basic Dry Cereal for Yogurt and Fruit

By preparing this high-fiber mix in advance, you'll have it ready to sprinkle over seasonal fresh fruit and low-fat or nonfat yogurt. Good fruit choices include apples, plums, peaches, bananas, blueberries, grapes, strawberries, cherries, oranges, pineapple, nectarines, and pears.

YIELD: 4 cups

PREPARATION TIME: 5 minutes

RDOB PER CUP: 38%

1 cup old-fashioned rolled oats

1 cup oat bran

1 cup wheat bran

2 tablespoons sesame seeds

2 tablespoons chopped walnuts

1/2 cup raisins, currants, or chopped dates

1 teaspoon cinnamon

1. Combine all ingredients in a bowl and mix well.
2. Keep refrigerated in an airtight container.

Orange-Apricot Muesli

Tangy apricots and orange juice give this muesli a real wake-up edge.

YIELD: 6 servings

PREPARATION TIME: 10 minutes, plus overnight standing time

RDOB PER SERVING: 25%

1 cup old-fashioned rolled oats	1/2 cup orange juice
1 cup oat bran	1/3 cup wheat germ
1 1/4 cups skim milk	1/4 cup honey
3/4 cup dried apricots, cut in quarters	

1. Mix all ingredients together in a large bowl.
2. Cover and refrigerate overnight.
3. Mix again before serving. Can be refrigerated in airtight containers for 1 day.

Portable Hot or Cold Cereal

An ideal take-along mix for eating on the road, in a hotel, or while camping. Keep a supply in your office desk, packed in an airtight container, for emergency meals and snacks.

YIELD: 7 cups

PREPARATION TIME: 15 minutes

RDOB PER CUP: 20%

3/4 cups rolled oats	1/2 cup chopped dried apricots
1 cup oat bran	1/2 cup chopped dried peaches
3/4 cup wheat flakes	1/3 cup unsalted raw sunflower seeds
1 1/2 cups nonfat dry milk powder	1/3 cup chopped almonds
3/4 cup wheat germ	
1/2 cup raisins	

1. Mix all ingredients together in a large bowl.

2. When ready to serve, add boiling water for hot cereal or cold water for cold cereal.

3. Keep refrigerated in airtight containers.

Apple-Walnut Muesli

This moist muesli stays fresh and delicious for 2 or 3 days if refrigerated. It can be eaten right away, without soaking, if you can't wait. (A friend from Germany serves it this way as a quick family dinner.)

YIELD: 10 servings (3/4 cup)

PREPARATION TIME: 10 minutes, plus 3 hours or overnight soaking time

RDOB PER SERVING: 13%

1 1/2 cups old-fashioned rolled oats
1/2 cup oat bran
2 cups skim milk
4 apples, cored and grated
1 tablespoon lemon juice
2 teaspoons vanilla extract
1/2 teaspoon cinnamon

1/2 cup raisins
2 tablespoons honey
1/3 cup wheat germ
1/4 cup chopped walnuts
1/2 cup unsalted raw sunflower seeds

1. Mix oats, oat bran, milk, apples, lemon juice, vanilla, cinnamon, raisins, and honey together in a glass or ceramic bowl.

2. Let soak in refrigerator for at least 3 hours (or overnight). The resulting mixture will have a thick texture.

3. Add wheat germ, walnuts, and sunflower seeds and stir well. Serve with additional skim milk.

Yogurt-Berry Breakfast

Create this unusual breakfast dish by combining uncooked raw oats, yogurt, honey, walnuts, lemon juice, and the berries of your choice.

YIELD: 6 servings

PREPARATION TIME: 10 minutes

RDOB PER SERVING: 8%

1 cup old-fashioned rolled oats
1 cup low-fat or nonfat plain yogurt
3 tablespoons honey
1/4 cup ground walnuts

Juice of 2 lemons
1 quart blueberries (or strawberries, cut in half), washed and drained

1. Stir oats, yogurt, honey, walnuts, and lemon juice together in a large bowl.
2. Mix in berries and serve.
3. Keep refrigerated in an airtight container.

Banana-Orange Muesli

This fruited muesli is ready for you in the morning and is good with skim milk or low-fat or nonfat yogurt.

YIELD: 2 servings

PREPARATION TIME: 5 minutes, plus overnight soaking time

RDOB: 25%

1 cup old-fashioned rolled oats
1 cup orange juice
1 apple

1 banana
2 tablespoons raisins
1 tablespoon chopped walnuts

1. In a mixing bowl, soak oats in orange juice overnight.
2. Before serving, core and grate apple and slice banana.
3. Add apple, banana, raisins, and walnuts to oat/orange juice mixture and serve.

HOT CEREALS

Hot cereal is one of the keystones of oat cookery. In addition to being the most familiar oat dish, it offers a quick, efficient way to get a high percentage of your recommended daily quantity of oat bran.

Hot oat cereal can be made from oat bran, rolled oats, or steel-cut ("Irish" or "Scottish") oats. The following recipes are diverse enough to punch up any breakfast menu.

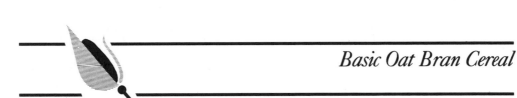

Basic Oat Bran Cereal

This dish offers the double advantage of a high RDOB and quick cooking. In two minutes, you can prepare a breakfast dish that will provide one third of your daily recommended oat bran intake.

YIELD: 2 servings

PREPARATION/COOKING TIME: 5 minutes

RDOB PER SERVING: 33%

2 cups water
1/8 teaspoon salt (optional)
2/3 cup oat bran

1. Bring water and salt (if desired) to a boil in a medium-size saucepan and slowly sprinkle in oat bran while stirring.
2. Lower heat and simmer for 2 minutes, stirring once or twice.
3. Serve with tub margarine and/or skim milk.

FRUIT BRAN CEREAL   Core a small apple and grate into cooked cereal. Add 2 tablespoons raisins or currants to boiling water right after the bran.

Creamy Oat Bran Cereal

This method makes a more liquid, creamier oat bran cereal, with the added nutritional advantage of skim milk.

YIELD: 2 servings

PREPARATION TIME: 12 minutes

RDOB PER SERVING: 25%

1 cup water	1/8 teaspoon salt (optional)
1 cup skim milk	1/2 cup oat bran

1. Bring water, milk, and salt (if desired) to a boil in a medium-size saucepan.
2. Slowly sprinkle in oat bran while stirring. Reduce heat and simmer for 10 minutes, stirring 2 or 3 times to prevent sticking.

Strawberries and "Cream" Oat Bran

YIELD: 2 servings

PREPARATION/COOKING TIME: 15 minutes

RDOB PER SERVING: 25%

1 cup evaporated skim milk	1/8 teaspoon salt (optional)
1 cup water or apple-strawberry juice	2 tablespoons pure-fruit strawberry preserves
1/2 cup oat bran	

1. Bring milk, water, and salt (if desired) to a boil in a medium-size saucepan.
2. Slowly sprinkle in oat bran while stirring. Reduce heat and simmer for 10 minutes, stirring 2 or 3 times.
3. Remove from heat and stir in preserves.

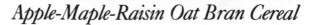

Apple-Maple-Raisin Oat Bran Cereal

YIELD: 2 servings

PREPARATION/COOKING TIME: 12 minutes

RDOB PER SERVING: 25%

1 cup apple juice

1 cup skim milk

1 teaspoon maple syrup or
brown sugar

1/8 teaspoon salt (optional)

1/4 cup raisins

1/2 cup oat bran

1. Bring apple juice, milk, syrup, salt (if desired), and raisins to a boil in a medium-size saucepan.

2. Slowly sprinkle in oat bran while stirring. Reduce heat and simmer for 10 minutes, stirring once or twice.

Creamy Maple Oat Bran Cereal

YIELD: 2 servings

PREPARATION TIME: 12 minutes

RDOB PER SERVING: 25%

1 cup water

1 cup evaporated skim milk

1 teaspoon maple syrup

1/4 cup raisins

1/8 teaspoon salt (optional)

1/2 cup oat bran

1. Bring water, milk, maple syrup, raisins, and salt (if desired) to a boil in a small saucepan.

2. Slowly sprinkle in oat bran while stirring. Reduce heat and simmer for 10 minutes, stirring 2 or 3 times.

Creamy Orange–Raisin Oat Bran

YIELD: 2 servings

PREPARATION/COOKING TIME: 15 minutes

RDOB PER SERVING: 25%

1 cup evaporated skim milk	1/2 cup oat bran
1 cup orange juice	1 teaspoon honey
1/8 teaspoon salt (optional)	1/4 cup raisins

1. Combine milk, juice, and salt (if desired) in a saucepan and simmer.
2. Slowly sprinkle in oat bran while stirring. Reduce heat. Add honey and raisins and simmer for 10 minutes, stirring 2 or 3 times.

Pear Porridge

YIELD: 4 servings

PREPARATION/COOKING TIME: 5 minutes

RDOB PER SERVING: 25%

3 cups pear nectar	1/2 teaspoon cinnamon
1/4 teaspoon salt (optional)	4 tablespoons raisins
1 cup oat bran	

1. Bring pear nectar and salt (if desired) to a boil in a medium-size saucepan. Slowly sprinkle in oat bran while stirring.
2. Reduce heat and simmer for 2 minutes until thickened.
3. Stir in cinnamon and raisins.

Pineapple-Apricot Oat Bran Cereal

YIELD: 2 servings

PREPARATION TIME: 12 minutes

RDOB PER SERVING: 25%

1 cup pineapple juice	1/4 cup chopped, dried apricots
1 cup skim milk	1/8 teaspoon salt (optional)
1 teaspoon honey	1/2 cup oat bran

1. Bring pineapple juice, milk, honey, apricots, and salt (if desired) to a boil in a medium-size saucepan.
2. Slowly sprinkle in oat bran while stirring. Reduce heat and simmer for 10 minutes, stirring 2 or 3 times.

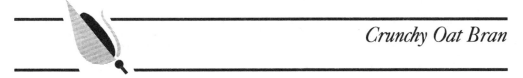

Crunchy Oat Bran

Toasted oat groats give contrasting texture to this maple-flavored dish.

YIELD: 2 servings

PREPARATION/COOKING TIME: 15 minutes

RDOB PER SERVING: 25%

1 cup skim milk	1/2 cup oat bran
1 cup water	1 teaspoon maple syrup
1/8 teaspoon salt (optional)	2 tablespoons oat groats

1. Bring milk, water, and salt (if desired) to a boil in a medium-size saucepan.
2. Slowly sprinkle in oat bran while stirring. Reduce heat. Add maple syrup and simmer for 10 minutes.
3. Toast oat groats in a dry skillet over low heat for 3 to 5 minutes.
4. Stir into cooked oat bran and serve.

Creamy Rolled Oat Cereal

This longer cooking method that starts with cold water and milk makes a smooth, blended cereal. Serve it with freshly cut fruit, honey, maple syrup, or tub margarine.

YIELD: 4 servings

PREPARATION/COOKING TIME: 10 minutes

RDOB PER SERVING: 25%

2 cups rolled oats	2 cups skim milk
2 cups water	1/4 teaspoon salt (optional)

1. Combine oats, water, milk, and salt (if desired) in a large saucepan. Bring to a boil.
2. Lower heat and simmer for 10 minutes, stirring 2 or 3 times.

Breakfast Crunch

The toasted flavor of this textured oatmeal is a nice surprise.

YIELD: 4 servings

PREPARATION/COOKING TIME: 20 minutes

RDOB PER SERVING: 17%

1 1/3 cups old-fashioned rolled oats	1/4 teaspoon salt (optional)
2 cups skim milk	1/4 cup chopped walnuts
1 cup water	1 teaspoon maple syrup

1. Toast oats in a dry skillet for 5 minutes, stirring frequently, or place them on a baking sheet and bake for 15 minutes at 350°F.
2. Combine milk and water in a medium-size saucepan. Heat, stirring to keep milk from sticking to the pan. Add oats, salt (if desired), walnuts, and maple syrup. Simmer for 6 minutes, stirring as needed.
3. Cover and set aside for 2 minutes. Serve hot.

Country Breakfast Oats

Make this creamy oatmeal and let it stand while you get dressed in the morning.

YIELD: 4 servings

PREPARATION/COOKING TIME: 20 minutes

RDOB PER SERVING: 13%

1 cup rolled oats	1/8 teaspoon cinnamon
3 cups water	2 sliced bananas
1/4 teaspoon salt (optional)	Skim milk
1/4 cup raisins or currants	

1. Stir oats and salt (if desired) into boiling water in a large saucepan. Lower heat and cook for 3 minutes.
2. Remove pan from heat.
3. Add raisins and cinnamon. Cover and let stand in a warm spot for 12 to 15 minutes.
4. Serve with sliced bananas and skim milk.

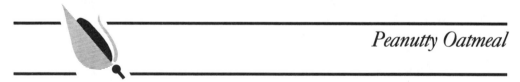

Peanutty Oatmeal

Peanut butter makes a surprise appearance in this rolled oat cereal. Try serving with sliced bananas, honey, and skim milk.

YIELD: 4 servings

PREPARATION/COOKING TIME: 6 minutes

RDOB PER SERVING: 17%

3 cups water	2 tablespoons unhydrogenated peanut butter
1 1/3 cup rolled oats	
1/4 teaspoon salt (optional)	

1. Bring water to a boil in a large saucepan. Add oats and salt (if desired) and stir over medium heat for 1 minute.
2. Add peanut butter. Continue cooking, stirring, until the oatmeal has thickened, about 2 to 5 minutes.

Allspice Oat Cereal

Apples and spice flavor this combination of both rolled oats and oat bran.

YIELD: 2 servings

PREPARATION/COOKING TIME: 5 minutes

COOKING TIME: 6 to 8 minutes

RDOB PER SERVING: 31%

2 cups water	1/4 cup oat bran
1/2 large apple, chopped	1 tablespoon maple syrup
3/4 cup old-fashioned rolled oats	1 teaspoon tub margarine
1/8 teaspoon salt (optional)	
Dash each nutmeg, cinnamon, and allspice	

1. Bring water to a boil in a medium-size saucepan. Add apples. Stir in rolled oats and salt (if desired). Reduce heat and simmer for 5 minutes.
2. Add nutmeg, cinnamon, and allspice. Stir in oat bran.
3. Remove from heat, cover, and let sit for 2 minutes. Add maple syrup and margarine right before serving.

Banana-Walnut Oatmeal

Toasted nuts provide a crunchy contrast in this blend of oats, bananas and raisins.

YIELD: 2 servings

PREPARATION/COOKING TIME: 10 minutes

RDOB PER SERVING: 17%

1/4 cup chopped walnuts	1/8 teaspoon salt (optional)
1/4 cup raisins	1 banana, sliced
1 1/2 cups water	1/2 teaspoon cinnamon
	2/3 cup quick rolled oats

1. Toast walnuts in a dry heavy skillet over medium heat for 3 to 5 minutes until lightly browned. Set aside.

2. Place raisins in water in a medium-size saucepan and bring to a boil. Stir in oats and salt (if desired). Reduce heat and simmer 1 minute until mixture has thickened. Remove from heat.

3. Stir in walnuts, sliced bananas, and cinnamon.

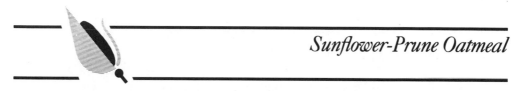

Sunflower-Prune Oatmeal

When serving try substituting orange juice for milk in this delightful melange of seeds, prunes, honey, and oats.

YIELD: 2 servings

PREPARATION/COOKING TIME: 10 minutes

RDOB PER SERVING: 17%

1 1/2 cups water	1/8 teaspoon cinnamon
2/3 cup rolled oats	1 tablespoon unsalted raw sunflower seeds
1/8 teaspoon salt (optional)	
6 pitted prunes, chopped	1 tablespoon honey

1. Bring water to a boil in a medium-size saucepan. Stir in oats, salt (if desired), prunes, and cinnamon.

2. Lower heat and simmer 4 to 5 minutes until thick. Stir in sunflower seeds and honey.

Sesame-Cinnamon Oatmeal

The sesame seeds add a bit of light flavor and texture to this oatmeal.

YIELD: 2 servings

PREPARATION/COOKING TIME: 12 minutes

RDOB PER SERVING: 13%

1 cup water
1/4 cup raisins
1/2 cup old-fashioned rolled oats
1/8 teaspoon salt (optional)

1/4 teaspoon vanilla extract
1/2 teaspoon cinnamon
1/4 cup unsalted sesame seeds

1. Bring water and raisins to a boil in a small saucepan.
2. Stir oats and salt (if desired).
3. Lower heat and simmer for 5 minutes, stirring as needed. Add vanilla and cinnamon.
4. Spoon into serving bowls and top with sesame seeds.

SUNFLOWER-CINNAMON OATMEAL   Substitute 1/4 cup unsalted raw sunflower seeds for the sesame seeds.

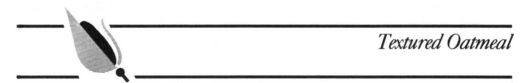

Steel-Cut Porridge

Also called Irish oatmeal, steel-cut oats offer a nuttier, firmer, and more textured change of pace.

YIELD: 2 servings

PREPARATION/COOKING TIME: 25 to 30 minutes

RDOB PER SERVING: 25%

2 cups water   1/8 teaspoon salt
1 cup steel-cut oats

1. Bring water to a boil in a medium-size saucepan. Stir in oats and salt (if desired).
2. Lower heat, cover pan, and simmer for 25 to 30 minutes, stirring once or twice.
3. Serve with tub margarine, skim milk, and honey, or with the traditional accompaniment, fresh buttermilk.

Textured Oatmeal

If you prefer your oatmeal with more texture and "chew," and you don't like creamy porridge, try this cooking method.

YIELD: 2 servings

PREPARATION/COOKING TIME: 6 minutes

RDOB PER SERVING: 25%

1 cup old-fashioned rolled oats   1 1/2 cups boiling water
1/4 teaspoon salt (optional)

1. Put oats and salt (if desired) in a warm dish.
2. Pour boiling water over oats and stir well.
3. Cover tightly and let stand for 5 minutes before serving.

For a different way to enjoy your morning oatmeal, try this pioneer standard. Prepare the oatmeal the day before, or, even better, use leftover oatmeal that has been stored in the refrigerator.

YIELD: 6 servings

PREPARATION TIME: 20 minutes, plus 24 hours chilling time

RDOB PER SERVING: 21%

3 3/4 cups water

2 cups rolled oats

1/4 teaspoon salt (optional)

2 tablespoons maple syrup

1/2 teaspoon cinnamon

1/2 cup raisins

1/4 cup oat bran

3 tablespoons peanut or safflower oil

1. Oil a 9×5-inch loaf pan.
2. Bring water to a boil in a large saucepan and stir in oats and salt (if desired). Lower heat and simmer for 5 minutes, stirring once or twice.
3. Remove from heat and stir in maple syrup, cinnamon, and raisins.
4. Pour into loaf pan and refrigerate for 24 hours.
5. Cut into 1/2-inch slices and dust lightly with oat bran.
6. Sauté in oil in a skillet over medium heat until crisp and lightly browned. Serve hot with yogurt, all-fruit preserves, or unsweetened applesauce.

Oat Pancakes

With the extra nutty flavor of oats, these are simply delicious. Make these quickly because the batter thickens as it sits. Add a little liquid at the end if becomes too stiff. Serve them hot with syrup, all-fruit jam, applesauce, or fresh fruit.

YIELD: 12 pancakes

PREPARATION TIME: 10 minutes

COOKING TIME: 5 minutes

RDOB FOR 4 PANCAKES: 25%

1 1/3 cups milk
  2 egg whites or 1 whole egg
  2 tablespoons peanut oil

1 tablespoon honey or maple syrup
1 tablespoon baking powder
1/4 teaspoon salt
1 1/2 cups oat flour (page 47)

1. Put milk, eggs, oil, honey, baking powder, salt, and finally oat flour into the blender or food processor and blend until mixed. If no blender is available, combine ingredients in a large bowl and beat with an egg beater or a wire whisk for a few minutes. Batter can be a little lumpy.

2. Pour batter by 1/4 cups onto lightly greased hot griddle or skillet. Turn when bubbles have popped and steam has stopped rising. Brown lightly on the second side.

Banana and lemon flavors make these a rich and unusual breakfast treat. Serve with spiced yogurt, fruit, applesauce, or a little honey or syrup.

YIELD: 9 pancakes

PREPARATION TIME: 10 minutes

COOKING TIME: 10 minutes

RDOB FOR 3 PANCAKES: 17%

2 egg whites

2 tablespoons peanut or safflower oil

1 1/2 cups mashed, ripe bananas (about 3 bananas)

2 teaspoons fresh lemon juice

1/3 cup water

1/4 teaspoon salt (optional)

1 cup oat flour (page 47)

1. Beat egg whites with a whisk or fork in a large bowl. Add oil, bananas, lemon juice, water and salt (if desired) and beat 1 minute.

2. Using a wooden spoon, mix in oat flour. Batter should be wet enough to spread a little when poured onto pan; add a little water if it is too stiff.

3. Pour 1/3 cup batter on lightly oiled medium-hot griddle or skillet. Cook 2 or 3 pancakes at a time, depending on size of pan. Cook until browned, about 1 minute on each side.

Puréed Fruit Pancakes

Here's an unusual and great way to make silver dollar pancakes and use up leftover pumpkin after the Halloween pumpkin has been carved or Thanksgiving dinner is over.

YIELD: 32 pancakes (4 servings)

PREPARATION TIME: 15 minutes, plus 20 minutes soaking time

COOKING TIME: 15 minutes

RDOB FOR 8 PANCAKES: 19%

1/2 cup old-fashioned rolled oats

1 2/3 cups skim milk

3 egg whites, beaten

1 tablespoon peanut or safflower oil

1/2 cup puréed pumpkin, apples, peaches, or pears

1/2 cup oat bran

1/4 cup whole wheat pastry flour

1/4 cup unbleached all-purpose flour

2 tablespoons wheat germ

1 teaspoon brown sugar

1. In a large bowl, pour 1 1/3 cups milk over oats and let soak for 20 minutes.

2. Add egg whites, oil, pumpkin, and remaining 1/3 cup milk. Stir well.

3. Combine oat bran, flours, wheat germ, and sugar in a separate bowl. Add to pumpkin mixture.

4. Pour 2 tablespoons batter on a lightly oiled hot griddle or skillet. When bubbles on the top side begin to break, turn and brown the second side.

Try topping these with applesauce or a mixture of raw apples, nuts, and raisins. You might also serve them with fresh berries and yogurt or sliced fresh peaches.

YIELD: 8 pancakes

PREPARATION TIME: 10 minutes

COOKING TIME: 10 minutes

RDOB FOR 4 PANCAKES: 44%

2 cups skim milk

1/4 cup rolled oats

3/4 cup oat bran

1 teaspoon grated lemon peel

1/4 teaspoon salt (optional)

1 teaspoon brown sugar

2 tablespoons peanut or safflower oil

3 egg whites, stiffly beaten

1. Pour milk into a saucepan and bring to a boil. Lower heat and add oats and oat bran. Cook for about 1 minute, until mixture thickens.

2. Add lemon peel, salt (if desired), brown sugar, and oil.

3. Fold in egg whites. Add milk if you prefer a thinner batter.

4. Pour batter on lightly oiled hot griddle or skillet, 1/3 cup for each pancake. When bubbles begin to break on the pancake's surface, turn over and brown the second side.

English Breakfast "Pancake"

An English friend calls this a pancake, but it is also like a big, flat, hearty oat scone. Eat it hot with margarine and syrup or cold as a snack for a high oat bran boost.

YIELD: 4 servings

PREPARATION TIME: 10 minutes

COOKING TIME: 25 minutes

RDOB PER SERVING: 38%

3 tablespoons tub margarine	1 egg white
1/3 cup maple syrup, golden syrup, or molasses	1 1/2 cups oat bran
1/3 cup skim milk	1/2 cup unbleached all-purpose flour
	1/8 teaspoon salt

1. Lightly oil a 9-inch square pan and dust with oat bran. Preheat oven to 375°F.

2. Melt margarine in a 1-quart saucepan. Add syrup, milk, and egg white and beat well.

3. Add oat bran, flour, and salt and mix.

4. Spread in prepared pan and smooth surface. Bake for 25 minutes until very lightly browned.

CRUNCHY BREAKFAST "PANCAKE"   For even more crunch, add 2 tablespoons sunflower seeds or sesame seeds.

Apple Bran Pancakes

Wheat germ, sunflower seeds, and lemon combine with chopped apple to create a hearty, thick pancake batter. Make this recipe quickly because the batter will thicken as it stands.

YIELD: 12 pancakes

PREPARATION TIME: 15 minutes

COOKING TIME: 10 minutes

RDOB FOR 3 PANCAKES: 25%

1 cup whole wheat pastry flour
1 cup rolled oats
1/2 cup oat bran
1/4 cup wheat germ
2 tablespoons unsalted raw sunflower seeds
4 teaspoons baking powder
1/8 teaspoon cinnamon

1 1/2 cups skim milk
3 egg whites, lightly beaten
1 tablespoon peanut or safflower oil
1 teaspoon vanilla extract
1 apple, chopped
1 teaspoon grated lemon peel

1. Mix together flour, oats, oat bran, wheat germ, sunflower seeds, baking powder, and cinnamon in a large bowl.

2. Combine milk, egg whites, oil, and vanilla in a second bowl. Stir in apple and lemon peel. Add to flour mixture and mix.

3. Pour 3 tablespoons batter per pancake on a lightly oiled hot griddle; since the batter is extremely thick, spread with a spatula right after you pour them. Add milk if too thick. Cook over low heat until lightly browned. Turn and brown the second side.

Gingerbread Pancakes

These spicy pancakes are seasoned with molasses, cinnamon and ginger. The prepared batter will keep in the refrigerator for two days.

YIELD: 12 pancakes

PREPARATION TIME: 15 minutes

COOKING TIME: 15 minutes

RDOB FOR 3 PANCAKES: 19%

1 1/2 cups skim milk

3/4 cup oat bran

1 cup unbleached all-purpose flour

1 1/2 teaspoons baking powder

3/4 teaspoon ground cinnamon

1/4 to 1/2 teaspoon ground ginger

1/4 teaspoon baking soda

3 egg whites

2 tablespoons peanut or safflower oil

2 tablespoons molasses

1. Scald milk in a small saucepan over low heat. Slowly stir in oat bran. Remove pan from heat and let stand 5 minutes.

2. Combine flour, baking powder, cinnamon, ginger, and baking soda in a large bowl. Set aside.

3. Beat together egg whites, oil, and molasses in a second bowl. Stir into oat mixture.

4. Add oat mixture to flour mixture and stir until moistened.

5. For each pancake, pour 1/4 cup batter on lightly greased hot griddle or skillet. (Add water, a tablespoon at a time, if batter is too thick to pour.) Cook until lightly browned. When surface bubbles begin to burst and edges are set, turn and cook other side until golden brown.

6. Serve with sliced fruit, low-fat yogurt mixed with a little cinnamon and vanilla, or pure fruit jam or marmalade.

These delicate Scandinavian-style pancakes are slightly thicker than crepes but are also traditionally filled and rolled, then topped with yogurt. Fill them with fresh fruit or mashed bananas, spread with honey, or peanut butter, or roll them without a filling and sprinkle the yogurt topping with nuts or maple syrup. They can also be simply enjoyed in a stack.

YIELD: 8 pancakes

PREPARATION TIME: 25 minutes

COOKING TIME: 10 minutes

RDOB FOR 4 PANCAKES: 38%

2 egg whites, beaten
1 cup skim milk
3/4 cup oat bran

2 tablespoons peanut or safflower oil
1 tablespoon honey

1. Combine all ingredients in a mixing bowl and whisk together until smooth. Let stand 15 minutes.
2. Pour 1/4 cup batter on a lightly oiled hot griddle or skillet. Cook about 1 minute, until bubbles on top begin to break. Turn and brown the second side for 30 seconds.
3. Stack pancakes on a warm plate as you cook. Keep the plate covered or wrapped in foil.

Oat Crepes

Making crepes will be a snap after you've done it a couple of times. Prepared crepes can be kept in a warm oven for a short period of time. Or do as the French do: Prepare them in the morning, stack and reheat them later in the day. Try serving these crepes with crushed fresh fruit, all-fruit preserves, or nonfat plain yogurt with a little cinnamon or maple syrup stirred in. As a main dish, serve rolled with fillings made from minced vegetables, seafood, or poultry.

YIELD: 6 crepes

PREPARATION TIME: 5 minutes, plus 30 minutes standing time

COOKING TIME: 15 minutes

RDOB PER CREPE: 13%

1/2 cup cold milk

1/2 cup cold water

2 egg whites plus 1 whole egg

2 tablespoons peanut or safflower oil

1/2 cup quick rolled oats

1/2 cup oat bran

2 tablespoons unbleached all-purpose flour

1/4 teaspoon salt (optional)

1. Place milk and water in blender container. Add rest of ingredients and blend at high speed for 30 seconds. Use a rubber spatula to loosen any flour that sticks to the container.

2. Cover and let stand for 30 minutes. The batter should be like thick cream; if it seems too thick, add 1 or 2 tablespoons milk. Stir before using.

3. Lightly oil a heavy 7-inch skillet or French crepe pan, or use a nonstick pan. Heat pan over a medium-high heat until hot.

4. Pour 1/3 cup batter into the pan. Quickly tip the pan, causing the batter to run and fill up the bottom with a thin layer. Cook for 1 or 2 minutes.

5. Gently loosen the edges with a wide spatula or cake turner and check the underside. If browned, gently slide the spatula under the crepe and flip over quickly. Brown for 1 more minute.

6. Continue to make crepes until batter is used.

Oat waffles are crisp and light if made quickly and with a hot waffle iron. The batter will thicken as it sits, so stir lightly before pouring each one.

YIELD: 8 waffles

PREPARATION TIME: 15 minutes

COOKING TIME: 15 minutes

RDOB PER WAFFLE: 9%

3/4 cup oat bran

1 cup unbleached all-purpose or whole wheat pastry flour

2 teaspoons baking powder

1 1/2 cups skim milk

3 tablespoons peanut or safflower oil

1 whole egg, separated

2 egg whites

1. Mix oat bran, flour, and baking powder in a large bowl.
2. Add milk, oil, and 1 egg yolk and mix until moistened.
3. Lightly oil waffle iron and turn on.
4. Beat the 3 egg whites until stiff and fold into batter.
5. Pour batter onto hot waffle iron and cook until lightly browned. Check after 1 or 2 minutes (when steam subsides) to see if done.

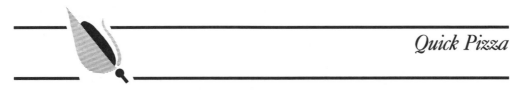

VEGETARIAN AND DAIRY MAIN DISHES

Quick Pizza

A crispy quick-bread crust and rich sauce make this a real pleaser that is well worth making. For variety, try any—or all—of the following toppings: 1/4 pound sliced ripe olives; 1/2 cup blanched broccoli or cauliflower pieces; 1/4 pound cooked chopped beef, lean Italian sausage, or sliced pepperoni. For the best crust, bake in a pizza pan with small holes in the bottom or on a pizza baking stone. The crust recipe can be doubled. (Roll out one round, and freeze the other half in a plastic bag for later use.)

YIELD: 6 servings

PREPARATION TIME: 30 minutes

COOKING TIME: 30 minutes

RDOB PER SERVING: 6%

CRUST:

- 3/4 cup oat flour (page 47)
- 3/4 cup whole wheat flour
- 3/4 cup unbleached all-purpose flour
- 1 teaspoon baking powder
- 1/4 teaspoon salt (optional)
- 2/3 cup milk
- 1/4 cup peanut or safflower oil

TOPPING:

- 1 small green pepper, cut into strips, or 1/2 green and 1/2 sweet red pepper
- 1 small onion, sliced into rings
- 8 ounces low-fat mozzarella cheese
- 6 or 7 fresh mushrooms, sliced
- 8 ounces spaghetti or pizza sauce
- Oregano, basil, and red peppers (optional)

1. Preheat oven to 425°F.
2. Combine oat, whole wheat, and all-purpose flours, baking powder, and salt (if desired) into a large bowl and mix well. Add milk and oil and mix to form a ball.

3. Knead dough about 10 times on a lightly floured surface. Use a rolling pin or long bottle to roll out into a thin circle the size of your pan (12-14 inches) and place on pan. Bake in lowest part of the hot oven for 15 minutes. (It will be partially baked.)

4. While crust is baking, cover peppers and onion with water in a sauce-pan and simmer for 5 minutes. Drain.

5. Grate mozzarella cheese by using a potato masher or grater with large holes.

6. Remove crust from the oven. Spread spaghetti sauce over the surface with a large spoon, sprinkle cheese loosely on top, and then add the peppers, onions, and mushrooms. Sprinkle on oregano, dried basil, and red peppers, if desired.

7. Return to oven and bake an additional 15 minutes, until cheese is bub-bly.

Vegetable Pizza

This pizza is made with quick-rising yeast which allows you to create a freshly baked crust in a hurry. While the dough rests, you're preparing the topping.

YIELD: 2 pizzas (8 servings)

PREPARATION TIME: 40 minutes

COOKING TIME: 15 minutes

RDOB PER SERVING: 9%

CRUST:

- 1 package (1/4 ounce) quick-rising yeast
- 1 cup warm water
- 4 tablespoons olive or safflower oil
- 1/2 teaspoon salt
- 1/2 cup oat bran
- 1/2 cup oat flour (page 47)
- 1 1/2 cups unbleached all-purpose flour
- 3/4 cup whole wheat flour

TOPPING:

- 1 onion, sliced or 1/2 cup sliced scallions
- 1 clove garlic, minced
- 2 celery stalks, thinly sliced
- 3/4 cup thinly sliced eggplant
- 2 tablespoons olive oil
- 1 can (16 ounces) Italian plum tomatoes
- 1 teaspoon dried basil
- 1 teaspoon dried oregano
- 3/4 cup chopped broccoli
- 3/4 cup chopped cauliflower
- 2 cups shredded low-fat mozzarella cheese (use a grater with large holes)
- 1/2 cup grated Parmesan cheese

1. Dissolve yeast in water in a medium-size bowl.

2. Add 3 tablespoons olive oil, salt, oat bran, and the three flours. Blend thoroughly.

3. Turn mixture out onto a floured surface and knead for 7 minutes. Let dough rest for 5 minutes.

4. Meanwhile, sauté onions, garlic, celery, and eggplant in olive oil in a large skillet until tender and lightly browned.

5. Add tomatoes, basil, and oregano and simmer 10 minutes.

6. In a covered saucepan, steam broccoli and cauliflower in a steamer basket in 1 inch boiling water until crisply tender, approximately 5 minutes.

7. Preheat oven to 475°F.

8. Divide dough into 2 parts and roll into two 11-inch circles. Place on two 11-inch pizza pans and brush with remaining 1 tablespoon olive oil.

9. Spoon tomato mixture over dough, then sprinkle mozzarella cheese evenly over tomato mixture.

10. Arrange broccoli and cauliflower on top of cheese. Sprinkle with Parmesan cheese.

11. Bake for 15 minutes in the lowest part of the oven. Let sit for 5 minutes before slicing.

QUICHES

Because quiches are generally made with high-fat ingredients such as cream, bacon, cheeses, and whole eggs, we've included some lighter alternatives here. Our quiches, which are baked in our Basic Oat Bran Pie Crust, include an egg yolk. Since there is only one used in six portions, you should be able to afford the milligrams of cholesterol unless you are on an extremely restricted diet. Because we're using fewer egg yolks and skim milk in these quiches, they may take slightly longer to set than quiches made with several yolks, whole milk, or cream, but the oat bran acts as an additional thickening agent.

To avoid spills, put the crust on a baking sheet in the hot oven and pour the milk mixture directly into the crust.

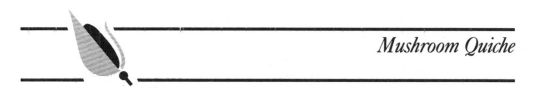

Mushroom Quiche

YIELD: 6 servings

PREPARATION TIME: 35 minutes

COOKING TIME: 40 minutes

RDOB PER SERVING: 12%

CRUST:

Dough for 1 Basic Oat Bran Pie Crust (page 272), omitting sugar

FILLING:

1 cup sliced mushrooms	1/4 grated Parmesan cheese
1 clove garlic, minced	1 whole egg plus 2 egg whites
1/2 cup onion, finely chopped	1 cup skim milk or buttermilk
1 tablespoon peanut or olive oil	1/4 cup oat bran
1 cup grated reduced-fat Swiss cheese or 1% cottage cheese	1/8 teaspoon black pepper
	1/4 teaspoon salt (optional)
	1/8 teaspoon nutmeg

1. Prepare crust and bake for 10 minutes only. Set aside to cool. Lower oven temperature to 375°F.

2. Sauté mushrooms, garlic, and onions in oil in a skillet until tender. Add Swiss cheese and Parmesan cheese and stir until well mixed.

3. Spread half the mixture on the bottom of the partially baked pie shell.

4. Beat eggs, milk, oat bran, pepper, salt, and nutmeg with a wire whisk or egg beater (or combine in blender or food processor until smooth if using cottage cheese). Pour over mushroom/cheese mixture in pie shell. Top with other half of mushroom/cheese mixture. Bake for 30 minutes until set. Let stand for 5 minutes before cutting and serving.

BROCCOLI QUICHE   Substitute 1 cup chopped steamed broccoli for the mushrooms. Add after garlic and onions are cooked.

Spinach Quiche

YIELD: 6 servings

PREPARATION TIME: 35 minutes

COOKING TIME: 40 minutes

RDOB PER SERVING: 13%

CRUST:

Dough for 1 Basic Oat Bran Pie Crust (page 272), omitting sugar

FILLING:

1/2 pound fresh spinach, trimmed and washed well

1 tablespoon safflower oil

1/2 cup finely chopped onion

1 cup grated reduced-fat Swiss cheese or 1% cottage cheese

1/4 cup grated Parmesan cheese

1 whole egg plus 2 egg whites

1 cup skim milk or buttermilk

1/4 cup oat bran

1/8 teaspoon black pepper

1/4 teaspoon salt (optional)

1/8 teaspoon nutmeg

1. Prepare crust and bake for 10 minutes only. Set aside to cool. Lower oven temperature to 375°F.

2. In a covered heavy-bottomed saucepan, cook spinach in 1/4 cup boiling water for 15 seconds to wilt. Drain well and squeeze out excess liquid. Chop well.

3. Heat oil in skillet and purée onion until soft. Add spinach and toss lightly. Remove from heat.

4. Combine Swiss and Parmesan cheese in a bowl. Sprinkle on bottom of partially baked pie shell. Spread spinach/onion mixture on top.

5. Beat eggs in a second bowl with a wire whisk or egg beaters. Add milk, oat bran, pepper, salt, and nutmeg (or combine in a blender or food processor until smooth if using cottage cheese). Carefully pour mixture over spinach and cheese in pie shell. Bake for 30 minutes until set. Let stand for 5 minutes before cutting and serving.

Ratatouille Flan

Served with some crusty French bread, this nutty, rich-flavored pie is a meal in itself.

YIELD: 4 servings

PREPARATION TIME: 25 minutes

COOKING TIME: 20 minutes

RDOB PER SERVING: 12%

CRUST:

Dough for 1 Basic Oat Bran
Pie Crust (page 272)

FILLING:

- 1 large onion, chopped
- 2 tablespoons olive or safflower oil
- 1 red pepper, thinly sliced
- 1 green pepper, thinly sliced
- 1 pound zucchini, sliced (unpeeled)
- 1 can (14 ounces) plum tomatoes
- 1 large clove garlic, crushed
- 1 teaspoon basil
- 1 teaspoon tarragon
- 1/4 teaspoon salt
- 1/8 teaspoon black pepper
- 1/4 cup oat bran
- 1/4 cup water
- 1 tablespoon minced parsley

1. Prepare crust and bake for 10 minutes only. Set aside to cool. Reduce oven temperature to 375°F.

2. While the crust is baking, sauté onions in oil in a large skillet for 5 minutes, stirring once or twice. Add peppers and zucchini and cook for 10 more minutes, stirring 2 or 3 times.

3. Add tomatoes (crush to break up whole pieces), garlic, basil, tarragon, salt, and pepper and simmer until vegetables are softened and sauce is a little thicker.

4. Add parsley, oat bran, and water and mix. Spoon filling into baked crust. Heat for 5 to 10 minutes. Serve hot.

Note: Filled pie can be frozen, then baked at 375°F. for 40 to 45 minutes.

The quick, easy filling is also puréed and used as a sauce for these satisfying crepes. You can make the ratatouille in advance to allow the flavors to blend.

YIELD: 6 crepes

PREPARATION TIME: 30 minutes

COOKING TIME: 55 to 60 minutes

RDOB PER CREPE: 15%

Batter for Oat Crepes (page 163)
1/3 cup olive oil
3 cloves garlic, minced
1 medium onion, chopped
3 zucchini, thinly sliced
1 medium eggplant, quartered and thinly sliced

2 tablespoons oat bran
2 green peppers, chopped
4 tomatoes, chopped
1 teaspoon dried basil
1 teaspoon dried oregano
1/2 cup grated Parmesan cheese
1/2 cup skim milk (optional)

1. Prepare Oat Crepes batter and let stand.
2. Heat oil and sauté garlic and onions until translucent. Set aside.
3. In a flat soup plate or plastic bag, toss zucchini and eggplant in oat bran. Add to onions.
4. Stir in peppers, tomatoes, basil, and oregano. Cover and cook 35 to 40 minutes until vegetables are tender.
5. Lightly oil a 9 × 13-inch baking pan. Preheat oven to 375°F.
6. Prepare six 7-inch crepes.
7. Place 2 to 3 tablespoons ratatouille on spotted (second) side of each crepe and sprinkle with 1 tablespoon Parmesan cheese. Roll up and place seam side down in baking dish. Repeat for remaining crepes and sprinkle with remaining Parmesan cheese. Bake for 20 minutes until bubbly.
8. Purée remaining ratatouille in a blender or food processor. Transfer to a saucepan and heat over a low heat. Add water if you prefer a thinner sauce.
9. Remove crepes from oven and pour sauce over them. Top with remaining Parmesan cheese. Serve hot.

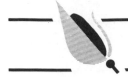

Crepes with Florentine Filling

This inexpensive yet elegant dish is made with our Oat Crepes recipe and is a subtle blend of spinach, fresh mushrooms, and cottage cheese. Double or triple the recipe for a brunch or dinner party.

YIELD: 6 crepes

PREPARATION TIME: 1 hour

COOKING TIME: 20 to 25 minutes

RDOB PER CREPE: 15%

Batter for Oat Crepes (page 163)

2 tablespoons tub margarine

3 tablespoons finely chopped onions

1 clove garlic, minced

1/2 cup chopped fresh mushrooms

2 tablespoons plus 1 teaspoon oat bran

1 1/4 cup skim or 1% milk

1 1/2 cups tightly packed chopped fresh spinach or 1 package chopped frozen spinach, defrosted

3/4 cup grated reduced-fat Swiss or mozzarella cheese

1/4 teaspoon ground black pepper

1/4 teaspoon ground fresh nutmeg

1/4 cup unsalted raw sunflower seeds

1 egg

1/2 cup 1% cottage cheese

1. Prepare Oat Crepes batter.

2. While letting batter stand, heat margarine in a heavy-bottomed, 2-quart saucepan. Add onions, garlic, and mushrooms and sauté for about 5 minutes until vegetables are softened.

3. Stir in oat bran. When mixture bubbles, add milk and bring to a simmer, stirring. Allow to simmer over low heat for 10 minutes, stirring occasionally.

4. Meanwhile, put fresh spinach in heavy-bottomed saucepan with 1/4 cup water and simmer, covered, for 1 minute. Then drain, squeeze out excess liquid, chop well. If using defrosted frozen spinach, do not cook but simply squeeze out excess liquid. Place spinach in a medium-size bowl.

5. Add 1/2 cup Swiss cheese, pepper, nutmeg, and sunflower seeds. Mix well.

6. Combine egg and cottage cheese in a separate bowl. Add to the spinach filling.

7. Stir half the oat/mushroom mixture into the spinach filling.

8. Prepare six 7-inch Oat Crepes.

9. Lightly oil a 9 × 13-inch baking pan. Preheat oven to 375°F.

10. With the spotted (second) side of the crepe up, put about 2 heaping tablespoons of the spinach mixture on one end of the crepe and roll up. Place in baking pan, seam side down. Repeat for remaining crepes, sprinkle with cheese, and top with remaining oat/mushroom mixture.

11. Bake for 20 to 25 minutes until bubbly.

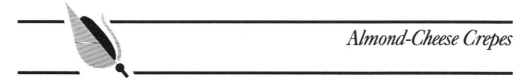

Almond-Cheese Crepes

Ground almonds and nutmeg flavor the fluffy cheese-yogurt filling. Try serving this dish with tomato soup and a salad of lettuce and oranges.

YIELD: 6 crepes

PREPARATION TIME: 45 minutes

COOKING TIME: 30 minutes

RDOB PER CREPE: 13%

Batter for Oat Crepes (page 163)

12 ounces skim ricotta cheese or 1% cottage cheese

4 egg whites

3/4 cup finely chopped almonds

1/2 cup freshly grated Parmesan cheese

1 cup low-fat or nonfat plain yogurt

1/4 teaspoon nutmeg

1. Prepare Oat Crepes batter and let stand.

2. Preheat oven to 325°F. Lightly oil a 9 × 13-inch baking pan.

3. Combine ricotta cheese and egg whites in blender at medium speed for 1 minute or with an egg beater in a mixing bowl until well combined.

4. Add almonds, Parmesan cheese, yogurt, and nutmeg. Mix well by hand.

5. Prepare six 7-inch crepes.

6. With spotted (second) side up, spread 2 tablespoons of the ricotta/almond mixture on one end of each crepe and roll up.

7. Place the crepes in prepared baking pan, seam side down, and cover.

8. Bake for 30 minutes, until bubbly.

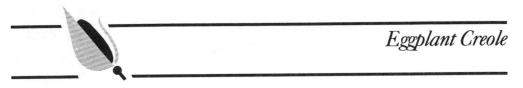

Eggplant Creole

Oat groats, celery, cloves, and walnuts are mixed with vegetables to produce a highly flavored stuffing for baked eggplant.

YIELD: 4 servings

PREPARATION TIME: 20 minutes

COOKING TIME: 1 1/2 to 1 3/4 hours

RDOB PER SERVING: 25%

2 cups oat groats, cooked in chicken broth (page 49)

1 medium to large eggplant

1 medium onion, chopped

1 green pepper, chopped

1/2 cup chopped celery

2 tablespoons olive or safflower oil

2 large tomatoes, chopped

2 tablespoons chopped walnuts

1/8 teaspoon cloves

1/8 teaspoon cayenne pepper

1/3 cup grated reduced-fat cheddar cheese

1 tablespoon tub margarine

1. Prepare oat groats.

2. Lightly oil an 8-inch square glass baking dish.

3. Cut stem off eggplant. Slice eggplant lengthwise; scoop out pulp and set aside. Brush hollow center of each eggplant with a little oil.

4. In a large skillet, sauté onion, green pepper, and celery in 2 tablespoons oil for 5 minutes until tender. Stir in tomatoes. Simmer on low heat for 5 minutes.

5. Preheat oven to 375°F.

6. Add walnuts, cloves, cayenne, and oat groats to vegetable mixture. Chop up reserved eggplant pulp and combine with mixture.

7. Place eggplant halves in baking dish. Stuff with vegetable/groat mixture. Sprinkle with cheese and dot with margarine.

8. Bake for 50 to 60 minutes until eggplant is tender.

Eggplant Parmigiana

This rich, filling dish can be assembled in advance, covered with plastic wrap, and refrigerated before baking. Serve with green salad and a fruit dessert.

YIELD: 4 servings

PREPARATION TIME: 15 minutes

COOKING TIME: 45 minutes

RDOB PER SERVING: 19%

1 medium eggplant

2 tomatoes, chopped

2/3 cup tomato juice

1/2 cup old-fashioned rolled oats

1/2 cup oat bran

2 tablespoons minced fresh basil or 1 teaspoon dried basil

1/4 teaspoon dried oregano

2 cloves garlic, minced

1/2 cup grated reduced-fat mozzarella cheese (use a large-hole grater)

2 tablespoons grated Parmesan cheese

1. Lightly oil a 1 1/2-quart casserole. Preheat oven to 350°F.

2. Cut eggplant into 1/2-inch slices. Place in overlapping layers in casserole dish; top with tomatoes.

3. Combine tomato juice, oats, oat bran, basil, oregano, and garlic in a small bowl. Spread over eggplant and tomatoes.

4. Sprinkle with mozzarella cheese, then with Parmesan.

5. Bake for 35 to 40 minutes or until lightly browned.

These baked boats make an excellent accompaniment to chicken or fish.

YIELD: 4 servings

PREPARATION TIME: 20 minutes

COOKING TIME: 30 to 40 minutes

RDOB PER SERVING: 19%

4 medium-size zucchini, washed and stem removed

1 clove garlic, minced

1/4 cup chopped onion

1/4 cup sliced fresh mushrooms

3 tablespoons olive or safflower oil

1 large tomato, chopped

1/2 cup shredded reduced-fat mozzarella cheese

3/4 cup oat bran

1/4 teaspoon dried oregano or 1/2 teaspoon finely chopped fresh oregano

1. Cut a slice lengthwise off each zucchini. Chop removed slices and set aside.
2. Scoop out the pulp of each zucchini, chop, and combine with reserved chopped slices. Set the hollowed shells aside.
3. Oil a 9×13-inch glass baking dish. Preheat oven to 375°F.
4. In a skillet, sauté 1/2 cup reserved chopped zucchini with garlic, onions, and mushrooms in 2 tablespoons oil until the onion is softened.
5. Add tomato, cheese, oat bran, and oregano and cook over medium heat, stirring well, until bubbly. If mixture seems dry, add 2 or 3 tablespoons water.
6. Brush zucchini shells with remaining oil. Fill with tomato/zucchini mixture. Place in baking dish and cover with foil.
7. Bake for about 40 minutes or until zucchini is tender.

Zucchini, Mozzarella, and Tomato Casserole

This excellent casserole can be prepared in advance and refrigerated. To reheat from room temperature in a conventional oven, heat at 300°F. for about 15 minutes; in a microwave, heat wedges on High (100%) for at least 1 minute.

YIELD: 6 servings

PREPARATION TIME: 45 minutes

COOKING TIME: 30 to 35 minutes

RDOB PER SERVING: 17%

1 pound zucchini, unpeeled
1 tablespoon olive oil
1/2 cup chopped onion
1 large clove garlic, minced
2 egg whites, beaten
2 cups tomato sauce
1 teaspoon dried basil

1/4 teaspoon salt (optional)
1/4 teaspoon freshly ground black pepper
1 cup oat bran
1/2 cup shredded part-skim mozzarella cheese

1. Lightly oil an 8-inch round baking dish. Preheat oven to 375°F.
2. Grate zucchini (you should have about 3 cups) and place in a collander to drain.
3. Heat oil in a 12-inch skillet over medium heat. Add onions and garlic and sauté until onions are transparent.
4. Combine egg whites, tomato sauce, basil, salt (if desired), and pepper in a large bowl.
5. Add zucchini to the onion mixture. Stir for a few minutes until it is glazed with the oil.
6. Combine all the ingredients, except the cheese, in the large bowl. Pour into baking dish and sprinkle the cheese evenly over the top.
7. Bake for 30 to 35 minutes until lightly browned.
8. Remove from oven and allow to sit for 10 minutes before cutting and serving.

Zucchini-Vegetable Casserole

Like most of our vegetarian main dishes, this casserole can be the centerpiece of a meatless meal, and hot pepper sauce can add an unexpected dimension. It's a good choice to take along to a pot luck supper.

[handwritten: the spices must be mixed with eggs, not added last, no distribution]

YIELD: 6 servings

PREPARATION TIME: 30 minutes

COOKING TIME: 35 to 40 minutes

RDOB PER SERVING: 8%

1 medium zucchini (about 1 cup)

1 medium onion, peeled

1 medium carrot, peeled (about 1/2 cup)

1 stalk celery (about 1/2 cup)

1 whole egg plus 4 egg whites

1 can (14 ounces) whole kernel corn, drained (set aside 1/3 cup of the liquid)

5 drops hot red pepper sauce (optional)

2 small cloves garlic, minced

1/2 cup oat bran

1/2 cup grated reduced-fat cheddar cheese

1 tablespoon tub margarine, melted

1/2 teaspoon oregano

1/4 teaspoon cumin

1/4 teaspoon black pepper

1/4 teaspoon salt

1. Lightly oil an 8-inch round cake pan or casserole dish. Preheat oven to 345°F.

2. Combine zucchini, and onions, carrots and celery in food processor and process until finely chopped. Set aside.

3. Combine eggs with reserved corn liquid in a large bowl and beat together with a wire whisk. Add hot sauce (if desired).

4. Add chopped vegetables, corn, and garlic to egg mixture. Sprinkle in oat bran and mix.

5. Add cheese, margarine, oregano, cumin, pepper, and salt and mix well.

6. Pour into pan or casserole dish. Bake for 35 to 40 minutes until set. Cut and serve with a pie server.

Zucchini-Sunflower Bake

Each slice of this cheesy vegetable and sunflower loaf is rich in protein and both soluble and insoluble fiber.

YIELD: 6 servings

PREPARATION TIME: 15 minutes

COOKING TIME: 30 minutes

RDOB PER SERVING: 17%

1/2 cup finely chopped onion	4 egg whites, lightly beaten
1 tablespoon peanut or safflower oil	1/2 cup wheat germ
2 cups old-fashioned rolled oats	1/2 cup unsalted toasted or raw sunflower seeds
3 cups grated zucchini	1/4 teaspoon nutmeg
3/4 cup grated reduced-fat Swiss cheese	

1. Preheat oven to 350°F. Lightly oil an 8 1/2 × 4-inch loaf pan.
2. Sauté onions in oil for 3 minutes or until softened.
3. Combine oats, zucchini, cheese, egg whites, wheat germ, sunflower seeds, and nutmeg in a mixing bowl. Add onions and mix lightly.
4. Press into loaf pan. Bake for 30 minutes. Slice and serve.

A friend in England who is a teacher eats this quick-to-prepare "roast" for an evening meal and then takes a piece with her to school for an afternoon pick-me-up. Its rich, nutty flavor is satisfying and unusual.

YIELD: 4 servings

PREPARATION TIME: 10 minutes

COOKING TIME: 25 to 30 minutes

RDOB PER SERVING: 9%

1 medium onion, finely chopped (about 3/4 cup)

3 tablespoons olive oil

3/4 cup rolled oats

1 cup unsalted raw sunflower seeds

1/2 teaspoon dried thyme

1/2 teaspoon dried rosemary, crumbled

1 teaspoon Marmite yeast extract or instant dried bouillon

1/2 cup warm water

1/4 cup minced parsley

1. Lightly oil a 5×7-inch small loaf pan. Preheat oven to 400°F.
2. In a small skillet, sauté onions in oil for 5 minutes, stirring once or twice.
3. While onions are cooking, combine oats, sunflower seeds, thyme, and rosemary in a medium-size bowl. Set aside.
4. Dissolve yeast or instant broth in warm water in a separate bowl. Add to onions when they are cooked. Add parsley and stir.
5. Add onion mixture to oat/seed mixture and mix lightly.
6. Turn into pan and press down firmly to make a denser layer. Bake for 25 to 30 minutes until lightly browned. Serve hot or at room temperature.

NOTE: Marmite is available in larger supermarkets and in health food stores.

Grain burgers made with oats instead of the traditional soybeans are a nice change of pace.

YIELD: 4 servings

PREPARATION TIME: 15 minutes

COOKING TIME: 20 minutes

RDOB PER SERVING: 12%

1 large carrot, peeled
2 tablespoons onions or chives
1 slice green pepper (1 inch wide)
1 stalk celery
1 tablespoon parsley
1 cup steel-cut oats, ground in blender to consistency of coarse cornmeal

2 egg whites
Juice of 1/2 lemon
1 tablespoon olive or safflower oil
1/8 teaspoon dried basil
1/4 cup tomato juice

1. Combine vegetables in food processor and process until finely chopped.
2. Lightly oil an 8-inch square baking pan. Preheat oven to 350°F.
3. Combine oats, chopped vegetables, egg whites, lemon juice, oil, basil, and tomato juice in a large bowl.
4. Shape into 4 hamburger-size patties. (If mixture is too crumbly to allow the patties to hold their shape, add tomato juice.)
5. Place in a shallow baking pan and bake for 15 minutes until tops are browned. Turn and brown for 5 minutes.

Tofu Burgers

Here's another meatless burger alternative. If you enjoy tofu, you'll find this dish spicy and satisfying. Serve on warm rolls with lettuce and tomato.

YIELD: 4 servings

PREPARATION TIME: 20 minutes

COOKING TIME: 10 minutes

RDOB PER SERVING: 19%

1 pound firm tofu
1 carrot, peeled and grated
1 stalk celery, diced
2 tablespoons chopped green pepper
2 tablespoons minced parsley
1 tablespoon chopped onion
1 clove garlic, minced

2 tablespoons wheat germ
1 tablespoon low-sodium soy sauce
1 tablespoon sesame oil
2 egg whites, beaten
3/4 cup oat bran
1/4 cup peanut or safflower oil

1. Mash tofu in a large bowl. Add carrot, celery, green pepper, parsley, onion, garlic, wheat germ, soy sauce, sesame oil, and egg whites and mix well.

2. Stir in oat bran and mix again. Form into hamburger-shaped patties. Refrigerate for 30 minutes.

3. Heat oil in a skillet. Brown burgers on both sides.

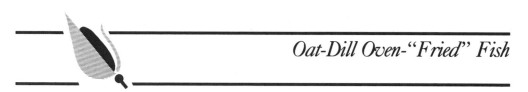

Oat-Dill Oven-"Fried" Fish

You can also use the bran-cornmeal topping in this recipe to prepare sautéed fillets.

YIELD: 6 servings

PREPARATION TIME: 10 minutes

COOKING TIME: 25 minutes

RDOB PER SERVING: 12%

3/4 cup oat bran

1/4 cup cornmeal

1/2 teaspoon dill

2 egg whites, beaten

1/4 cup skim milk

3 tablespoons tub margarine

3 pounds fish fillets

1 lemon, sliced, for garnish

1/4 cup fresh parsley for garnish

1. Combine oat bran, cornmeal, and dill in a shallow bowl or soup plate. Combine egg whites and milk with a fork in a second shallow bowl.

2. Preheat oven to 375°F. Melt margarine in a shallow roasting pan.

3. Pat fish with paper towels and dip into bran mixture to coat, then into egg mixture, then into bran mixture again.

4. Place fish on top of margarine in roasting pan and bake for 15 minutes. Turn and continue baking 10 minutes until second side is lightly browned. Serve hot, garnished with lemon slices and parsley.

Fish Creole

Peppers, tomatoes, basil, and thyme accent this zesty entrée, which is baked with a cheese and oat topping. Serve with crusty bread and a green salad. It's one of our favorites!

YIELD: 4 servings

PREPARATION TIME: 25 minutes

COOKING TIME: 20 to 25 minutes

RDOB PER SERVING: 12%

1 large green pepper, sliced
1 large red pepper, sliced
1 large onion, sliced
1 teaspoon dried basil
1 teaspoon dried thyme
1 can (16 ounces) tomatoes
6 drops hot red pepper sauce
1/4 teaspoon salt (optional)
1/8 teaspoon black pepper
1 pound fillet of scrod, cod, whiting, haddock, or other white fish
2 tablespoons oat bran

TOPPING:

2/3 cup old-fashioned rolled oats
1/4 cup whole wheat flour
2 tablespoons olive oil
  Salt and pepper (optional)
1/2 cup grated reduced-fat Swiss cheese

1. Combine peppers, onions, basil, thyme, tomatoes, hot sauce, salt (if desired), and pepper in a skillet and simmer, covered, over a low heat for 20 minutes. Set aside.

2. Preheat oven to 400°F.

3. Cut fish into 1- to 2-inch pieces and place in an oiled 7- or 8-inch casserole dish.

4. Make the topping by combining oats, flour, oil, salt and pepper (if desired) in a mixing bowl. Add cheese and toss lightly.

5. Mix oat bran with the tomato mixture and pour it over the fish. Sprinkle the oat/cheese topping over the sauce.

6. Bake for 20 to 25 minutes until the topping is bubbly and browned.

Bran-Cornmeal Crisp Fish

The oat bran and cornmeal make a good coating for any fish fillet. Be sure to dip the fillets in the oat mixture twice as the recipe suggests for an especially crispy result.

YIELD: 3 servings

PREPARATION TIME: 10 minutes

COOKING TIME: 6 minutes

RDOB PER SERVING: 17%

1/2 cup oat bran

1/4 cup cornmeal

2 teaspoons dry mustard

1 teaspoon paprika

2 egg whites, beaten

1/4 cup skim milk

1/4 cup olive, peanut, or safflower oil

3 fish fillets

1 lemon, sliced, for garnish

1/4 cup fresh parsley for garnish

1. Mix together oat bran, cornmeal, mustard, and paprika in a shallow bowl or soup plate. In a second shallow bowl, beat egg whites and milk with a fork until combined.

2. Heat oil in large skillet.

3. Pat fish with paper towels and dip into bran mixture to coat, then into egg mixture, then into bran mixture again.

4. Heat oil in a large skillet and sauté fish over medium heat until lightly browned on each side, turning once. Drain well on paper towels. Garnish with lemon slices and parsley.

A nutty oat bran and basil coating perks up the scallops' subtle flavor in this quick luncheon or supper dish.

YIELD: 2 servings

PREPARATION TIME: 10 minutes

COOKING TIME: 5 to 10 minutes

RDOB PER SERVING: 25%

1/2 cup oat bran

1/4 teaspoon dried basil or tarragon

Dash black pepper and salt (optional)

1/2 pound bay scallops, or 1/2 pound sea scallops, cut in half

2 tablespoons tub margarine

1. Mix oat bran, basil, pepper and salt (if desired) in a shallow bowl or soup plate, or place in a plastic bag.

2. Put half the scallops in the bran mixture. Toss with a spoon or shake in the bag to coat well. Repeat with remaining scallops until all are coated.

3. Heat margarine in a heavy-bottomed skillet over medium heat. Sauté scallops 5 to 10 minutes until browned, stirring frequently with a spatula. Serve hot.

Fish fillets taste fresh and light if they're soaked first in milk. The browned coating adds some crunch to the smooth fish.

YIELD: 4 servings

PREPARATION TIME: 15 minutes, plus at least 1 hour refrigeration time

COOKING TIME: 6 minutes

RDOB PER SERVING: 16%

2 fish fillets of equal size (about 2 pounds total)

1% or skim milk to cover

2 egg whites

2/3 cup oat bran

1/8 teaspoon salt (optional)

1/8 teaspoon black pepper

3 tablespoons peanut or safflower oil

Lemon wedges for garnish

1. Place fillets in a shallow dish and cover with milk. Refrigerate for 1 hour or more until ready to use.

2. Place egg whites in a shallow dish or soup plate and beat with a fork until combined. In a second dish, combine oat bran, salt (if desired), and pepper.

3. Drain fillets and pat with paper towels. Dip in the egg whites, then the oat bran to coat well.

4. Heat oil in a large skillet until hot. Add the fillets, lower the heat to medium, and sauté for 3 minutes on each side or until nicely browned. Serve hot with lemon wedges.

Baked Flounder Parmigiana

Delicate flounder fillets are lightly breaded in an oat-Parmesan mixture accented with cayenne pepper.

YIELD: 4 servings

PREPARATION TIME: 15 minutes, plus 15 minutes soaking time

COOKING TIME: 20 minutes

RDOB PER SERVING: 19%

2 tablespoons peanut or safflower oil	1/8 teaspoon cayenne pepper
1 pound flounder fillets	1 small onion, finely chopped
1/2 cup skim milk	1 lemon, cut into wedges, for garnish
3/4 cup oat bran	1/4 cup chopped fresh parsley for garnish
1/2 cup grated Parmesan cheese	

1. Preheat oven to 375°F. Spoon oil into an 8-inch square glass baking dish.
2. Cut flounder into 4 serving portions. Soak in milk in a large bowl for 15 minutes.
3. Combine oat bran, Parmesan cheese, and cayenne in a shallow bowl.
4. Dip fish in bran mixture to coat both sides well.
5. Spread onions in the baking dish. Place fillets on top. Sprinkle remaining bran mixture over fish.
6. Bake for 20 minutes or until fish flakes with a fork. Garnish with lemon wedges and parsley.

Oat groats have become one of our favorite foods. Once you've tasted them in recipes like this one, we're sure you'll agree. Combined with vegetables and spices, they are a great replacement for rice. You can also use the groat mixture as a stuffing for a whole fish or fillets.

YIELD: 4 servings

PREPARATION TIME: 25 minutes

COOKING TIME: 1 1/4 to 1 1/2 hours

RDOB PER SERVING: 13%

1/3 cup chopped celery	1/4 teaspoon dried thyme
2 tablespoons chopped green pepper	1/8 teaspoon dried sage
1 clove garlic, minced	1/8 teaspoon black pepper
1/4 cup tub margarine	2 tablespoons lemon juice
2 cups cooked oat groats (page 49)	1 1/2 pounds cleaned whole white fish or fish fillets

1. Sauté celery, green pepper, and garlic in margarine in a medium-size skillet for 10 minutes until softened.

2. Lightly oil a 9 × 13-inch baking dish. Preheat oven to 350°F.

3. Add oat groats, thyme, sage, pepper, and lemon juice to the sautéed vegetables, stir, and remove from heat.

4. If cooking whole fish, place in the baking dish and stuff the cavity with the groat mixture. If cooking fillets, place half in the baking dish and spoon on the groat mixture, then top with remaining fillets. Sprinkle lemon juice over fish.

5. Bake about 30 minutes for fillets and 35 to 45 minutes for whole fish, until the fish flakes when tested with a fork.

Spinach-Stuffed Sea Trout

Sea trout fillets are wrapped around a mushroom-spinach stuffing seasoned with onions and lemon juice.

YIELD: 6 servings

PREPARATION TIME: 20 minutes

COOKING TIME: 25 minutes

RDOB PER SERVING: 13%

1 package (10 ounces) frozen chopped spinach, or 10 ounces fresh spinach

1 cup sliced mushrooms

1/2 cup onions, sliced

2 tablespoons olive, peanut, or safflower oil

1/2 cup old-fashioned rolled oats

1/2 cup oat bran

2 egg whites

1/4 cup lemon juice

6 sea trout fillets (about 2 pounds)

1. Defrost spinach, saving package liquid, or wash, drain, and chop fresh spinach. Preheat oven to 375°F. Lightly oil a 13×9-inch baking dish.

2. In a medium-size skillet, sauté mushrooms and onions in oil over medium heat. Stir in oats, oat bran, egg whites, 2 tablespoons lemon juice, spinach and its liquid (add 2 tablespoons water if using fresh spinach).

3. Divide spinach mixture into 6 portions and spread on fish fillets, leaving a 1/2-inch margin around edges. Roll up fillets and place, seam down, in baking dish. Sprinkle fillets with remaining lemon juice. Bake 25 minutes or until fish flakes easily.

Salmon Loaf with Tomato Sauce

The sweet richness of the tomato sauce contrasts beautifully with the savory fish in this entrée. This is an easy and delicious way to combine oat fiber and Omega-3 fish oil. Leftovers can be served cold as an appetizer, spread on crackers as you would a pâté. Use a quality red salmon; remember, the redder it is, the higher the Omega-3 oil content.

YIELD: 6 servings

PREPARATION TIME: 20 minutes

COOKING TIME: 45 to 55 minutes

RDOB PER SERVING: 13%

LOAF:

1 can (16 ounces) good-quality red salmon, including liquid

1/2 cup rolled oats

1/2 cup oat bran

1/2 cup bread cubes or coarse bread crumbs (leftover oat bread if possible)

3/4 cup skim milk

2 egg whites or 1 whole egg, lightly beaten

1 small onion, finely chopped

1 stalk celery, finely chopped

2 tablespoons lemon juice

2 tablespoons minced fresh parsley

2 tablespoons minced fresh dill or 1 teaspoon dried dill

1/8 teaspoon black pepper

1/4 teaspoon salt (optional)

Lemon wedges for garnish

SAUCE:

1 tablespoon minced onion

1 teaspoon tub margarine

1 can (8 ounces) tomato sauce

1. Lightly oil in a 6-inch casserole dish. Preheat oven to 350°F.

2. In a medium-size bowl, flake fish with a fork and mix with salmon liquid, oats, oat bran, and bread cubes.

3. Stir in milk and egg whites.

4. Add remaining ingredients and mix well. Turn into casserole dish.

5. Bake for 45 to 55 minutes until set.

6. While loaf is baking, make the sauce by sautéing onions in margarine for 5 minutes until softened. Add tomato sauce and simmer 10 minutes.

7. Remove loaf from oven and cool for 5 minutes. If desired, invert after cooling. Garnish with lemon wedges and serve with a small pitcher of the sauce.

TUNA LOAF WITH TOMATO SAUCE   Substitute 2 cans (7 ounces each) water-pack tuna for the canned salmon. Use white albacore tuna for highest Omega-3 oil content.

CUCUMBER SAUCE   Try this low-fat sauce instead of the tomato sauce:

1 cup low-fat or nonfat plain
  yogurt
1 cucumber, finely chopped
2 tablespoons chopped chives
1 tablespoon lemon juice

1. To prepare sauce, stir yogurt, cucumber, chives, lemon juice, and dill together.
2. Serve warm or cold in a small pitcher with the loaf.

Dilled Salmon Cakes

These salmon cakes are easy to prepare and require a very short cooking time. We recommend using a quality red salmon; the redder the salmon, the higher it is in Omega-3 oil.

YIELD: 6 cakes (3 servings)

PREPARATION TIME: 15 minutes

COOKING TIME: 10 to 12 minutes

RDOB FOR 2 CAKES: 17%

1 can (8 ounces) red salmon
3 egg whites
1/2 cup oat bran
1/2 cup chopped celery
1/4 cup chopped onion

1 tablespoon minced fresh dill
  or 1 teaspoon dried dill
1 tablespoon lemon juice
1 tablespoon skim milk
3 tablespoons olive or safflower
  oil

1. Combine salmon, egg whites, oat bran, celery, onions, dill, lemon juice, and milk in a bowl and mix well.
2. Shape into 6 cakes.
3. Heat oil in skillet and sauté cakes until well browned.

Classic crab cakes are pan-fried, or they can be broiled until browned if you want to avoid the extra calories from margarine.

YIELD: 6 crab cakes (3 servings)

PREPARATION TIME: 15 minutes, plus 2 hours chilling time

COOKING TIME: 10 to 12 minutes

RDOB FOR 2 CAKES: 25%

3 to 4 tablespoons tub margarine
2 tablespoons minced onion
3/4 cup oat bran
3 egg whites, beaten
1/2 cup skim milk
2 cups crabmeat
1/2 cup finely chopped celery

1/2 teaspoon dry mustard
1/2 teaspoon lemon juice
2 tablespoons chopped fresh parsley
1/2 teaspoon paprika

1. Melt 2 tablespoons margarine in a skillet. Add onions and 1/2 cup oat bran. Stir and cook gently for 3 minutes.
2. Combine egg whites, milk, crabmeat, celery, mustard, lemon juice, parsley, and paprika in a bowl. Add onion/bran mixture.
3. Chill for 2 hours.
4. Shape into cakes and dust lightly with the remaining 1/4 oat bran. Melt 1 to 2 tablespoons margarine in skillet over medium-high heat. Brown crab cakes quickly on both sides. Lower heat and cook slowly for 6 additional minutes.

POULTRY

Chicken Salsa

Sautéed chicken cutlets are topped with spicy salsa and cheese and toasted in the broiler. The result is a great blend of flavors and an unexpected tang.

YIELD: 4 servings

PREPARATION TIME: 25 minutes

COOKING TIME: 20 minutes

RDOB PER SERVING: 13%

2 whole chicken breasts, skinned, boned, and cut in half

1/2 cup oat bran

1 clove garlic, minced

1/2 teaspoon ground cumin

1/8 teaspoon cayenne pepper

4 egg whites

1/2 cup cornmeal

2 tablespoons olive or safflower oil

2 slices low-fat mozzarella cheese, cut in half diagonally

SALSA:

1/2 green pepper, chopped

1/2 small onion, finely chopped

1 clove garlic, minced

3 sprigs parsley, minced

1/2 jalapeño pepper, minced

1 cup chopped drained canned tomatoes or fresh tomatoes

2 teaspoons wine vinegar

1 tablespoon lime juice

1. Place chicken cutlets between 2 sheets of waxed paper and pound to 1/2-inch thickness.

2. Combine oat bran, garlic, cumin, and pepper in a shallow bowl. Beat eggs in a separate bowl. Place cornmeal into a third bowl.

3. Dip chicken into bran mixture, then into eggs, then into cornmeal to coat evenly on both sides. Chill while making the salsa.

4. To make salsa, mix together green pepper, onions, garlic, parsley, jalapeño pepper, tomatoes, vinegar, and lime juice in a medium-size bowl. Set aside.

5. In a large skillet, sauté chicken cutlets in hot oil for about 4 minutes on each side or until lightly browned.

6. Transfer chicken to a heatproof serving dish. Spoon salsa over cutlets and top with cheese. Toast in broiler or toaster oven until cheese is melted.

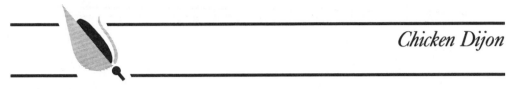

Chicken Dijon

These tender chicken breasts in a tangy mustard sauce can be prepared quickly on the top of the stove.

YIELD: 4 servings

PREPARATION TIME: 10 minutes

COOKING TIME: 15 minutes

RDOB PER SERVING: 13%

2 whole chicken breasts, skinned, boned, and cut in half	1/2 cup oat bran
	3 tablespoons tub margarine
1/4 teaspoon black pepper	1 cup 1% or skim milk
3 tablespoons Dijon-style mustard	

1. Place chicken pieces between 2 sheets of waxed paper and pound to 1/4-inch thickness. Season with pepper.

2. Spread 2 tablespoons mustard on both sides of chicken pieces.

3. Place oat bran in a shallow dish. Dip chicken to coat evenly on both sides.

4. Melt margarine in a 9-inch skillet over medium heat. Place chicken in skillet and brown 3 minutes on each side. Remove with a slotted spoon to a warm dish.

5. Add milk to skillet and simmer for 2 minutes while stirring and scraping from the bottom. Remove skillet from heat. Stir in remaining 1 tablespoon mustard.

6. Return chicken to the skillet and heat over medium heat for 2 minutes, basting with the sauce while cooking. Serve immediately.

Chicken is crisped in oat bran and served with spicy gumbo sauce. Served over oat groats instead of the usual rice, this dish makes a complete meal.

YIELD: 4 servings

PREPARATION TIME: 20 minutes

COOKING TIME: 1 hour 15 minutes

RDOB PER SERVING: 25%

1 cup oat groats	1/2 cup sliced mushrooms
2 cups chicken broth	1/2 cup chopped green pepper
1/2 cup oat bran	1/2 cup chopped onion
1 teaspoon dried thyme	1 clove garlic, minced
1/4 teaspoon cayenne pepper	2 to 3 bay leaves
2 egg whites	1 cup tomato sauce
2 whole chicken breasts, skinned, boned, and split in half	1/2 cup dry cooking wine
3 tablespoons peanut, olive, or safflower oil	1 teaspoon ground gumbo filé (sassafras and thyme leaves) (optional)

1. Toast oat groats in a dry skillet for 5 minutes, stirring frequently. Transfer to a 1-quart saucepan and cook in broth for 40 minutes until tender.

2. While groats are cooking, put oat bran, thyme, and cayenne in blender container and blend to give bran a more flourlike consistency. Transfer mixture to a shallow dish.

3. Put egg whites in a second dish. Pound chicken breasts between two sheets of waxed paper until an even thickness. Dip each breast in oat bran, then in egg, then in oat bran again to coat well on both sides.

4. Sauté chicken in oil in a large skillet for 15 minutes, turning once. Remove and keep warm.

5. Add mushrooms, pepper, onions, garlic, and bay leaves to the skillet and sauté 10 minutes until tender. Stir in tomato sauce and wine and simmer 5 more minutes.

6. Remove from heat and stir in gumbo filé if desired.

7. Put cooked oat groats on a serving plate. Pour sauce over groats and arrange chicken on top. Serve at once.

A coating of oat bran and herbs is a tasty alternative to the packaged varieties made with sugars and preservatives. Serve this dish hot with salad and crusty bread for a classic meal or cold for an excellent picnic.

YIELD: 6 pieces

PREPARATION TIME: 10 minutes

COOKING TIME: 40 minutes

RDOB PER PIECE: 13%

3/4 cup oat bran
1/2 teaspoon dried basil
1/2 teaspoon dried tarragon
1/4 teaspoon paprika

1/8 teaspoon black pepper
1/8 teaspoon salt (optional)
6 chicken pieces (6 thighs, 6 legs, or 3 breasts split in half), skin removed

1. Preheat oven to 350°F.
2. Place all the dry ingredients in a plastic bag and shake to mix.
3. Rinse chicken in cold water and pat dry with paper towels.
4. Place 1 piece of chicken at a time in the bag and shake to coat well.
5. Arrange chicken pieces in a shallow baking dish or cookie sheet. Bake for 20 minutes on each side, turning once, until bubbly and browned.

GARLIC SHAKE-AND-COAT CHICKEN   Replace basil with 1/2 teaspoon garlic powder.

Chicken Roma

The oat bran, tomato sauce, and cheese create a rich chicken dish. It is excellent served over pasta.

YIELD: 4 servings

PREPARATION TIME: 25 minutes

COOKING TIME: 40 minutes

RDOB PER SERVING: 13%

1/2 cup oat bran

2 tablespoons all-purpose flour

1 teaspoon dried oregano

1/4 teaspoon black pepper

2 egg whites

2 whole chicken breasts, skinned, boned, and split in half

1 clove garlic, minced

2 tablespoons olive or safflower oil

8 ounces tomato sauce

1 teaspoon dried basil or 2 tablespoons minced fresh basil

1/2 cup grated reduced-fat skim-milk mozzarella cheese (use a grater with large holes)

1. Combine oat bran, flour, oregano, and pepper in a shallow bowl.
2. Beat egg whites in a second shallow bowl.
3. Dip chicken first in bran mixture, then in egg, then in bran again to coat evenly on both sides.
4. Sauté garlic briefly in oil in large skillet. Add chicken and sauté 10 minutes on each side until browned.
5. Add tomato sauce and basil. Cover and simmer 15 minutes.
6. Sprinkle cheese over chicken and cover. Continue cooking until cheese is melted.

The cheese combines with the oat bran for a richly coated chicken. Serve hot or cold with salads and pastas.

YIELD: 4 servings

PREPARATION TIME: 20 minutes

COOKING TIME: 40 minutes

RDOB PER SERVING: 25%

1 cup oat bran

1/3 cup grated Parmesan cheese

1/4 teaspoon salt (optional)

1/2 teaspoon paprika

1/4 teaspoon black pepper

1/3 cup 1% or skim milk

8 chicken pieces (thighs, legs, or breasts split in half), skin removed

1. Preheat oven to 375°F.
2. Combine oat bran, cheese, salt, paprika, and pepper in a shallow bowl.
3. Put milk in a second shallow bowl.
4. Dip each piece of chicken in oat bran, then in milk, then in oat bran again to coat evenly on both sides.
5. Place in a baking pan and bake for 20 minutes a side, turning once, until nicely browned.

Green peppers are stuffed with a mixture of ground chicken and vegetables and baked in a tomato sauce with Italian spices.

YIELD: 6 servings

PREPARATION TIME: 40 minutes

COOKING TIME: 45 minutes

RDOB PER SERVING: 19%

6 medium green peppers
1 1/4 cups water
2 cups tomato juice
6 ounces tomato paste
1 teaspoon dried oregano
1 clove garlic, minced
1/2 teaspoon dried basil

1 pound ground or finely chopped chicken or turkey breast
3/4 cup oat bran
3/4 cup rolled oats
1 tomato, chopped
1/4 cup grated peeled carrot
1/4 cup grated onion

1. Lightly oil a 9 × 13-inch baking dish. Preheat oven to 350°.
2. Cut peppers in half lengthwise. Discard membrane and seeds.
3. In a medium-size saucepan, simmer water, 1 cup tomato juice, tomato paste, oregano, garlic, and basil over low heat for 15 minutes.
4. Meanwhile, place chicken, remaining 1 cup tomato juice, oat bran, oats, tomato, carrots, and onions in a separate bowl and mix.
5. Fill each pepper half with 1/3 cup of the chicken mixture. Place filled peppers in baking dish. Distribute sauce around peppers.
6. Bake for 45 to 50 minutes until bubbly.

BEEF AND PEPPERS MARINARA   Substitute 1 pound very lean ground beef for the chicken or turkey.

This is a variation of a favorite Chinese dish. Serve with rice and stir-fried broccoli.

YIELD: 6 servings

PREPARATION TIME: 30 minutes

COOKING TIME: 15 minutes

RDOB PER SERVING: 13%

SAUCE:

1 cup pure fruit orange marmalade

1/2 cup fresh lemon juice

2 teaspoons grated lemon peel

BATTER:

3/4 cup oat bran, finely ground to a flourlike consistency

1 teaspoon peanut or safflower oil

1/2 cup water

2 egg whites

CHICKEN:

3 whole chicken breasts, skinned, boned, and split in half

1/4 teaspoon black pepper

Peanut oil

Shredded lettuce for serving platter

Lemon wedges for garnish

1. Simmer marmalade, lemon juice, and lemon peel in a saucepan over low heat for about 15 minutes. Stir as needed to prevent burning. Set aside to cool.

2. Put oat bran in a shallow bowl. Mix oil, water, and egg whites well in a second shallow bowl.

3. Place chicken pieces between two sheets of waxed paper and pound to an even thickness. Sprinkle with pepper.

4. Dip each chicken piece in oat bran, then in egg mixture, then in oat bran again to coat evenly. Heat peanut oil in a skillet or wok over high heat. When oil is hot, lower temperature to medium and place chicken in skillet. Sauté until both sides are browned.

5. Line a large serving platter with crisp shredded lettuce. Add chicken, pour the sauce over the top, and garnish with lemon wedges.

This quiche is baked in our basic oat bran crust and can be made with either fresh or canned asparagus.

YIELD: 6 servings

PREPARATION TIME: 30 minutes

COOKING TIME: 40 minutes

RDOB PER SERVING: 13%

CRUST:

    Dough for 1 Basic Oat Bran Pie Crust (page 272), omitting sugar

FILLING:

10 spears fresh or canned asparagus

1 green pepper, thinly sliced

1 1/2 cups thinly sliced fresh mushrooms

1 small chicken breast, steamed, skinned, and boned

1 egg plus 2 egg whites

1 1/2 cups skim milk

1/4 cup oat bran

1 tablespoon chopped parsley

1/8 teaspoon black pepper

1. Bake Basic Oat Bran Pie Crust.

2. While crust is baking, chop 6 asparagus spears and the cooked chicken breast. (If using fresh asparagus, poach with 1 cup water in a large covered skillet for 5 minutes until fork-tender.)

3. Arrange chicken and asparagus in baked crust. Lower oven temperature to 375°F.

4. Beat together eggs, skim milk, and oat bran in a mixing bowl. Add parsley and pepper.

5. Pour milk mixture over chopped asparagus and chicken.

6. Arrange remaining 4 asparagus spears on top of quiche. Place peppers and sliced mushrooms between asparagus.

7. Bake for 30 minutes or until quiche filling is firm.

This delicious recipe calls for chicken baked with herbs, vegetables, olives, and sherry.

YIELD: 4 servings

PREPARATION TIME: 30 minutes

COOKING TIME: 55 minutes

RDOB PER SERVING: 13%

2 egg whites

1/2 cup oat bran

1/8 teaspoon black pepper

1/4 teaspoon dried oregano

1/4 teaspoon dried basil

1/2 teaspoon dried parsley

2 chicken breasts split in half or 4 chicken thighs, skin removed

3 tablespoons olive or safflower oil

1 onion, chopped

1 clove garlic, crushed

2 cups canned tomatoes

1 cup canned corn

1 cup cooking sherry

8 stuffed green olives

1. Preheat oven to 350°F.

2. Beat egg whites in a shallow bowl.

3. Combine oat bran, pepper, and herbs in a second shallow bowl. Dip chicken pieces in oat bran, then in egg whites, then in oat bran again to coat evenly on both sides.

4. In a large skillet, sauté chicken in 1 tablespoon oil until lightly browned on both sides. Transfer to a 3-quart casserole dish and cover.

5. In same skillet, sauté onions and garlic in the remaining 2 tablespoons until translucent. Add tomatoes, corn, sherry, and olives. Cook over medium heat until the mixture comes to a boil. Pour over chicken.

6. Bake, covered, for 55 minutes.

Baked Chicken with Whole Oats

The toasted groats take on the texture of wild rice as they bake with the chicken.

YIELD: 4 servings

PREPARATION TIME: 20 minutes

COOKING TIME: 30 to 40 minutes

RDOB PER SERVING: 28%

1 1/4 cups oat groats, rinsed and drained

1/2 cup oat bran

2 chicken breasts split in half or 1 broiling chicken cut into quarters, skin removed

1 teaspoon low-sodium soy sauce

2 tablespoons safflower oil

2 cups chicken broth

1/8 teaspoon black pepper

1. Brown half the oat groats in a large dry skillet over medium heat. Stir and shake the skillet to prevent the groats from burning. Repeat with the remaining groats. Transfer to a large ovenproof casserole dish.

2. Place oat bran in a shallow bowl. Sprinkle chicken with soy sauce and dip in oat bran to coat evenly on both sides.

3. Preheat oven to 350°F.

4. Heat the oil in the skillet and brown the chicken pieces on both sides. Place chicken on top of groats in casserole.

5. Combine chicken broth and pepper in the skillet and bring to a boil. Pour over chicken and groats.

6. Bake for 30 to 40 minutes until tender.

Be sure to try this delectable chicken-vegetable mixture baked in flaky pastry.

YIELD: 3 servings

PREPARATION TIME: 30 minutes

COOKING TIME: 25 to 30 minutes

RDOB PER SERVING: 19%

PASTRY:

> Dough for 1 Basic Oat Bran Pie Crust (page 272), omitting sugar

FILLING:

1 cup cooked chopped chicken breast

1 small onion, chopped

1 tablespoon olive or safflower oil

1/2 cup 1% cottage cheese

2/3 cup canned corn, drained (set aside 2 tablespoons liquid)

12 stuffed green olives, chopped

1/4 teaspoon white pepper

1 tablespoon oat bran

1 tablespoon minced fresh parsley or 1/2 teaspoon dried parsley

Skim milk for glaze

1. Prepare Basic Oat Bran Pie Crust dough. Cover and chill.

2. Sauté chicken and onions in oil in a medium-size skillet until onions are tender.

3. Mix together cottage cheese, corn and liquid, olives, pepper, oat bran, and parsley in a medium-size bowl.

4. Lightly oil a baking pan. Preheat oven to 400°F.

5. Roll out dough into a 9- to 10-inch shape on a lightly floured work surface.

6. Spoon the chicken mixture onto half of the dough. Top with the cheese/corn mixture. Moisten the edge all the way around with water and fold the remaining half of the dough over the filled half.

7. Pinch the edges together firmly, crimp, and trim away any excess pastry. Carefully transfer to the baking pan.

8. Lightly brush with skim milk and bake for 25 to 30 minutes until crust is lightly browned.

Chicken breasts are flavored with lemon juice and dill and dipped in a light oat bran batter before baking.

YIELD: 6 servings

PREPARATION TIME: 10 minutes

COOKING TIME: 35 minutes

RDOB PER SERVING: 13%

3/4 cup oat bran

1 teaspoon black pepper

2 tablespoons minced fresh dill or 1 teaspoon dried dill

1 teaspoon lemon juice

2 egg whites

1/4 cup water

3 whole chicken breasts, skinned, boned, and split in half

2 tablespoons peanut or safflower oil

1. Lightly oil a 9 × 13-inch baking dish. Preheat oven to 375°F.
2. Combine oat bran, pepper, and dill in a shallow bowl.
3. Beat together lemon juice, egg whites, and water in a separate bowl.
4. Place chicken between 2 sheets of waxed paper and pound to an even thickness.
5. Dip chicken in bran mixture, then in egg mixture, then again in bran mixture to coat evenly on both sides.
6. Arrange in the baking dish and drizzle with oil. Bake for 35 minutes.

MEAT LOAF AND OATS

Beef and oats make an excellent combination for meat loaf. The texture is airy yet holds together, and they bring out each other's flavor. Serve the following dishes hot for hearty suppers or slice, cold, for excellent sandwiches. Save time by putting skewered baking potatoes in the oven next to the meat loaf and bake at the same time.

Savory Meat Loaf

Rolled oats and oat bran lend texture and fiber to this classic recipe. It can be served cold, sliced, for excellent sandwiches or hot for a hearty meal rich with herbs.

YIELD: 8 servings

PREPARATION TIME: 20 minutes

COOKING TIME: 1 hour

RDOB PER SERVING: 9%

2 pounds lean ground beef

1 medium onion, finely chopped

2 stalks celery, finely chopped

1 teaspoon each dried rosemary, tarragon, and thyme

2 teaspoons minced fresh parsley

1/4 teaspoon black pepper

10 drops hot red pepper sauce

2 egg whites, beaten

1 cup tomato sauce, plus 2 tablespoons for garnish

1 cup rolled oats

1/2 cup oat bran

2/3 cup skim milk

1. Preheat oven to 350°F.

2. Place all ingredients in a large bowl and mix with a large wooden spoon.

3. Pour into a 9×5-inch loaf pan and pat into mounded shape. Make a shallow trough across the length of the loaf and fill with 2 tablespoons tomato sauce.

4. Bake for 1 hour or until the top is browned and the meat loaf has slightly pulled away from the sides of the pan.

5. Let stand in the pan for 10 to 15 minutes to allow juices to settle before serving.

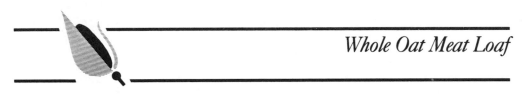

Whole Oat Meat Loaf

The whole-grain oat groats give the meat loaf an extra texture and taste that is similar to wild rice.

YIELD: 6 servings

PREPARATION TIME: 1 hour 15 minutes

COOKING TIME: 1 hour 30 minutes

RDOB PER SERVING: 8%

1 cup oat groats, rinsed and drained

1 3/4 cups water

1 small onion, chopped

1 tablespoon tub margarine

1/2 cup seeded chopped green pepper

2 egg whites, beaten

1 pound very lean ground beef

1 tablespoon chopped parsley

1 teaspoon dried thyme

1 teaspoon dried basil or oregano

1/2 teaspoon black pepper

1. Preheat oven to 325°F.

2. In a medium-size saucepan, cook groats in water over low heat for 30 minutes. Drain.

3. In a medium-size skillet, sauté groats and onions in margarine for 5 minutes. Add green pepper. Cook until pepper is softened.

4. Transfer groat mixture to a large bowl. Add egg whites, beef, parsley, thyme, basil, and black pepper and mix. Form a loaf and place in baking dish. Bake for 1 hour. Let stand for a few minutes before serving.

Each little meat loaf is served topped with cheese and tomato sauce and makes a special meal for guests. They take less time to cook than the larger versions and can be reheated at 350°F. for 15 to 20 minutes for a quick meal.

YIELD: 4 servings

PREPARATION TIME: 20 minutes

COOKING TIME: 25 minutes

RDOB PER SERVING: 13%

1 egg white
1 pound lean ground beef
1/2 cup oat bran
1 can (8 ounces) tomato sauce
2 tablespoons minced onion
1 tablespoon minced fresh parsley
1 teaspoon chili powder (optional)

1/2 teaspoon salt (optional)
1 teaspoon dried thyme or rosemary
1 cup water
1 clove garlic, minced, or 1/8 teaspoon garlic powder
1/2 cup shredded reduced-fat Swiss or mild cheddar cheese

1. Preheat oven to 375°F.

2. Beat egg white in a mixing bowl. Add beef, oat bran, half the tomato sauce, 1 tablespoon onions, parsley, chili powder and salt (if desired), and thyme. Mix well.

3. Form into 4 small loaves and place in an 8-inch square baking pan. Bake for 20 minutes.

4. While the loaves are baking, combine the rest of the tomato sauce and onions, water, and garlic in a small saucepan and simmer for 5 minutes.

5. When meat has cooked for 20 minutes, remove loaves from oven, top with the tomato sauce mixture, sprinkle with cheese, and return to the oven for 5 to 10 minutes until well heated and bubbly.

Oat bran and herbs give these burgers a smooth texture and rich flavor.

YIELD: 4 servings

PREPARATION TIME: 10 minutes

COOKING TIME: 10 minutes

RDOB PER SERVING: 8%

1 clove garlic, minced
1 small onion, minced
1 tablespoon olive or safflower oil
1 pound lean ground beef
1/3 cup oat bran
1/3 cup tomato sauce

2 egg whites
Dash hot red pepper sauce
Several pinches of dried herbs (thyme, basil, rosemary, oregano, sage, and/or parsley to taste)

1. In a medium-size skillet, sauté garlic and onions in oil for 2 to 3 minutes until softened.

2. Combine remaining ingredients in a bowl. Add garlic and onions and mix well. Form into 4 patties.

3. Cook the hamburgers in the skillet for about 5 minutes on each side until done to taste. Or broil, turning once, 4 to 5 minutes a side for medium well done.

Pork Chops with Whole Oats

You can indulge in an occasional pork chop on your lower-fat diet by shopping carefully for lean meat and trimming away fat before cooking. The pork, thyme, and oat groat trio is a delicious way to increase your RDOB.

YIELD: 4 servings

PREPARATION TIME: 15 minutes

COOKING TIME: 1 hour to 1 hour 15 minutes

RDOB PER SERVING: 31%

4 pork chops, 3/4 inch thick, trimmed of fat

1/4 teaspoon black pepper

1/4 teaspoon thyme

1/4 cup oat bran

1 tablespoon peanut or safflower oil

1 cup sliced onion

2 cups whole oat groats, rinsed and drained

4 cups chicken broth

1. Sprinkle pork chops with pepper, thyme, and oat bran. Place in very lightly oiled skillet and brown on both sides. Transfer chops to a plate.

2. In the same skillet, sauté onions in oil until tender.

3. Preheat oven to 350°F.

4. Place 1 cup oat groats in the bottom of a heavy casserole dish. Add pork chops, then onions, then remaining cup of groats.

5. Pour chicken broth in a small saucepan and bring to a boil. Pour over the casserole.

6. Cover and bake for 1 hour to 1 hour 15 minutes until chops and oats are tender.

Grecian Village Lamb Stew

This Mediterranean favorite, rich with rosemary and tomatoes, is a complete meal in itself or goes well with crusty bread and a Greek salad.

YIELD: 6 servings

PREPARATION TIME: 30 minutes

COOKING TIME: 2 hours

RDOB PER SERVING: 6%

3/4 cup chopped onion	2 cups water
2 tablespoons olive oil	2 cups canned tomatoes
2 pounds lean shoulder or breast of lamb, cut into 1-inch pieces	4 medium potatoes (1 1/2 pounds), peeled and cubed
1 teaspoon minced garlic	2 cups green beans, cut in 1-inch pieces
2 teaspoons dried rosemary	1/4 teaspoon black pepper
1/3 cup oat bran	2 tablespoons minced parsley for garnish
1 cup chicken broth	

1. Sauté onions in olive oil in a heavy-bottomed 3- to 4-quart pot until lightly browned. Transfer to a separate dish.

2. Sauté lamb in remaining hot oil for 12 minutes, turning until all sides are browned. Drain oil from skillet. Sprinkle garlic, rosemary, and oat bran over meat and stir to coat.

3. Add broth, water, and tomatoes and stir well. Cover and simmer for 1 hour, stirring 2 or 3 times.

4. While lamb is cooking, place potatoes and green beans in a steamer basket over 1 inch of boiling water in a 2-quart saucepan. Cover and steam until just tender, about 12 minutes.

5. Add onions to the lamb and cook for 15 minutes. Add the potatoes, green beans and pepper and cook until the potatoes are warmed through. Sprinkle with parsley and serve.

Veal Mexicana

Veal and Mexican spices are nicely complemented with cornbread and a salad of mixed greens.

YIELD: 6 servings

PREPARATION TIME: 15 minutes

COOKING TIME: 35 minutes

RDOB PER SERVING: 6%

6 cups canned tomatoes

1/4 cup minced garlic

3 tablespoons olive oil

3 tablespoons chili powder

1 tablespoon cumin

2 egg whites

1 pound ground lean veal

1/3 cup oat bran

1/4 cup skim or 1% milk

2 tablespoons minced parsley

1/4 teaspoon black pepper

1. Break up tomatoes into 1-inch pieces. Simmer in a 2-quart saucepan over medium heat for 15 minutes.

2. In a skillet, sauté garlic in 1 tablespoon olive oil for 1 minute while stirring. Stir in chili powder and cumin. Add mixture to the tomatoes.

3. Beat egg whites in a large bowl. Add veal, oat bran, milk, parsley, and black pepper and mix well. Shape into 2-inch balls.

4. Sauté veal balls in remaining 1 tablespoon olive oil in skillet until brown on all sides.

5. Add to tomato mixture and simmer for 20 minutes.

Breadsticks, pasta, and a green salad tossed with olive oil and wine vinegar are excellent with this Italian classic.

YIELD: 3 servings

PREPARATION TIME: 1 hour 15 minutes

COOKING TIME: 15 minutes

RDOB PER SERVING: 17%

1 1/2 pounds veal cutlet, 1/4 inch thick

1/4 cup lemon juice

1 can (16 ounces) tomatoes

2 tablespoons tomato paste

1 teaspoon dried basil

2 tablespoons grated onion

1/2 cup oat bran

1/2 cup Parmesan cheese

1/4 teaspoon paprika

1/4 teaspoon chives

2 egg whites, beaten

3 to 4 tablespoons tub margarine

1. Soak veal cutlet in lemon juice in a shallow dish for 1 hour. Dry well with paper towels.

2. Slice into 2×2-inch pieces. Pound until each slice measures 3 inches by 3 inches.

3. Combine tomatoes with tomato paste, basil, and onions in a saucepan. Bring to a boil and simmer for 10 minutes.

4. Meanwhile, combine oat bran, Parmesan cheese, paprika, and chives in a shallow bowl. Place egg whites in a second bowl. Dip veal slices in oat bran mixture, then in egg whites, then again in oat bran mixture to coat evenly on all sides.

5. Sauté veal slices in margarine in a large skillet for 2 minutes on each side until crisp. Serve with tomato sauce.

SIDE DISHES, STUFFINGS, AND SALADS

Sesame-Baked Vegetables

An oat–sesame seed topping provides a crisp accent for a medley of vegetables, which are first steamed and then baked.

YIELD: 6 servings

PREPARATION TIME: 15 minutes

COOKING TIME: 20 minutes

RDOB PER SERVING: 6%

1 cup sliced carrots
1 cup broccoli florets
1 cup sliced celery
1 cup canned or fresh corn
1 onion, chopped
1/2 teaspoon dried dill
2 tablespoons chopped fresh parsley

3 tablespoons tub margarine
1/4 cup chicken broth

TOPPING:

2/3 cup rolled oats
2 tablespoons sesame seeds
4 tablespoons peanut, olive, or safflower oil
1/4 teaspoon black pepper

1. Lightly oil a 2-quart baking dish. Preheat oven to 375°F.

2. In a saucepan, place carrots, broccoli, and celery in a steamer basket over 1 inch of boiling water. Cover and steam until crisp tender, approximately 5 minutes.

3. Combine carrots, broccoli, and celery with corn, onions, dill, parsley, margarine, and broth in a large bowl. Mix well. Spread in baking dish.

4. Mix together oats, sesame seeds, oil, and pepper. Spread evenly over vegetable mixture.

5. Bake for 20 minutes. The topping should be crisp and lightly browned.

Stir-fried vegetables are simmered with cooked oat groats and tomatoes.

YIELD: 4 servings

PREPARATION TIME: 15 minutes

COOKING TIME: 1 hour

RDOB PER SERVING: 13%

1 cup oat groats, rinsed and drained	1/2 cup chopped mushrooms, preferably fresh
4 1/2 cups chicken broth	1 cup cauliflower florets
1 small onion, sliced	2 tablespoons safflower oil
1 clove garlic, minced	1/4 teaspoon cayenne pepper
1/2 cup chopped celery	1 cup tomatoes, chopped and drained

1. Place oat groats in 2 cups chicken broth in a saucepan and bring to a boil. Lower heat, cover, and simmer for 40 minutes. Drain.

2. Stir-fry onion, garlic, celery, mushrooms, and cauliflower in oil in a large pot. Stir in cayenne and 2 1/2 cups chicken broth.

3. Add groats and bring broth mixture to a boil. Lower heat, cover, and simmer for 10 minutes. Stir in tomatoes and cook for 5 more minutes.

Tomato halves are stuffed with a jalapeño-flavored corn mixture and baked—a perfect choice when summer tomatoes and corn are abundant.

YIELD: 4 servings

PREPARATION TIME: 15 minutes

COOKING TIME: 30 minutes

RDOB PER SERVING: 25%

1 medium green pepper, chopped

1/4 cup water

4 large tomatoes (about 2 pounds)

1/2 jalapeño pepper, chopped

1 cup oat bran

1 cup cooked fresh or canned corn

3/4 cup thinly sliced scallions

2 egg whites

1 tablespoon olive or safflower oil

1/2 teaspoon dried basil

1/2 teaspoon dried oregano

2 tablespoons chopped fresh parsley for garnish

1. Lightly oil a 13×9-inch baking dish. Preheat oven to 350°F.

2. Simmer green pepper in water in a small saucepan for 2 to 3 minutes. Drain.

3. Slice tomatoes in half. Scoop out pulp and chop.

4. Combine tomato pulp with green and jalapeño peppers, oat bran, corn, scallions, egg whites, oil, basil, and oregano.

5. Place tomato halves in baking dish. Fill each with corn mixture. Bake for 30 minutes or until hot. Garnish with parsley.

Green Bean Cheddar Bake

Steamed green beans and sautéed onions are baked with whole oats and cheese.

YIELD: 6 servings

PREPARATION TIME: 15 minutes

COOKING TIME: 1 hour

RDOB PER SERVING: 10%

1 cup oat groats, rinsed and drained

1 cup water

1 cup vegetable or chicken broth

2 cups cut green beans (1-inch pieces)

2 cups chopped celery

1/4 cup chopped onions

1/2 teaspoon celery seed

2 tablespoons olive or safflower oil

1 cup grated reduced-fat or imitation cheddar cheese

1/2 cup oat cracker crumbs

1. Place oat groats, water, and broth in a heavy-bottomed saucepan and bring to a boil. Reduce heat and simmer gently for 45 minutes or until groats are tender and liquid is absorbed.

2. In a separate saucepan place green beans in a steamer basket over 1 inch of boiling water. Cover and steam for 5 minutes until just tender.

3. Preheat oven to 375°F.

4. Sauté celery, onions, and celery seed in oil in a large skillet for 4 minutes, stirring frequently. Add groats and stir for 1 minute to heat.

5. Add green beans and 3/4 cup of the cheddar cheese to the groat mixture. Transfer to a 3-quart casserole dish.

6. Sprinkle with cracker crumbs and remaining cheese. Bake for 15 minutes until bubbly.

Carrots and apples spiced with ginger and cinnamon go well with baked or barbecued chicken.

YIELD: 8 servings

PREPARATION TIME: 20 minutes

COOKING TIME: 30 to 35 minutes

RDOB PER SERVING: 13%

1 teaspoon lemon juice

1 teaspoon brown sugar

1/2 teaspoon ground dried ginger or 1 teaspoon ground fresh ginger

1/2 teaspoon cinnamon

1/2 cup water

2 apples, pared, cored, and cut into small cubes

6 carrots, grated

1 cup oat bran

2 egg whites, lightly beaten

1. Lightly oil a 9-inch square baking pan. Preheat oven to 350°F.
2. Combine lemon juice, brown sugar, ginger, cinnamon, and water in a bowl. Stir in apples, carrots, and oat bran and mix well.
3. Stir in egg whites. Transfer mixture to baking dish. Seal top with foil.
4. Bake for 30 to 35 minutes until carrots are tender.

This old-fashioned standard for leftover or freshly cooked potatoes is browned for extra crunch.

YIELD: 4 servings

PREPARATION TIME: 20 minutes (add 20 minutes if boiling potatoes)

COOKING TIME: 10 minutes

RDOB PER SERVING: 13%

1/2 cup skim milk
1/2 cup oat bran
1/2 teaspoon salt (optional)
3/4 cup mashed potatoes
1 teaspoon baking powder
2 egg whites, beaten

2 teaspoons minced fresh dill or 1/2 teaspoon dried dill
2 tablespoons chopped fresh parsley
1 tablespoon olive oil

1. Scald milk in a medium-size saucepan. Stir in oat bran and salt and cook 2 minutes until thickened.
2. Stir in remaining ingredients. Form into 4 patties.
3. Sauté each on lightly oiled nonstick skillet until browned.

Oat bran gives these pan-toasted potatoes a crunchy coating.

YIELD: 4 servings

PREPARATION TIME: 15 minutes

COOKING TIME: 20 minutes

RDOB PER SERVING: 19%

2 egg whites

2 tablespoons skim milk

3/4 cup oat bran

16 small potatoes (1 pound), well scrubbed, with skins on

2 tablespoons olive or safflower oil

1 tablespoon minced fresh parsley or 1/2 teaspoon dried parsley

1/8 teaspoon black pepper

1/4 teaspoon salt (optional)

1. Place potatoes in just enough boiling water to cover and simmer for 15 minutes until done when tested with a fork. Drain and cut into quarters.

2. Beat egg whites and milk together in a shallow bowl.

3. Put oat bran in a second shallow bowl.

4. Dip potatoes first in bran, then in egg mixture, then again in bran.

5. Brown potatoes on all sides in hot oil in a large skillet, stirring frequently. Sprinkle with parsley, pepper, and salt, toss well, and serve immediately.

Oat "Rice"

Oat groats are an excellent substitute for rice or potatoes. With their nutty, hearty flavor, they're as tasty as wild rice—and much less expensive. Make them with water, broth, or milk to accompany meats, poultry, and vegetable dishes; made with milk they go well with sweets, too.

YIELD: 4 servings

PREPARATION TIME: 10 minutes

COOKING TIME: 40 minutes

RDOB PER SERVING: 13%

1 cup oat groats

2 cups water, broth, or skim milk

1/4 teaspoon salt (optional)

METHOD I
1. Rinse and drain oat groats.
2. Place water, broth, or milk in a heavy-bottomed pot and bring to a boil.
3. Stir in the oat groats and salt (if desired). Lower heat, cover the pot with a snug fitting lid, and cook for 40 minutes, until liquid is absorbed.

METHOD II (produces a fluffier cooked groat and reduces the possibility of scorching)
1. Rinse and drain oat groats.
2. Place water, broth, or milk in a heavy-bottomed pot and bring to a boil.
3. Stir in the oat groats. Lower heat, cover the pot with a snug-fitting lid, and cook for 15 minutes. Turn off the heat and allow to stand, covered, for 45 minutes longer.

METHOD III (reduces total cooking time)
1. Rinse oat groats and soak in 3 cups of water overnight.
2. Transfer mixture to a heavy-bottomed pot. Bring to a boil and cook for 25 minutes until liquid is absorbed.

Toasted steel-cut oats make this an excellent accompaniment to main dishes.

YIELD: 4 servings

PREPARATION TIME: 10 minutes

COOKING TIME: 35 minutes

RDOB PER SERVING: 13%

1 cup steel-cut oats

1 small onion, diced

3 cups chicken or vegetable broth

2 tablespoons tub margarine

1 tablespoon minced parsley or scallions for garnish (optional)

1. Place oats in a heavy saucepan and toast, while stirring, over a medium-low heat for 3 to 5 minutes. When fragrant and lightly browned, add onions and stir.

2. Add broth and bring to a quick boil. Reduce heat and simmer, covered, for 30 minutes until liquid is absorbed. Check the pan after 25 minutes. If dry, add 1/4 to 1/2 cup more liquid.

3. Add margarine. Fluff mixture with a fork. Serve hot, garnished with parsley or scallions if desired.

Beautiful, puffy cheese soufflés make any meal special.

YIELD: 6 servings

PREPARATION TIME: 30 minutes

COOKING TIME: 30 minutes

RDOB PER SERVING: 8%

1 1/2 cups chicken or beef broth
  1 teaspoon dry yeast
1/2 cup oat bran
1/2 cup grated reduced-fat cheddar cheese

3/4 cup skim milk
  1 tablespoon whole wheat flour
  1 whole egg, separated, plus 4 egg whites

1. Lightly oil 6 custard cups or small baking dishes.
2. Bring broth to a boil in top half of double boiler placed directly over heat.
3. Bring 1 inch of water to a boil in the bottom of double boiler. Put double boiler together. Stir in yeast and oat bran and gently cook for 15 minutes until oat bran has absorbed the broth.
4. Preheat oven to 350°F.
5. Turn off heat under double boiler. Add cheese, milk, flour, and egg yolk and mix well.
6. Beat egg whites until stiff. Remove top of double boiler from water and fold egg whites into cheese mixture.
7. Spoon into custard cups and bake for 30 minutes until very lightly browned. Serve immediately.

Oats with Vegetables and Herbs

Freshly made or leftover cooked oats are the basis for this colorful, delicious side dish.

YIELD: 4 servings

PREPARATION TIME: 20 minutes

COOKING TIME: 15 minutes; if cooking oats, add 30 to 40 minutes

RDOB PER SERVING: 25%

2 cups cooked oat groats (page 49)

4 tablespoons olive oil

1 medium onion, diced

1 green pepper, diced

1 stalk celery with leaves, diced

1 carrot, peeled and grated

1/2 teaspoon powdered sage

1/2 teaspoon dried thyme

1 teaspoon low-sodium soy sauce

1/4 teaspoon black pepper

2 teaspoons minced parsley for garnish

1. In a heavy skillet, sauté oats in 2 tablespoons of the oil for 5 minutes. Remove from skillet and set aside.

2. Heat remaining oil in the same skillet and sauté onions and green pepper for 5 minutes, stirring frequently.

3. Add remaining ingredients and stir. Cover and cook for 3 to 5 minutes, until softened.

4. Return oats to the skillet and heat through, stirring to combine. Serve hot. Sprinkle with parsley for garnish.

Crunchier than regular rice, this hearty dish is closer to the taste of wild rice and even more nutritious. Steel-cut oats can be substituted for groats.

YIELD: 4 servings

PREPARATION TIME: 20 minutes

COOKING TIME: 55 minutes

RDOB PER SERVING: 13%

1 cup oat groats, washed and drained

1 tablespoon peanut, olive, or safflower oil

1 medium onion, finely chopped

1/3 pound mushrooms, sliced (about 1 1/2 cups)

2 cups chicken or vegetable broth (see Note)

1/4 teaspoon ground black pepper

3 tablespoons minced fresh parsley

1. In a heavy-bottom saucepan, sauté groats in the oil for 3 to 4 minutes, stirring frequently. (They will begin to toast and smell very nutty.)

2. Add onions and sauté 3 more minutes.

3. Add mushrooms and sauté 5 more minutes.

4. Add broth and pepper and bring to a boil. Lower heat and cover. Simmer for 40 minutes, stirring once or twice until liquid is absorbed. Check pan after 35 minutes, and add 1/4 to 1/2 cup water if too dry, or remove cover if too wet.

5. Remove from the heat, stir in parsley, and serve.

NOTE: Use homemade broth, or add enough water to a 13 3/4-ounce can of broth to make 2 cups of liquid.

You vary the vegetables to include whatever you happen to have in your refrigerator.

YIELD: 6 servings

PREPARATION TIME: 20 minutes

COOKING TIME: 1 hour

RDOB PER SERVING: 10%

1 1/4 cups oat groats, rinsed and drained

2 1/4 cups water

2 tablespoons peanut or safflower oil

1 onion, chopped

1 clove garlic, minced

2 stalks celery, thinly sliced

1 small zucchini, thinly sliced

1 large red pepper, seeded and chopped

1/2 cup sliced mushrooms

4 tablespoons dry sherry

1/4 teaspoon black pepper

2 teaspoons dried basil

1. Simmer oat groats in water in a saucepan over low heat for 40 to 45 minutes until liquid is absorbed.

2. Stir-fry onions and garlic in oil in a skillet until soft. Add the remaining vegetables and stir-fry for 2 or 3 minutes.

3. Add the oat groats to the skillet. Season with sherry, pepper, and basil. Cook over low heat for 5 minutes longer.

Savory Oats

Also called "Poorman's Wild Rice," this is especially good with chicken or pork; it's also delicious cold, tossed with greens in a salad. Steel-cut oats can be substituted if you can't find groats.

YIELD: 6 servings

PREPARATION TIME: 10 minutes

COOKING TIME: 40 to 45 minutes

RDOB PER SERVING: 8%

2 cups chicken or vegetable broth

1 cup oat groats, rinsed and drained

1 tablespoon peanut or safflower oil

1/2 teaspoon crushed caraway seeds or celery seeds

3 tablespoons minced parsley for garnish

1. Bring broth to a boil in a heavy-bottomed pot.
2. Add groats, oil, and caraway seeds and stir.
3. Lower heat, cover, and simmer for 40 to 45 minutes until liquid is absorbed.
4. Garnish with parsley.

Oats and Toasted Almonds

Don't let the simplicity of this dish fool you—the almonds bring out the subtle sweetness of the oats.

YIELD: 6 servings

PREPARATION TIME: 10 minutes

COOKING TIME: 30 minutes

RDOB PER SERVING: 8%

1 cup steel-cut oats

3 cups water

1/4 teaspoon salt

1/2 cup slivered almonds

Low-sodium soy sauce

1. Combine oats, water, and salt in a medium-size saucepan. Bring to a boil and simmer, uncovered, for 25 minutes until water is absorbed. Stir 2 or 3 times.

2. Toast almonds in a heavy dry skillet over medium heat until lightly browned, stirring frequently.

3. Transfer oats to a serving dish. Top with almonds and sprinkle with soy sauce.

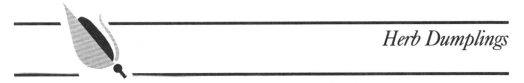

Herb Dumplings

These moist oat dumplings are reminiscent of matzoh balls. Start with a thin soup because they will thicken the stew or soup they are cooking in.

YIELD: 4 servings

PREPARATION TIME: 10 minutes

COOKING TIME (DUMPLINGS ONLY): 12 minutes

RDOB PER SERVING: 8%

2/3 cup oat flour (page 47)

2/3 cup unbleached all-purpose flour

1 tablespoon plus 1 teaspoon baking powder

1 tablespoon chopped fresh chives

1 tablespoon chopped fresh parsley

3/4 cup skim milk

1. Mix oat flour, all-purpose flour, and baking powder in a small bowl. Add chives and parsley.

2. Add milk and mix briefly (batter can be a little lumpy).

3. Drop batter into simmering stew or soup, 1 tablespoon at a time.

4. Adjust heat to a low boil, cover soup pot, and cook for 12 minutes. (Do not uncover pot while dumplings are cooking.) Finished dumplings should be puffy and moist on the outside and dry in the middle.

Small, golden fritters are prepared with a hint of nutmeg, and provide a high share of RDOB.

YIELD: 16 small fritters; 4 servings

PREPARATION TIME: 10 minutes

COOKING TIME: 15 minutes

RDOB PER SERVING: 25%

1 cup canned cream-style corn

3 egg whites, beaten

1 cup oat bran

1/2 teaspoon baking powder

1/4 teaspoon salt

Dash nutmeg

3 tablespoons tub margarine

1. Mix together corn, egg whites, oat bran, baking powder, salt, and nutmeg in a large bowl.

2. Melt margarine in a skillet. Add corn batter by the tablespoon. Brown and turn to brown the reverse side. Serve immediately.

A spicy, creamy blend of winter squash, apples, and oats, this makes a wonderful side dish with roast chicken or turkey.

YIELD: 8 servings

PREPARATION TIME: 30 minutes

COOKING TIME: 1 hour 45 minutes

RDOB PER SERVING: 25%

2 cups old-fashioned rolled oats

1 cup oat bran

5 cups water

2 1/2 cups skinned cubed acorn or butternut squash

3 apples, pared and grated

3 tablespoons chopped almonds

1/2 cup whole wheat pastry flour

1/2 teaspoon cinnamon

1/4 teaspoon nutmeg

1. Preheat oven to 350°F. Generously oil a 2-quart casserole dish.

2. Place rolled oats, oat bran, water, and squash in a large pot and bring to a boil. Lower heat and simmer for 15 minutes.

3. Cool mixture slightly and purée in a blender, food mill, or food processor.

4. Stir apples, almonds, flour, cinnamon, and nutmeg into the purée. Pour the mixture into the casserole dish. Bake for 1 1/2 hours.

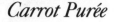

You can make this smooth-textured dish, laced with ginger and cinnamon, ahead of time and reheat in a casserole dish for 30 minutes at 375°F.

YIELD: 4 servings

PREPARATION/COOKING TIME: 20 minutes

RDOB PER SERVING: 25%

1 cup water
4 cups sliced carrots (about 8 carrots)
1 cup oat bran
1/2 cup skim milk
2 tablespoons brown sugar

1 tablespoon peanut or safflower oil
1/2 teaspoon cinnamon
1/8 teaspoon nutmeg
2 tablespoons chopped walnuts

1. Boil water in a large saucepan. Add carrots, cover, and simmer 10 minutes, until tender.
2. Process carrot/water mixture, a half at a time, in blender or food processor until smooth.
3. Add oat bran, milk, sugar, oil, cinnamon, and nutmeg, and mix well.
4. Transfer to a serving bowl, sprinkle with walnuts, and serve hot.

This carrot-corn casserole is baked with dill and topped with wheat germ and oats.

YIELD: 4 servings

PREPARATION TIME: 20 minutes

COOKING TIME: 20 minutes

RDOB PER SERVING: 17%

4 cups sliced carrots

1 tablespoon tub margarine

1/2 teaspoon dried dill or 1 tablespoon minced fresh dill

1 cup canned corn

1 tablespoon minced fresh parsley or 1 teaspoon dried parsley

1/3 cup chicken broth

1/8 teaspoon black pepper

2/3 cup oat bran

4 tablespoons wheat germ

4 tablespoons olive or safflower oil

1. In a saucepan, place carrots in a steamer basket over 1 inch of boiling water. Cover tightly and steam for 5 minutes.

2. Lightly oil a 9 × 13-inch baking dish. Preheat oven to 375°F.

3. Combine carrots, margarine, dill, corn, parsley, broth, and pepper in a large bowl. Pour into baking dish.

4. Combine oat bran, wheat germ, and oil in a separate bowl. Sprinkle on vegetables.

5. Bake for 20 minutes until topping is crisp.

This easy-to-prepare recipe is an excellent source of oat bran. You can use either fresh or frozen cauliflower.

YIELD: 4 servings

PREPARATION/COOKING TIME: 20 minutes

RDOB PER SERVING: 19%

1/2 cup water	1/4 cup skim milk
4 cups chopped cauliflower	1 tablespoon tub margarine
3/4 cup oat bran	1/4 teaspoon white pepper

1. Boil water in a large saucepan. Add cauliflower, cover, and simmer for 7 to 8 minutes, until tender.
2. Blend cauliflower and water, half at a time, with remaining ingredients in a blender or food processor until smooth.
3. Transfer to a serving bowl and serve hot.

BROCCOLI PURÉE   Substitute 4 cups chopped broccoli for the cauliflower.

STUFFINGS

Stuffing can be made from oat groats, leftover oat bread, rolled oats, or granola; these are a few examples of each in the recipes that follow. Cook it in poultry, thick chops, or breast of veal, or add enough liquid to moisten and bake it separately.

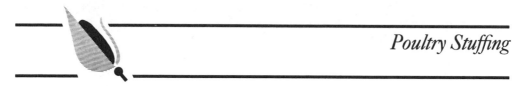

Poultry Stuffing

The rich, nutty flavor will remind you of wild rice stuffing.

YIELD: Stuffing for a 12-pound bird
(6 servings)

PREPARATION TIME: 45 minutes

COOKING TIME: Follow roasting directions
for poultry

RDOB PER SERVING: 8%

Giblets from poultry
1 1/4 teaspoons dried thyme
1 1/2 cups water
1 cup oat groats
2 cups dry bread stuffing or bread cut into small cubes (use leftover oat bread if possible)
1 tablespoon tub margarine, melted
1 teaspoon dried tarragon

1/2 cup currants
1/4 cup chopped walnuts (optional)
2 stalks celery, chopped
1 small onion, chopped (about 1/2 cup)
1 tablespoon olive, peanut, or safflower oil
1 1/2 cups broth
1/4 teaspoon each salt and pepper (optional)

1. In a small saucepan, cover giblets with water. Add 1/4 teaspoon thyme, cover, and simmer for 30 minutes.

2. In a large bowl, combine oat groats, bread stuffing, margarine, tarragon, remaining thyme, currants, and walnuts (if desired).

3. Sauté celery and onion in oil in a small skillet for 5 minutes, until softened. Add to oat mixture.

4. Remove giblets from water. Strain the water and add this broth to the oat mixture.

5. Chop the liver and heart finely, pick the meat off the neck and chop, and discard the gizzard. Add chopped meat to the bread mixture, add salt and pepper if desired, and mix lightly but well with a wooden spoon. (Mixture should be moist but not wet.)

6. Stuff dressing into the neck and chest cavities, using a wooden spoon. Do not force a tightly packed cavity because the bread and oats need a little room to expand.

7. Follow baking instructions for the poultry. Add enough water to moisten and bake any extra stuffing in a covered dish next to the poultry for 1 hour.

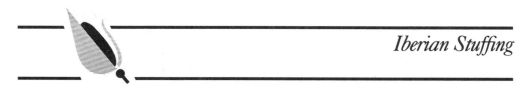

Iberian Stuffing

Leftover oat bread is the starting point for an unusual raisin-almond stuffing.

YIELD: Stuffing for a 12-pound turkey (16 half cup servings)

PREPARATION TIME: 20 minutes

COOKING TIME: Follow roasting directions for turkey

RDOB PER SERVING: 6%

3 tablespoons peanut or safflower oil

1 medium onion, chopped

1/2 pound chopped fresh mushrooms

2 green peppers, chopped

6 cups cubed leftover oat bread, such as No-Frills Oat Bran Bread (page 125)

1/2 cup finely chopped almonds or sunflower seeds

1/2 cup raisins or currants

1 teaspoon dried thyme

1/2 teaspoon dried marjoram

1/2 cup chopped fresh parsley

2 egg whites, beaten

1/4 cup dry sherry or cider

1. Sauté onions, mushrooms and peppers in oil in a skillet until soft.

2. Combine bread, almonds, raisins, thyme, marjoram, and parsley in a large mixing bowl. Add sautéed vegetables.

3. Add egg whites and sherry and toss to mix. Stuff turkey lightly; do not pack as stuffing will swell. Follow cooking directions for the turkey. Add enough water to moisten and bake extra stuffing in a covered dish next to the poultry for 1 hour.

The nutty flavor comes from old-fashioned oats that are toasted and then added to a traditional mixture of celery, thyme, parsley and onion.

YIELD:	Stuffing for an 8- to 10-pound turkey (8 cups)
PREPARATION TIME:	30 minutes
COOKING TIME:	Follow roasting directions for turkey if cooking inside bird. Bake for 25 to 30 minutes if cooking separately.
RDOB FOR 1/2 CUP SERVING:	19%

6 cups old-fashioned rolled oats
2 cups finely chopped celery
1 cup finely chopped onion
2 tablespoons minced fresh parsley

1/4 teaspoon dried thyme
1/8 teaspoon black pepper
1/2 cup tub margarine, melted
1/4 to 1/3 cup water

1. Toast oats on a baking sheet at 350°F. for 20 minutes, stirring once or twice.

2. Combine with celery, onion, parsley, thyme, and pepper in a large bowl. Mix thoroughly and stir in margarine and water to blend.

3. Stuff turkey and bake according to poultry directions. Add enough water to moisten and bake extra stuffing in a covered dish next to the poultry for the last 25 to 30 minutes of roasting time.

HOLIDAY STUFFING   Add 1/2 cup chopped apples or roasted chestnuts.

Apricot–Whole Oat Stuffing

This unique combination of apricots, whole oats, vegetables, cinnamon, savory, and mace can be used either as a poultry stuffing or a side dish.

YIELD: Stuffing for a 6- to 8-pound turkey (6 cups)

PREPARATION TIME: 20 minutes

COOKING TIME: 40 minutes for oat groats. Follow roasting directions for poultry if cooking inside bird. Bake for 25 to 30 minutes if cooking separately

RDOB FOR 1/2 CUP: 6%

1 1/2 cups oat groats, rinsed and drained

3 cups chicken broth

2 tablespoons peanut or safflower oil

1/2 cup sliced fresh or canned mushrooms

1 small onion, chopped

1/2 cup minced parsley

1 cup chopped unsweetened canned apricots, drained, or 1/3 cup dried chopped apricots that have simmered in 2/3 cup water for 20 minutes

1/2 cup chopped celery

1 cup fresh orange juice

1/2 teaspoon dried savory

1/8 teaspoon cinnamon

1/8 teaspoon mace

1. Bring oat groats and broth to a boil in a 4-quart saucepan. Reduce heat and simmer for 40 minutes.

2. Heat oil in a small skillet and sauté mushrooms and onions for 5 minutes until browned.

3. Add mushrooms and onions to the groats. Stir in parsley, apricots, celery, orange juice, savory, cinnamon, and mace.

4. Stuff turkey and roast according to poultry directions. Add enough water to moisten and bake extra stuffing in a covered dish next to the poultry for the last 30 minutes of roasting time.

Make this trio of stuffings with Basic Granola and use them with roast poultry, fish, or pork, or serve as a side dish. Follow recipe directions for poultry, fish, or pork for cooking temperatures and times.

Granola-Celery Stuffing

YIELD: 4 cups

RDOB FOR 1/2 CUP SERVING: 16%

1 tablespoon whole wheat flour
1/4 teaspoon black pepper
1/4 teaspoon dried dill
2 cups Basic Granola (page 129)

2 cups diced celery
1/2 cup warm skim milk
1/2 cup tub margarine, melted

1. Mix together flour, pepper, and dill in a bowl. Stir in granola.
2. Add celery, milk, and margarine and toss to mix.

Granola-Rice Stuffing

YIELD: 4 cups

RDOB FOR 1/2 CUP SERVING: 12%

2 cups chicken or vegetable broth
1 cup chopped onion
1 cup brown rice, uncooked
3 tablespoons peanut or safflower oil

1 1/2 cups Basic Granola (page 129)
1/4 teaspoon black pepper
3 tablespoons minced fresh parsley or 1 teaspoon dried parsley
1 teaspoon dried tarragon

1. In a small skillet, sauté onions and rice in oil for 10 minutes.
2. Heat broth to a simmer over medium heat in a large saucepan.
3. Stir rice and onions into broth. Cover and simmer for 20 minutes.
4. Stir in granola, pepper, parsley, and tarragon and mix well.

Granola-Apple Stuffing

YIELD: 4 cups

RDOB FOR 1/2 CUP SERVING: 16%

2 egg whites
3 apples, peeled, cored, and grated
1/2 onion, grated
1/2 cup chopped celery
1 clove garlic, minced
1/3 cup apple cider or water
2 cups Basic Granola (page 129)
1/4 cup reduced-fat or imitation cheddar cheese
1 tablespoon honey
3 tablespoons minced fresh parsley or 1 teaspoon dried parsley
1/4 teaspoon ground cloves

1. Beat egg whites in a large bowl.
2. Add apples, onions, celery, garlic, cider, granola, cheese, honey, parsley, and cloves. Toss to mix well.

Mixed Green Salad with Parmesan Oats

Garlic- and cheese-flavored toasted oats are used in place of croutons to provide added crunch to mixed greens.

YIELD: 4 servings

PREPARATION TIME: 15 minutes

COOKING TIME: 15 minutes

RDOB PER SERVING: 14%

1 cup old-fashioned rolled oats

1/4 cup tub margarine, melted

1/3 cup grated Parmesan cheese

1 clove garlic, minced

3 cups romaine lettuce leaves, washed and torn into bite-size pieces

3 cups spinach leaves, washed, stems removed, and torn into bite-size pieces

1 1/2 cups sliced fresh mushrooms

1 medium red or Bermuda onion, sliced into thin rings

2 tomatoes, cut in wedges

1 teaspoon oat bran

1. Preheat oven to 350°F. Combine oats, margarine, cheese, and garlic in a small bowl. Bake on an unoiled baking sheet for 15 minutes.

2. While oats are baking, toss romaine, spinach, mushrooms, onions, and tomatoes in a large bowl.

3. Top with warm Parmesan oats. Add 1 teaspoon oat bran to your favorite salad dressing, shake well, and toss with salad.

Oat groats replace bulgur wheat in this nutritious and delicious Middle Eastern specialty. Tabouli is particularly appealing in hot weather when served chilled.

YIELD: 4 servings

PREPARATION TIME: 10 minutes

COOKING TIME: 45 minutes

RDOB PER SERVING: 13%

1 cup oat groats, rinsed and drained

2 cups water

3 tablespoons olive oil

4 tablespoons lemon juice

1 teaspoon grated lemon peel

2 cloves garlic, crushed

6 scallions, sliced

1/8 teaspoon black pepper

1 tablespoon minced fresh mint or 1/2 teaspoon dried mint

3/4 cup loosely packed minced parsley

4 fresh tomatoes, chopped

1. Place oat groats and water in a saucepan and bring to a boil. Reduce heat, cover, and simmer for 45 minutes. Check after 35 minutes; add 1/4 cup water if dry. Rinse under cold water and drain well. Cool.

2. Mix oil, lemon juice, lemon peel, and garlic together in a bowl. Add scallions and pepper.

3. Stir oat groats, mint, and parsley together in a second bowl. Add lemon juice and dressing and mix. Toss with tomatoes and serve.

NOTE: You can also refrigerate this for an hour or more before serving.

Oat Sprout Salad with Lemon Garlic Dressing

While unhulled fresh oats for sprouting can be difficult to find, they are well worth the effort. Experiment and add the sprouts to your favorite salad.

YIELD: 6 servings

PREPARATION TIME: 30 minutes

RDOB PER SERVING: 9%

1 cup tightly packed oat sprouts (page 47)

1 cup mung or soy bean sprouts

2 tomatoes, chopped

2 stalks celery, chopped

2 scallions, thinly sliced

1 carrot, peeled and grated

1 cucumber, finely chopped

1/2 cup minced fresh parsley

DRESSING:

1/2 cup olive oil

1/2 cup lemon juice

1 clove garlic, minced

1 teaspoon oat bran

1/4 teaspoon low-sodium soy sauce

1. Combine sprouts, tomatoes, celery, scallions, carrots, cucumbers, and parsley in a large salad bowl and toss.

2. Combine all ingredients in a blender container and blend for 30 seconds.

3. Pour dressing over vegetables and marinate for 30 minutes before serving.

Fruit Salad

Rolled oats and oat bran toasted with brown sugar and cinnamon provide a sweet and crunchy topping for seasonal fruits.

YIELD: 4 servings

PREPARATION TIME: 15 minutes

RDOB PER SERVING: 13%

1/3 cup tub margarine, melted
1 cup old-fashioned rolled oats
2/3 cup oat bran
1 tablespoon brown sugar
1/2 teaspoon cinnamon
2 navel oranges, peeled and cubed

1/2 pink grapefruit, peeled and cubed
1 cup fresh or frozen blueberries
1 cup seedless red grapes
1 cup unsweetened pineapple chunks

1. Melt margarine in a skillet and add oats, oat bran, brown sugar, and cinnamon. Stir over medium heat for 5 minutes until lightly toasted. Cool.

2. Toss together oranges, grapefruit, blueberries, grapes, and pineapple in a serving bowl. Top with oats.

There's nothing better than oatmeal cookies, and the varieties are endless. A friend once said, "You haven't really lived if you haven't tasted real home-made oatmeal cookies," and we think she's right.

Wire racks for cooling cookies are handy, but if you don't have any, try using newspapers instead. A clever Norwegian friend always does this, and it's especially helpful with the tiny cookie "drops" that can fall through the wire racks.

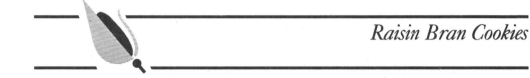

Raisin Bran Cookies

A variation on the familiar oatmeal raisin cookie, this soft cookie features oat bran instead of rolled oats. Unlike commercially baked oatmeal cookies, these have limited quantities of sugar, cholesterol, and fat.

YIELD: 24 cookies

PREPARATION TIME: 20 minutes

COOKING TIME: 10 to 12 minutes

RDOB FOR 2 COOKIES: 8%

1/2 cup tub margarine	1/2 teaspoon baking powder
1/3 cup brown sugar	1/2 teaspoon baking soda
4 egg whites	1/4 teaspoon salt
1/4 cup water	1 teaspoon cinnamon
1/2 teaspoon vanilla extract	1/2 cup raisins
3/4 cup all-purpose flour	
1 cup oat bran	

1. Lightly oil 2 baking sheets. Preheat oven to 375°F.
2. Beat margarine and sugar in electric mixer at medium speed until light and aerated. Add egg whites, water, and vanilla and mix for 1 more minute.
3. Combine flour, oat bran, baking powder, baking soda, salt, and cinnamon in a second bowl. Add to margarine mixture and beat at medium speed until well combined.
4. Remove mixer blades and stir in raisins.
5. Drop batter by tablespoons on the baking sheets. Bake until bottoms are very lightly browned. Cool on wire racks.

VARIATION: Add 1/3 cup finely chopped walnuts.

It's hard to believe that these moist, chewy treats are made without the usual sugars and additives found in most cookies.

YIELD: 24 cookies

PREPARATION TIME: 20 minutes

COOKING TIME: 20 minutes

RDOB FOR 2 COOKIES: 10%

3 very ripe bananas

1/3 cup peanut or safflower oil

1/8 teaspoon salt (optional)

1 teaspoon vanilla extract

1 1/2 cups rolled oats

1/2 cup oat bran

1 1/2 cups dried fruit (raisins, chopped dates, or other dried fruit, in any combination)

1/2 cup chopped walnuts or almonds

1. Oil 2 baking sheets. Preheat oven to 350°F.
2. Mash bananas well in a mixing bowl. Add oil, salt, and vanilla and mix.
3. Add oats, oat bran, fruit, and nuts and mix well.
4. Drop by rounded tablespoons on the baking sheets, flattening the batter slightly with the back of the spoon.
5. Bake for 20 to 25 minutes or until lightly browned. Turn out on wire racks to cool. Store in refrigerator after first day.

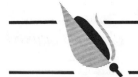

Soluble and insoluble fiber (in the form of rolled oats, whole wheat pastry flour, and wheat bran) unite with peanut butter, honey, nuts, and raisins in a chunky, great-tasting cookie.

YIELD: 30 cookies

PREPARATION TIME: 20 minutes

COOKING TIME: 12 to 15 minutes

RDOB FOR 3 COOKIES: 8%

2 egg whites	1 cup whole wheat pastry flour
1/2 cup honey	1 tablespoon baking soda
2 tablespoons peanut butter	1 1/2 cups rolled oats
1 teaspoon vanilla extract	1 cup wheat bran
1/2 cup water	1/2 cup raisins
3/4 cup peanut or safflower oil	1/2 cup walnuts or peanuts

1. Lightly oil 2 baking sheets. Preheat oven to 375°F.

2. Combine egg whites, honey, peanut butter, vanilla, water, and oil in a blender or with a whisk.

3. Mix flour and baking soda in a large bowl. Stir in oats and wheat bran.

4. Add the wet ingredients to the flour mixture and blend well. Fold in raisins and nuts. Drop by rounded tablespoons on the baking sheets.

5. Bake for 10 minutes or until lightly browned. Turn out on wire racks to cool.

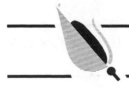

Serve these crisp, thin cookies with coffee, tea, or fresh fruit and keep them fresh in the refrigerator or cookie jar. Design your own shapes for special occasions.

YIELD: 20 hearts, circles, or squares

PREPARATION TIME: 30 minutes

COOKING TIME: 20 minutes

RDOB FOR 5 COOKIES: 13%

1 cup whole wheat pastry flour	1 cup quick rolled oats
1/8 teaspoon salt	3 tablespoons brown sugar
1 teaspoon baking powder	2 egg whites, lightly beaten, or
1/3 cup tub margarine, cold	1 whole egg, lightly beaten

1. Lightly oil 2 baking sheets. Preheat oven to 350°F.

2. Sift together flour, salt, and baking powder into a large bowl. Include any bran from the flour that may be left in sifter if screen is fine.

3. Add margarine and cut into flour mixture with a pastry blender or 2 forks until it resembles coarse crumbs.

4. Add oats and sugar and mix well. Add beaten egg.

5. Knead dough into a smooth ball, turn out onto a well-floured surface, and roll to 1/4 inch thick with a floured rolling pin. (If dough appears too crumbly to roll, add 1 teaspoon water.)

6. Cut into shapes with a 2 1/2-inch cookie cutter circle or heart or cut into squares with a knife. Use all of the dough by rerolling the scraps.

7. Transfer to the baking sheet with a spatula and bake for 20 minutes until very lightly browned and crisped. Turn out on wire racks to cool.

VARIATION: Use 1/2 cup oat bran and 1/2 cup quick rolled oats for an RDOB of 19%.

Though light in color and texture, these cookies are rich in flavor.

YIELD: 18 cookies

PREPARATION TIME: 20 minutes

COOKING TIME: 20 minutes

RDOB FOR 2 COOKIES: 6%

3/4 cup unbleached all-purpose flour

1/4 cup brown sugar substitute

1/2 teaspoon cinnamon

1/4 teaspoon baking powder

1/4 cup peanut or safflower oil

2 egg whites

1 teaspoon vanilla extract

1 cup rolled oats

1/2 cup chopped walnuts

1/4 cup raisins

1. Lightly oil 2 baking sheets. Preheat oven to 375°F.

2. Combine flour, sugar substitute, cinnamon, and baking powder in a large bowl and mix.

3. Add oil, egg whites, and vanilla and mix with an electric mixer or by hand until well combined.

4. Stir in oat bran, walnuts, and raisins.

5. Drop by tablespoons onto the baking sheets, 2 inches apart. Flatten with a fork. Bake for 10 minutes or until lightly browned. Turn out on wire racks to cool and store in an airtight container.

Wheat Germ Oatmeal Cookies

You'll get both oat bran and rolled oats as well as insoluble fiber in the form of wheat germ from these tasty cookies.

YIELD: 48 cookies

PREPARATION TIME: 20 minutes

COOKING TIME: 12 minutes

RDOB FOR 4 COOKIES: 19%

1/2 cup old-fashioned rolled oats for toasting
1/2 cup peanut or safflower oil
1/2 cup honey
2 egg whites
2 teaspoons vanilla extract
1/2 cup water

1/2 teaspoon cinnamon
1/4 teaspoon nutmeg
1 cup wheat germ
1 1/2 cups oat bran
1 cup old-fashioned rolled oats
1 cup raisins
1/2 cup whole wheat pastry flour

1. Use 1/2 cup prepared toasted oats or put 1/2 cup rolled oats in a dry heavy skillet and cook over medium heat for 5 minutes, stirring frequently, until browned.

2. Lightly oil 2 baking sheets. Preheat oven to 350°F.

3. Cream oil and honey together in a mixing bowl. Beat in egg whites, vanilla, and water. Stir in cinnamon, nutmeg, toasted oats, wheat germ, oat bran, 1 cup rolled oats, raisins, flour, and the remaining oats and mix well.

4. Drop by teaspoons onto the baking sheets about 1 inch apart.

5. Bake for 10 to 12 minutes. Turn out on wire racks to cool. Store in airtight container.

Easy-to-prepare and high in oat bran content, these drop cookies make a great snack with skim milk, decaffeinated coffee, or herbal tea.

YIELD: 24 cookies

PREPARATION TIME: 35 to 40 minutes

COOKING TIME: 9 to 11 minutes

RDOB PER COOKIE: 10%

1/2 cup peanut or safflower oil	1/2 teaspoon cinnamon
1/2 cup honey	1 cup oat bran
1/2 cup water	3 cups old-fashioned rolled oats
4 egg whites	1/2 cup finely chopped dried apricots
1/2 teaspoon vanilla extract	1/2 cup finely chopped walnuts
1 1/4 cups unbleached all-purpose flour	1/2 teaspoon grated orange peel
1 teaspoon baking powder	

1. Lightly oil 2 baking sheets. Preheat oven to 350°F.

2. Beat together oil, honey, and water in a large bowl. Add egg whites and vanilla and beat well.

3. Combine flour, baking powder, and cinnamon in a separate bowl. Add to liquid mixture and mix well.

4. Stir in oat bran, oats, apricots, walnuts, and orange peel.

5. Drop by rounded teaspoons onto baking sheets. Bake for 9 to 11 minutes or until lightly browned. Turn out on wire racks to cool.

Dates give these soft cookie drops their wonderful chewy texture.

YIELD: 72 cookies

PREPARATION TIME: 25 minutes

COOKING TIME: 20 minutes

RDOB FOR 2 COOKIES: 5%

1 package (8 ounces) date pieces (1 1/4 cups)	1 teaspoon vanilla extract
1/2 cup water	1/2 cup chopped walnuts
1 cup grated apple, with skins	1/4 teaspoon salt (optional)
3/4 cup peanut or safflower oil	2 cups rolled oats
	1 cup oat bran

1. In a saucepan, simmer 1 cup of the date pieces in water for 5 minutes. Mash with a fork into a purée.

2. Add apple and oil and beat well with a wooden spoon until mixture is smooth.

3. Add remaining ingredients and mix well. Let stand 10 minutes to thicken.

4. Mix well and drop by level teaspoons onto dry baking sheets. (Batter does not spread when baking, so cookies can be placed next to each other.)

5. Bake for 20 minutes until lightly browned around edges. Turn out on newspapers to cool.

Quick to prepare, these cookies are excellent with tea.

YIELD: 36 cookies

PREPARATION TIME: 10 minutes

COOKING TIME: 17 minutes

RDOB FOR 2 COOKIES: 6%

2 cups quick rolled oats	2 egg whites
3/4 cup brown sugar	1/4 teaspoon salt
1/2 cup peanut or safflower oil	1/2 teaspoon almond extract

1. Oil 2 baking sheets well. Preheat oven to 325°F.
2. Mix oats and sugar in a large bowl. Add oil and toss until well mixed.
3. Beat egg whites, salt, and almond extract in a small bowl until frothy. Add to oat mixture and combine well.
4. Drop by rounded teaspoons onto the baking sheets.
5. Bake for 17 to 20 minutes until set. Let cool for 5 minutes, then remove from pans with a spatula and cool on wire racks.

NOTE: This is very sticky dough, so you might prefer making the cookies on foil-lined baking sheets; let cool, then peel off foil.

Tiny, fruit-rich cookies are reminiscent of little fruit cakes.

YIELD: 100 drops

PREPARATION TIME: 45 minutes

COOKING TIME: 15 to 20 minutes for
each of 2 batches

RDOB FOR 4 DROPS: 4%

1/2 cup dark brown sugar

1 cup evaporated skim milk

1/2 cup low-sugar or all-fruit
orange marmalade

1 cup whole wheat pastry flour

1/2 cup plus 2 tablespoons oat
bran

1/2 cup rolled oats

1/4 cup toasted wheat germ

1/2 teaspoon baking powder

1 package (6 ounces) mixed
dried fruit bits (1 cup)

1. Oil 4 sheets of foil and dust with oat bran. Line 2 baking sheets at a time with foil. Preheat oven to 350°F.

2. Combine brown sugar, milk, and marmalade in a large bowl.

3. Mix together flour, 1/2 cup oat bran, oats, wheat germ, and baking powder in a separate bowl. Stir into milk mixture.

4. Sprinkle 2 tablespoons oat bran over fruit bits in a small bowl and mix to coat. Add to batter and mix well.

5. Drop batter by teaspoons onto sheets, 25 cookies per tray.

6. Bake 2 sheets at a time for 15 to 20 minutes until dough is set.

7. Remove with spatula immediately and cool on newspapers.

The unexpected combination of peaches, cinnamon, and peanuts will make these tasty treats a welcome addition to your cookie jar or lunch box.

YIELD: 48 cookies

PREPARATION TIME: 15 minutes

COOKING TIME: 15 to 20 minutes

RDOB FOR 3 COOKIES: 6%

1/4 cup honey

1/2 cup safflower oil

2 egg whites, beaten

3/4 cup finely chopped drained unsweetened canned peaches

2 cups whole wheat pastry flour

1/2 cup oat bran

1 cup rolled oats

1/2 teaspoon cinnamon

1/2 cup chopped unsalted dry-roasted peanuts

1. Lightly oil 2 baking sheets. Preheat oven to 375°F.

2. Blend honey and oil in a large bowl. Stir in egg whites and peaches.

3. Mix together flour, oat bran, oats, and cinnamon in a separate bowl. Add to wet ingredients and mix well. Stir in peanuts.

4. Drop by teaspoons onto baking sheets. (If batter is too thick to drop, add additional fruit; if too thin, stir in more flour.) Bake for 15 to 20 minutes until lightly browned. Turn out on wire racks to cool.

A combination of spices and oats gives standard peanut butter cookies an added punch. The white wine is a variation from a Portuguese recipe.

YIELD: 40 cookies

PREPARATION TIME: 20 minutes

COOKING TIME: 20 minutes

RDOB FOR 4 COOKIES: 5%

8 ounces unhydrogenated peanut butter

1/4 cup tub margarine

1/4 cup sugar

1/2 cup oat bran

1 cup unbleached all-purpose flour

3 tablespoons white wine or water

1/4 teaspoon nutmeg

1/4 teaspoon cinnamon

1/4 teaspoon ground cloves

Confectioners sugar (optional)

1. Cream together peanut butter, margarine, and sugar in a large bowl.
2. Add remaining ingredients and mix together, first with a spoon and then with your hands, to form a dough.
3. Preheat oven to 350°F.
4. On a flat surface dusted with oat bran, form 2 logs, 1 1/2 inches in diameter.
5. Cut into 1/4-inch slices using a sharp knife that has been dipped in flour. Arrange on an unoiled cookie sheet.
6. Bake for 20 minutes, until very lightly browned. Dust lightly with confectioners sugar if desired. Turn out on wire racks to cool.

Peanut Butter and Jelly Oat Cookies

Reminiscent of the simple pleasures of a peanut butter and jelly sandwich, these small oat-enriched cookies are filled with a combination of natural peanut butter and pure fruit preserves.

YIELD: 36 cookies

PREPARATION TIME: 20 minutes

COOKING TIME: 12 to 14 minutes

RDOB FOR 2 COOKIES: 8%

1/4 cup brown sugar

1/2 cup tub margarine

2 egg whites

1/2 cup unhydrogenated peanut butter

1 1/2 cups oat bran, finely ground in blender or processor

1 cup unbleached all-purpose flour

1/2 teaspoon baking powder

1/2 teaspoon baking soda

1/3 cup pure-fruit grape preserves

1. Preheat oven to 350°F.

2. In a medium-size bowl, combine brown sugar and margarine with an electric mixer. Add eggs and peanut butter. Mix until well combined.

3. Combine oat bran, flour, baking powder, and baking soda in a large bowl. Add peanut mixture and mix to form dough.

4. Roll dough into balls 1 inch in diameter. Place on unoiled baking sheets 1 1/2 inches apart. Make a slight depression in the center of each ball with your thumb to flatten cookies.

5. Place a tiny dollop of preserves in the center of each cookie and bake for 12 minutes or until lightly browned. Turn out on wire racks to cool.

Hidden in these protein-packed cookies is the surprise of apples and raisins combined with a rich cheddar cheese flavor. They make a healthful snack.

YIELD: 24 cookies

PREPARATION TIME: 30 minutes

COOKING TIME: 15 minutes

RDOB FOR 2 COOKIES: 9%

3/4 cup unbleached all-purpose flour

2/3 cup tub margarine

2 egg whites, beaten

1 teaspoon vanilla extract

2 teaspoons brown sugar

1/2 teaspoon cinnamon

1/2 teaspoon baking powder

3/4 cup old-fashioned rolled oats

3/4 cup oat bran

1 cup shredded reduced-fat cheddar cheese

3/4 cup raisins

1 cup finely chopped or grated apples

1. Preheat oven to 350°F.

2. Mix together flour, margarine, egg whites, vanilla, brown sugar, cinnamon, and baking powder in a large bowl.

3. Add oats, oat bran, cheese, and raisins and mix again. Add apples.

4. Spoon heaping tablespoons of batter onto unoiled baking sheets. Bake for 15 minutes until lightly browned. Turn out onto wire racks to cool. Keep refrigerated in airtight containers after the first day.

The tangy lemon-accented dough is mixed in a single bowl, shaped into balls, and pressed with a glass.

YIELD: 36 cookies

PREPARATION TIME: 15 minutes

COOKING TIME: 15 minutes

RDOB FOR 3 COOKIES: 11%

2/3 cup tub margarine

1/4 cup brown sugar

1 tablespoon lemon juice

2/3 cup unbleached all-purpose flour

1 cup oat bran

3/4 cup rolled oats

2 tablespoons sugar

1. Oil 2 baking sheets. Preheat oven to 325°F.

2. Blend margarine and brown sugar in a large bowl. Add lemon juice, flour, oat bran, and oats and mix well to form dough.

3. Roll dough into small balls (about 1 inch in diameter) and place on baking sheets. Moisten bottom of a glass, dip in sugar, and press down on each cookie to flatten.

4. Bake for 13 to 15 minutes. Turn out on wire racks to cool.

Orange-Walnut Thins

Save these tangy, lacy cookies for those occasions when you aren't counting calories and you're craving a sweet oat bran treat.

YIELD: 60 cookies

PREPARATION TIME: 15 minutes

COOKING TIME: 5 to 8 minutes

RDOB FOR 5 COOKIES: 8%

1 cup oat bran	2 egg whites
4 tablespoons whole wheat pastry flour	1/4 cup maple syrup
1/8 teaspoon baking soda	1/2 cup honey
1/2 cup ground walnuts	1 teaspoon vanilla extract
2 tablespoons finely grated orange peel	1/2 cup tub margarine, melted

1. Oil 2 baking sheets liberally with tub margarine. Preheat oven to 350°F.

2. Stir oat bran, flour, baking soda, walnuts, and orange peel together in a large bowl, combining well.

3. Beat egg whites with a wire whisk and combine with syrup, honey, vanilla, and margarine in a medium-size bowl.

4. Add egg/syrup mixture to oat bran mixture and mix well.

5. Drop batter by half teaspoons onto the baking sheets, about 2 inches apart. Bake for 5 to 8 minutes until edges are lightly browned. Remove sheets from oven and *immediately* loosen all cookies with a spatula; this must be done while the cookies are still quite soft. Turn out on wire racks to cool.

6. Repeat baking with remaining dough.

Pecan Crunch Cookies

The taste treat in these drop cookies is vanilla and orange juice.

YIELD: 48 cookies

PREPARATION TIME: 15 minutes

COOKING TIME: 12 to 15 minutes

RDOB FOR 2 COOKIES: 10%

1 cup unbleached all-purpose flour
1/4 teaspoon salt
1/2 teaspoon baking soda
2/3 cup tub margarine
1/2 cup brown sugar

2 egg whites
1/4 cup orange juice
1 teaspoon vanilla extract
2 cups old-fashioned rolled oats
1 1/2 cups oat bran
1/2 cup chopped pecans

1. Preheat oven to 350°F.
2. Mix flour, salt, and baking soda together in a small bowl.
3. Cream margarine and brown sugar together in a large bowl. Add egg whites, orange juice, and vanilla and mix well.
4. Stir flour mixture into margarine/sugar mixture. Stir in oats, oat bran, and pecans and mix well.
5. Drop batter by rounded teaspoons onto unoiled baking sheets. (If baking in several batches, cover the batter with plastic wrap to prevent drying.) Bake for 12 to 15 minutes. Cool briefly on sheets to harden, then turn out onto wire racks to finish cooling.

If you're a fan of carrot cake, you're sure to love these cookies, which deliver the same taste sensation without the extra sugar and fat calories.

YIELD: 32 cookies

PREPARATION TIME: 20 minutes

COOKING TIME: 10 to 12 minutes

RDOB FOR 2 COOKIES: 5%

1/4 cup peanut oil	1/2 teaspoon baking powder
1/4 cup honey or molasses	1/4 cup instant nonfat milk powder
2 egg whites, beaten	
1/2 cup oat flour (page 47)	1/4 teaspoon cinnamon
1/2 cup unbleached all-purpose flour	1 cup grated peeled carrots
	1 1/4 cups rolled oats
1/2 teaspoon baking soda	1/2 cup raisins

1. Lightly oil 2 baking sheets. Preheat oven to 400°F.

2. In a large bowl, mix oil, honey, and egg whites with a wire whisk or with an egg beater until well combined.

3. Mix together flours, baking soda, baking powder, milk powder, and cinnamon in a medium-size bowl.

4. Add flour mixture to honey mixture and blend well. Stir in carrots, oats, and raisins.

5. Drop by rounded teaspoons onto the baking sheets, 2 1/2 inches apart. Bake 10 to 12 minutes until set.

6. Cool on baking sheet for 1 minute, then turn out on wire racks to finish cooling. Store in airtight containers after the first day.

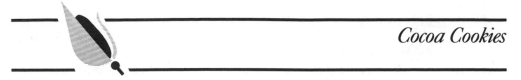
These moist and chewy peanut butter and cocoa cookies will keep well in the refrigerator or in an airtight container. They're higher in sugar than most of our recipes, so save for special days.

1/2 cup milk
1 cup sugar
3 tablespoons cocoa
1/3 cup tub margarine

1/2 cup chunky unhydrogenated peanut butter
3 cups quick rolled oats
1 teaspoon vanilla extract

Cocoa Cookies, No-Bake Version

YIELD: 24 cookies

PREPARATION TIME: 10 minutes

COOLING TIME: 20 minutes minimum

RDOB FOR 2 COOKIES: 13%

1. Combine milk, sugar, cocoa, margarine, and peanut butter in a large heavy-bottomed saucepan. Bring to a boil, stirring frequently.
2. Boil gently for 2 minutes while stirring.
3. Remove from heat. Stir in oats and vanilla and mix well.
4. Drop batter by tablespoons onto waxed paper. Let cool until firm.

Cocoa Cookies, Baked Version

Crisp and chocolaty, these little cookie drops will satisfy any sweet tooth.

YIELD: 100 small drops

PREPARATION TIME: 10 minutes

COOKING TIME: 10 minutes

RDOB FOR 5 DROPS: 8%

1. Follow recipe steps 1-3 for no-bake version.
2. Lightly oil 2 baking sheets. Preheat oven to 350°F.
3. Drop by half teaspoons on the baking sheets.
4. Bake for 10 to 12 minutes. Let sit 5 minutes, then remove with a spatula. Cool on newspapers.

Use your favorite flavor of pure-fruit preserves in these layered treats.

YIELD: 24 bars

PREPARATION TIME: 20 minutes

COOKING TIME: 25 minutes

RDOB FOR 2 BARS: 13%

1 1/2 cups unbleached all-purpose flour

1/2 teaspoon baking powder

3/4 cup tub margarine

1/3 cup brown sugar

1 cup old-fashioned rolled oats

1 cup oat bran

1 jar (12 ounces) pure fruit preserves

1. Lightly oil a 9 × 13-inch baking pan and dust with a little oat bran. Preheat oven to 400°F.

2. Combine flour and baking powder in a small bowl.

3. In a large mixing bowl, beat together margarine and sugar until fluffy and aerated. Add flour mixture and stir.

4. Add oats and oat bran and combine to form a crumbly mixture.

5. Press half the mixture on the bottom of the baking pan. Spread preserves on top. Cover with the other half of the oat mixture.

6. Bake for 25 minutes. Cool in pan for 5 minutes, then cut into bars.

Applesauce Bars

Easy to make, these versatile bars are full of raisins and nuts. They're good for a quick breakfast, lunch, or late-evening snack.

YIELD: 24 bars

PREPARATION TIME: 20 minutes

COOKING TIME: 25 to 30 minutes

RDOB FOR 2 BARS: 15%

1 2/3 cups old-fashioned rolled oats
1 cup oat bran
1 cup unbleached all-purpose flour
3/4 cup whole wheat flour
1/2 cup peanut or safflower oil
1/2 cup water
1/3 cup honey

1/4 teaspoon nutmeg
1 teaspoon cinnamon
1/8 teaspoon ground cloves
1/2 teaspoon baking powder
1 cup unsweetened applesauce
3/4 cup raisins
1/2 cup chopped walnuts or pecans

1. Lightly oil a 9 × 13-inch baking pan. Preheat oven to 400°F.

2. Combine oats, oat bran, flours, oil, water, honey, spices, and baking powder in a large mixing bowl. Beat by hand or with an electric mixer until crumbly.

3. Set aside 2 cups of mixture. Press remaining mixture on the bottom of the baking pan.

4. Combine applesauce, raisins, and nuts in a small bowl. Spread over oat mixture in pan. Cover with the reserved 2 cups of oat mixture.

5. Bake for 25 to 30 minutes or until browned. Cool in pan 5 minutes, then cut into 24 bars.

These chewy squares are a (healthful) alternative to brownies.

YIELD: 9 squares

PREPARATION TIME: 15 minutes

COOKING TIME: 30 minutes

RDOB PER SQUARE: 17%

1 cup oat bran
1 cup quick rolled oats
1/4 cup unsalted sesame seeds
1/4 cup shredded coconut
1/4 cup toasted wheat germ
1/2 cup chopped walnuts or pecans
1/4 teaspoon cardamom

1/4 teaspoon nutmeg
1/8 teaspoon salt
1/2 cup peanut oil
1 whole egg plus 3 egg whites, beaten
1/4 cup brown sugar
1 teaspoon vanilla extract

1. Preheat oven to 350°F.
2. Mix together oat bran, oats, sesame seeds, coconut, wheat germ, walnuts, cardamom, nutmeg, and salt in a large bowl. Spread on bottom of unoiled 9-inch square baking pan.
3. With a wire whisk or fork, mix together oil, eggs, sugar, and vanilla in a second bowl. Pour over oat mixture.
4. Bake for 30 minutes. Cut into squares and cool completely in pan before serving.

not true. Cocoa & even chocolate with cocoa butter is known to reduce cholesterol, where the most highly saturated coconut fat (solid at room temp) skyrockets cholesterol.

This old-fashioned cake is an oat bran-enriched variation of the "milkless-butterless" cake that was popular during World War II.

YIELD: 9 servings

PREPARATION TIME: 20 minutes

COOKING TIME: 25 to 30 minutes

RDOB PER SERVING: 14%

1/4 cup sugar

1/2 cup peanut or safflower oil

1 1/4 cups sifted unbleached all-purpose flour

3/4 cup oat bran

1 cup old-fashioned rolled oats

1 1/2 teaspoons baking soda

1 teaspoon cinnamon

1/4 teaspoon nutmeg

1/4 teaspoon ground cloves

1 cup water

1/2 cup chopped walnuts

1/2 cup raisins

4 egg whites

1. Lightly oil a 9-inch square baking pan and dust with a little oat bran. Preheat oven to 350°F.

2. Beat sugar and oil together with a wire whisk or fork in a large mixing bowl.

3. Combine flour, oat bran, oats, baking soda, cinnamon, nutmeg, and cloves in a separate bowl.

4. Alternately add flour mixture and water to oil mixture and mix well with a wooden spoon. Add walnuts and raisins.

5. Beat egg whites until stiff and fold into batter.

6. Pour batter into pan. Bake 25 to 30 minutes until a wooden toothpick inserted in the center of cake comes out clean. Cool in the pan. Cut into 9 squares.

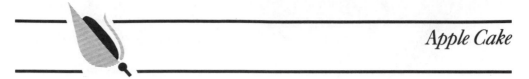

A lovely spiced cake, it tastes as good the second day as it does right out of the oven. Warmed, unsweetened apple sauce, spiced with a little cinnamon, makes a tasty topping on the cake squares.

YIELD: 9 servings

PREPARATION TIME: 25 minutes

COOKING TIME: 45 minutes

RDOB PER SERVING: 8%

1 1/4 cups sifted unbleached all-purpose flour

1 teaspoon baking powder

1 teaspoon baking soda

1/4 teaspoon salt

1 teaspoon cinnamon

1/2 teaspoon nutmeg

1/2 cup firmly packed brown sugar

1 cup rolled oats

1/4 cup oat bran

1/2 cup chopped walnuts (optional)

2 egg whites plus 1 whole egg, lightly beaten

1/3 cup milk

2 tablespoons tub margarine, melted

2 tablespoons peanut or safflower oil

1 1/2 cups shredded peeled apples (approximately 2 medium-size apples)

1. Lightly oil 8-inch square baking pan and dust with a little oat bran. Preheat oven to 350°F.

2. Sift together flour, baking powder, baking soda, salt, cinnamon, and nutmeg into a large mixing bowl. Add brown sugar, oats, oat bran, and walnuts (if desired) and mix.

3. Stir in eggs, milk, margarine, and oil. Add apples and stir briefly.

4. Spoon into the baking pan. Bake for 45 minutes or until lightly browned and pulled away from the sides of the pan. Cut into 9 squares. Cool in the pan.

Carrot-Banana-Nut Cake

For extra moistness, this spicy snack cake departs from traditional carrot cake recipes by adding bananas to the batter.

YIELD: 9 servings

PREPARATION TIME: 25 minutes

COOKING TIME: 40 minutes

RDOB PER SERVING: 14%

1 1/2 cups sifted unbleached all-purpose flour

2 teaspoons baking powder

1/2 teaspoon baking soda

1 teaspoon cinnamon

1/4 teaspoon ground cloves

1 cup mashed ripe bananas

1/4 cup sugar

2/3 cup peanut or safflower oil

4 egg whites

1 cup old-fashioned rolled oats

3/4 cup oat bran

1 cup grated peeled carrots

1/3 cup chopped walnuts

1. Lightly oil a 9-inch square baking pan and dust with a little oat bran. Preheat oven to 350°F.

2. Sift together flour, baking powder, baking soda, cinnamon, and cloves into a small bowl.

3. Briskly mix together bananas, sugar, oil, and egg whites in a large bowl.

4. Add flour mixture, oats, oat bran, and carrots to the banana mixture. Spread batter in the baking pan. Top with walnuts.

5. Bake for 40 minutes or until lightly browned and edges have pulled away from the sides of the pan. Cut into 9 squares and cool in the pan.

Petite Oat Fruitcakes

Bake a batch of these tiny cakes at holiday time to replace traditional sugar- and fat-laden desserts.

YIELD: 48 mini cakes

PREPARATION TIME: 30 minutes

COOKING TIME: 25 minutes per batch

RDOB FOR 3 CAKES: 5%

1 1/2 cups grated apple, with skin	1/2 cup whole wheat pastry flour
1/2 cup orange juice	1/2 cup raisins
1/4 cup peanut or safflower oil	1/2 cup chopped dried apricots
1 1/2 cups rolled oats	1/2 cup chopped dried pineapple
2 tablespoons grated orange peel	1/4 cup pecans
	24 dried cherries, cut in half

1. Preheat oven to 350°F. Lightly oil 24 gem mini muffin cups, or line with mini baking cups.

2. Combine apple, orange juice, and oil in a large bowl. Add oats, orange peel, and flour and mix well. Let stand for 10 minutes.

3. Add raisins, apricots, pineapple, and pecans to fruit mixture. Mix well.

4. Fill muffin cups with half the batter. Top each with half a dried cherry.

5. Bake for 20 to 25 minutes. Cool. Bake second half of batter. Store in airtight containers on the shelf for 1 to 2 days or in the refrigerator for longer.

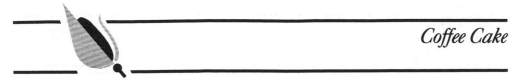

An adaptation of a favorite breakfast and afternoon tea cake, this version has rolled oats in its lovely browned topping and oat bran in the cake itself. Leftover pieces can be refrigerated or frozen.

YIELD: 9 servings

PREPARATION TIME: 20 minutes

COOKING TIME: 30 to 35 minutes

RDOB PER SERVING: 14%

CAKE:

- 2 tablespoons honey, or brown sugar, well packed
- 2 egg whites
- 1/4 cup peanut or safflower oil
- 1/4 teaspoon vanilla extract
- 1 cup buttermilk or skim milk
- 1 cup oat bran
- 1 1/4 cups unbleached all-purpose flour
- 2 teaspoons baking powder
- 1/2 teaspoon cinnamon
- 1/4 teaspoon salt (optional)

TOPPING:

- 1/2 cup rolled oats
- 1/2 cup walnuts
- 2 tablespoons brown sugar, well packed
- 1/2 teaspoon cinnamon
- 4 teaspoons tub margarine

1. Lightly oil an 8-inch square baking pan and dust with a little oat bran. Preheat oven to 375°F.

2. Beat together honey, egg whites, oil, and vanilla in a small bowl. Add buttermilk and beat again.

3. Combine oat bran, flour, baking powder, cinnamon, and salt in a large bowl.

4. Make a well in the middle of the flour mixture, add the milk mixture, and combine. Pour batter into baking pan.

5. To make the topping, combine oats, walnuts, sugar, and cinnamon in a small bowl.

6. Add margarine and mix with a fork or your fingers until all margarine is blended and mixture is crumbly. Sprinkle over cake batter.

7. Bake for 30 to 35 minutes until lightly browned and pulled away from the sides of the pan slightly. Serve warm or cooled. Cool in the pan.

PIE CRUSTS, PIES, AND CRISPS

PIE CRUSTS

The pie crusts we developed using oat products were among the most pleasant surprises we had while creating recipes for this book. After much experimentation, we selected four crusts that can be used as a base for a wide variety of sweet desserts and savory main dishes.

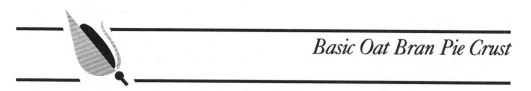

Basic Oat Bran Pie Crust

The end result is a flaky, rich crust that is perfect for both hot and cold dessert fillings. If you omit the brown sugar, you'll have a crust that is ideal for quiches and savory entrées. The dough is easy to handle and roll out.

YIELD: one 9-inch pie crust
(6 servings)

PREPARATION TIME: 15 minutes

COOKING TIME: 12 to 15 minutes

RDOB PER SERVING: 8%

3/4 cup unbleached all-purpose flour

1/2 cup oat bran

1/2 teaspoon salt (optional)

1 tablespoon brown sugar (omit when using savory fillings)

1/3 cup tub margarine, cold

3 tablespoons very cold water

1. Lightly oil a 9-inch pie pan. Preheat oven to 425°F.
2. Combine flour, oat bran, salt (if desired), and brown sugar. Using a pastry blender or 2 forks, cut in margarine until mixture is the texture of coarse crumbs.
3. Add water and stir until the dough takes on the shape of a ball.
4. Turn out on a floured surface and knead a few times. Shape into a well-formed ball.

5. Roll with a rolling pin to create a circle 10 inches in diameter. Place in pie pan, crimp the edges, and prick the bottom of the crust with a fork.

6. Bake for 12 to 15 minutes until lightly browned. Cool. (The crust is now ready to receive a cold filling. For fillings that are cooked in the crust, follow specific recipe directions.)

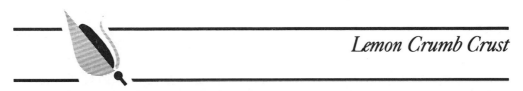

Lemon Crumb Crust

This versatile crust can be made in advance, frozen or refrigerated, then baked. It has a wonderful lemony flavor and a crunchy texture.

YIELD: crust for one 9-inch deep-dish pie or two 7-inch pie pans (6 servings)

PREPARATION TIME: 20 minutes

COOKING TIME: 15 minutes unfilled; 1 hour filled

RDOB PER SERVING: 10%

1/4 cup tub margarine, cold
1/4 cup honey
1 1/4 cups oat flour (page 47), or 1/4 cup rolled oats plus 1 cup oat flour

1/2 cup whole wheat pastry flour
1 tablespoon grated lemon peel
1/4 teaspoon salt

1. Lightly oil one 9-inch deep-dish or two 7-inch pie pans. Preheat oven to 350°.

2. Mix ingredients using a pastry blender or 2 forks until texture of coarse crumbs.

3. Line pie pan with the dough, pressing onto edges first and then the bottom.

4. Bake for 15 minutes until lightly browned. Cool. (The crust is now ready to receive a cold filling. For fillings that are cooked in the crust, follow specific recipe directions.)

Tarragon and basil make this an excellent crust for quiches and other savory main dish pies.

YIELD: one 9-inch crust (6 servings)

PREPARATION TIME: 5 minutes

COOKING TIME: 10 minutes

RDOB PER SERVING: 17%

1 cup oat bran
1/2 cup wheat germ
1/2 cup whole wheat bread crumbs
1/4 cup all-purpose flour

1/4 teaspoon salt (optional)
1/4 teaspoon dried tarragon
1/4 teaspoon dried basil
1/2 cup olive oil

1. Lightly oil a 9-inch pie pan, doing edges first. Preheat oven to 350°F.
2. Mix together all ingredients except oil in a medium-size bowl. Add oil and toss to mix well.
3. Press evenly into the pie pan. Bake for 10 minutes. Refrigerate or freeze crust for later use, or fill and continue baking according to filling's directions.

Moist and flaky, this recipe calls for both all-purpose and whole wheat flours and is flavored with cinnamon. It is particularly well-suited to fruit fillings.

YIELD: one 9-inch pie crust
(6 servings)

PREPARATION TIME: 15 minutes

COOKING TIME: 12 to 15 minutes

RDOB PER SERVING: 11%

1 cup unbleached all-purpose flour

1 cup whole wheat pastry flour

2/3 cup oat bran

2 teaspoons baking powder

1 tablespoon cinnamon

4 ounces tub margarine, cold

3 tablespoons low-fat or nonfat plain yogurt

1. Lightly oil a 9-inch pie pan. Preheat oven to 375°F.
2. Mix together the flours, oat bran, baking powder, and cinnamon in a medium-size bowl. Using a pastry blender or 2 forks, cut in margarine until the mixture is the texture of coarse crumbs. Add yogurt and stir to form a ball.
3. Sprinkle a little oat bran or flour on a sheet of waxed paper. Roll out dough until it is approximately 10 inches in diameter.
4. Line the pie pan with dough, pricking the bottom with a fork.
5. Bake for 12 to 15 minutes until lightly browned.

PIES

You can also add oat products to pie fillings to increase your RDOB; we've included a few recipes to get you started. Our selections also feature reduced-sugar calories and rely on fruit and nonfat special additions such as lemon juice and spices for flavor.

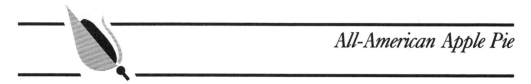

All-American Apple Pie

Traditional apple pie, rich with cinnamon and ginger, and a double oat crust, it can be served either hot or cold.

YIELD: 6 servings

PREPARATION TIME: 35 minutes

COOKING TIME: 35 to 40 minutes

RDOB PER SERVING: 22%

CRUST:

    Dough for 2 Basic Oat Bran Pie Crusts (page 272)

FILLING:

1/3 cup oat bran

1/2 teaspoon ground cinnamon

1/2 teaspoon ground ginger

1/8 teaspoon ground cloves

    Grated rind and juice from 1 lemon

5 medium apples, cored, peeled, and thinly sliced

2 tablespoons skim milk

1. Preheat oven to 400°F.
2. Combine oat bran, spices, lemon rind, and lemon juice in a mixing bowl. Add apples and toss lightly.
3. Roll out half the pie dough to a 10-inch circle. Fill with oat bran/fruit mixture.
4. Roll out the other half of the dough and cover the pie. Trim excess dough and seal the edges of the two crust layers together. Glaze top of pie with skim milk, and cut a vent in center.
5. Bake for 35 to 40 minutes.

Blueberries and oats seem to have a natural affinity for one another, as demonstrated by this citrus-flavored blueberry pie filling baked in an oat bran crust.

YIELD: 6 servings

PREPARATION TIME: 25 minutes

COOKING TIME: 45 minutes

RDOB PER SERVING: 18%

CRUST:

Dough for 2 Basic Oat Bran
Pie Crusts (page 272)

FILLING:

4 cups blueberries

1/4 cup honey

2 tablespoons lemon juice

2 tablespoons oat flour

1/4 cup orange juice

1. Preheat oven to 350°F. Lightly oil a 9-inch pie pan.
2. Refrigerate half the crust dough in a covered bowl.
3. Roll out the other half of the crust dough to a 10-inch circle and place in the pie pan. Bake for 5 minutes. Remove from oven.
4. Set oven at 450°F.
5. Rinse and sort blueberries. Combine with honey and lemon juice in a mixing bowl.
6. Dissolve oat flour in orange juice in a second bowl, then stir into berries. Transfer berry mixture to pie shell.
7. Roll out chilled dough and cut into 1/2-inch strips. Weave on pie to create a lattice topping.
8. Bake for 10 minutes. Reduce heat to 350°F. and bake for 30 more minutes.

A delicious chilled strawberry pie with a lemony tang.

YIELD: 6 servings

PREPARATION TIME: 35 to 40 minutes

COOKING TIME: 10 minutes

RDOB PER SERVING: 14% with Lemon Crumb Crust, 12% with Basic Oat Bran Pie Crust

CRUST:

1 prebaked Basic Oat Bran Pie Crust (page 272) or Lemon Crumb Crust (page 273)

FILLING:

3 tablespoons whole wheat pastry flour

1/3 cup brown sugar

1/4 cup Basic Granola (page 129)

3 1/2 cups sliced strawberries (cut from fresh or frozen whole strawberries)

1/2 cup evaporated skim milk

1/4 cup low-fat powdered milk

1 tablespoon lemon juice

1. In a medium-size saucepan, cook flour, sugar, Basic Granola, and 1 1/2 cups strawberries over medium heat for 10 minutes, stirring frequently. Chill in a covered bowl.

2. Place remaining 2 cups strawberries in baked 9-inch pie shell.

3. In a small mixing bowl, beat evaporated skim milk with electric mixer or egg beater until stiff. Fold in powdered milk and lemon juice.

4. Fold chilled strawberry mixture into milk mixture. Carefully pour over uncooked strawberries in crust. Chill until serving time.

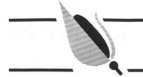

The flavor of the oat bran pie crust blends particularly well with a melange of spices and tangy pears. Apples can be substituted for the pears for variety.

YIELD: 6 servings

PREPARATION TIME: 30 minutes

COOKING TIME: 45 minutes

RDOB PER SERVING: 17%

CRUST:

Dough for 2 Basic Oat Bran Pie Crusts (page 272)

FILLING:

5 cups sliced ripe pears (preferably unpeeled) or unsweetened, drained canned pears

1/4 cup honey

1 tablespoon oat bran, dissolved in 3 tablespoons water

1/2 teaspoon cinnamon

1/2 teaspoon nutmeg

1/4 teaspoon allspice

1 teaspoon vanilla extract

1 tablespoon lemon juice

2 tablespoons skim milk mixed with 1/4 teaspoon cinnamon

1. Preheat oven to 350°F. Lightly oil a 9-inch pie pan.
2. Refrigerate half the crust dough in a covered bowl.
3. Roll out the other half of the crust dough and place in the pie pan. Bake for 5 minutes. Remove from oven.
4. Set oven at 450°F.
5. Combine sliced pears with honey, dissolved oat bran, cinnamon, nutmeg, allspice, vanilla, and lemon juice. Pour into pie shell.
6. Roll out chilled dough and place on top of the pears. Make a cut in the dough for a vent. Brush top of pie with milk/cinnamon mixture.
7. Bake for 10 minutes. Reduce heat to 350°F. and bake for 30 more minutes.

Rolled oats and nuts create an instant crust for desserts with your favorite flavor of frozen yogurt or frozen tofu prepared ice cream-type desserts.

YIELD: 6 servings

PREPARATION TIME: 15 minutes

COOKING TIME: 8 to 10 minutes

RDOB PER SERVING: 8%

1 cup rolled oats	1/2 teaspoon cinnamon
1/2 cup chopped walnuts	3 to 4 cups frozen yogurt or
1/3 cup brown sugar	frozen tofu prepared dessert
4 tablespoons tub margarine, melted	

1. Lightly oil a 9-inch pie dish. Preheat oven to 375°F.

2. Combine oats, 1/4 cup walnuts, sugar, margarine, and cinnamon in a bowl and mix well.

3. Press onto the sides and then the bottom of the pie pan. Bake for 8 to 10 minutes. Cool.

4. Fill with frozen yogurt or tofu dessert. Sprinkle with remaining nuts. Serve at once or freeze for future use.

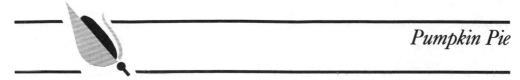

Although pumpkin pie is usually thought of as being high in fat, cholesterol, and calories, this delicious version can be included in a prudent diet thanks to the use of low-fat milk and only one egg yolk.

YIELD: one 9-inch pie (6 servings)

PREPARATION TIME: 25 minutes

COOKING TIME (INCLUDING CRUST): 55 minutes

RDOB PER SERVING: 14% with Lemon Crumb Crust; 12% with Basic Crust

CRUST:

    Dough for 1 Lemon Crumb Crust (page 273) or Basic Oat Bran Pie Crust (page 272)

FILLING:

1 whole egg plus 4 egg whites
1 can (16 ounces) pumpkin

2/3 cup honey
1/4 cup oat bran
1 teaspoon cinnamon
1 1/2 cups evaporated skim milk
1/2 teaspoon ginger
1/8 teaspoon cloves
1/4 teaspoon nutmeg

1. Preheat oven to 425°F.
2. In a large bowl, beat egg and egg whites with egg beater. Add pumpkin, honey, oat bran, cinnamon, milk, ginger, cloves, and nutmeg. Mix until thoroughly combined.
3. Transfer to uncooked pie shell. Bake for 10 minutes. Lower oven to 350°F. and bake for 45 to 50 minutes until center is set and pie is lightly browned.

CRISPS

One of the most popular uses of oat products in American kitchens has always been as a topping for baked fruit dishes or crisps. Our recipes use fresh and dried fruits, all made extra-tempting with the addition of a crunchy oat crumb topping. They go well with one of our dessert toppings (pages 50–51).

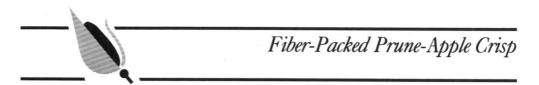

Fiber-Packed Prune-Apple Crisp

This recipe comes from the newsletter Diabetes and Nutrition News, *published by the HCF Diabetes Foundation.*

YIELD: 8 servings

PREPARATION TIME: 20 minutes

COOKING TIME: 1 hour 15 minutes

RDOB PER SERVING: 6%

1/2 cup oat bran
5 cups thinly sliced apples (peeled if desired)
1 cup unsweetened apple juice
1/2 cup finely chopped prunes

1/2 cup raisins
1/2 teaspoon cinnamon
1/4 teaspoon cloves
1/3 cup wheat bran flakes, crushed

1. Oil an 8-inch square baking pan. Preheat oven to 350°F.
2. Spread oat bran in the bottom of the pan. Place apple slices on top.
3. Pour apple juice over the bran and apples.
4. Toss prunes, raisins, cinnamon, and cloves to mix well. Sprinkle over apples.
5. Cover with foil and bake for 1 hour. Remove foil and sprinkle with wheat bran flakes. Bake 15 minutes longer.

Pear or Apple Crisp

This scrumptious, crunchy dessert is best served warm, with one of our dessert toppings (pages 50–51).

YIELD: 8 servings

PREPARATION TIME: 25 minutes

COOKING TIME: 45 minutes

RDOB PER SERVING: 9%

CRUSTS:

1 1/2 cups quick rolled oats

1/2 cup unbleached all-purpose flour

1/3 cup firmly packed brown sugar

2 teaspoons cinnamon

1/3 cup peanut or safflower oil

2 tablespoons tub margarine, melted (optional)

FILLING:

2 pounds cooking apples or pears (about 4 large pieces of fruit)

2 tablespoons sugar

1 tablespoon lemon juice

1 teaspoon grated lemon peel

1/4 teaspoon cinnamon

1. To make crusts, combine oats, flour, brown sugar, and cinnamon in a large bowl. Add oil and margarine (if desired, for a buttery taste), stirring with a fork until well mixed.

2. For filling, peel (if desired), core, and thinly slice apples or pears, saving as much of the juice as possible while cutting. Combine in a separate bowl with sugar, lemon juice, peel, and cinnamon and toss gently to mix.

3. Preheat oven to 350°F. Oil an 8-inch square baking pan.

4. Sprinkle half the oat mixture into the pan and pat down to form a bottom "crust."

5. Carefully pour the fruit mixture over the crust. Sprinkle the remaining oat topping over the fruit.

6. Bake for 45 minutes until lightly browned and bubbly.

Tart cranberries and sweet apples are a perfect blend in this crisp. Serve with milk or yogurt toppings (pages 50–51).

YIELD: 12 servings

PREPARATION TIME: 25 minutes

COOKING TIME: 40 minutes

RDOB PER SERVING: 5%

FILLING:

- 1 package (12 ounces) fresh cranberries
- 6 large apples, cored and sliced (peeled if desired)
- 2 teaspoons cinnamon
- 1/2 teaspoon nutmeg
- 1/2 cup brown sugar
- 2 tablespoons oat bran

TOPPING:

- 6 tablespoons peanut or safflower oil
- 3 tablespoons brown sugar
- 1 cup old-fashioned rolled oats
- 1/2 cup oat bran
- 1/2 cup chopped walnuts
- 1/4 cup whole wheat flour

1. Lightly oil a 2-quart shallow baking pan. Preheat oven to 375°F.
2. To make filling, mix cranberries, apples, cinnamon, nutmeg, sugar, and 2 tablespoons oat bran in a large bowl. Pour into baking pan.
3. To make topping, mix oil, sugar, oats, oat bran, walnuts, and flour in the same bowl. Sprinkle over fruit mixture.
4. Bake for 40 minutes or until lightly browned.
5. Let stand for 10 minutes.

Rhubarb Crisp

Remember this crisp recipe when you see fresh rhubarb in the produce bin. It's a great way to increase your oat bran consumption while enjoying one of nature's most unusual taste sensations.

YIELD: 6 servings

PREPARATION TIME: 20 minutes

COOKING TIME: 50 minutes

RDOB PER SERVING: 16%

1 1/2 cups whole wheat flour
1 cup old-fashioned rolled oats
1/3 cup brown sugar
1/2 cup + 2 tablespoons oat bran
1/2 teaspoon baking soda

1/2 cup tub margarine, cold
2 egg whites, beaten
3 cups rhubarb, cut into 1-inch pieces
1 teaspoon honey

1. Lightly oil an 8-inch square baking dish. Preheat oven to 350°F.
2. Combine flour, oats, sugar, 1/2 cup oat bran, and baking soda in a mixing bowl. Using a pastry blender or 2 forks, cut in margarine until mixture is the texture of coarse crumbs.
3. Place half the oat mixture in the bottom of the baking dish.
4. Combine egg whites, rhubarb, honey, and 2 tablespoons oat bran in a separate bowl. Pour on top of oat mixture in baking dish. Crumble the rest of the oat mixture on top of the rhubarb.
5. Bake for 50 minutes until lightly browned and bubbly. Serve warm.

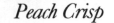

Peach Crisp

This dessert is particularly good when made with fresh, ripe peaches and served warm from the oven. You'll also enjoy preparing it with canned peaches when fresh fruit isn't in season. Save any leftovers for breakfast.

YIELD: 6 servings

PREPARATION TIME: 10 minutes

COOKING TIME: 35 minutes

RDOB PER SERVING: 21%

2 cups sliced fresh peaches or water-packed canned peaches, drained

1 cup oat bran

1/2 cup old-fashioned rolled oats

1/2 cup whole wheat pastry flour

1/2 cup tub margarine

1/4 cup finely chopped almonds

1. Lightly oil a 8-inch square baking dish. Preheat oven to 375°F.

2. Combine oat bran, oats, and flour in a mixing bowl. Using a pastry blender or 2 forks, cut in margarine until mixture is the texture of coarse crumbs. Stir in almonds.

3. Spread peaches in baking dish. Cover with oat topping and bake for 35 minutes until topping is lightly browned.

4. Serve warm.

Bananas, pineapple, and fruit preserves give a tropical twist to this traditional crisp preparation.

YIELD: 6 servings

PREPARATION TIME: 15 minutes

COOKING TIME: 20 minutes

RDOB PER SERVING: 13%

1 can (20 ounces) unsweetened pineapple cubes

2 cups sliced bananas (3 medium bananas)

2 tablespoons pure-fruit apricot or peach preserves

1/2 cup old-fashioned rolled oats

1/2 cup oat bran

1/4 cup brown sugar

3 tablespoons grated coconut (optional)

1/4 cup tub margarine, cold

1. Lightly oil a 1 1/2-quart baking dish. Preheat oven to 400°F.
2. Strain pineapple and set aside juice.
3. Combine bananas and pineapple in the baking dish.
4. Stir preserves into pineapple juice and pour over fruit.
5. Mix oats, oat bran, sugar, and coconut (if desired) in a medium-size bowl. Using a pastry blender or 2 forks, cut in margarine until mixture is the texture of very coarse crumbs. Spread over fruit.
6. Bake for 20 minutes or until topping is lightly browned. Serve warm.

Cranberry Crisp

Tart, fresh cranberries are briefly cooked until they pop, then combined with an oat crunch topping and baked.

YIELD: 6 servings

PREPARATION TIME: 20 minutes

COOKING TIME: 45 minutes

RDOB PER SERVING: 8%

1 pound fresh cranberries

1 teaspoon honey

1 cup old-fashioned rolled oats

1/2 cup whole wheat pastry flour

1/3 cup brown sugar

1/2 cup oat bran

1/2 cup tub margarine, cold

1. Cook fresh cranberries in a heavy-bottomed saucepan until they burst open. Stir in honey. Set aside.
2. Lightly oil an 8-inch square baking dish. Preheat oven to 350°F.
3. Combine oats, flour, sugar, and oat bran in a mixing bowl. Using a pastry blender or 2 forks, cut in margarine until mixture is the texture of coarse crumbs.
4. Put half the oat mixture in the bottom of the baking dish. Add the cranberries. Top with remaining oat mixture.
5. Bake for 45 minutes.

Like all tradition blueberry grunts, this recipe is made on top of the stove by dropping dumplings into a pot of simmering blueberries. Try making it with other berries as well.

YIELD: 6 servings

PREPARATION TIME: 25 minutes

COOKING TIME: 30 minutes

RDOB PER SERVING: 10%

1 pint fresh or frozen blueberries	1/2 cup unbleached all-purpose flour
1/4 cup sugar	3/4 cup rolled oats
1/2 cup water	1 teaspoon baking powder
1 tablespoon fresh lemon juice	1/4 teaspoon salt
1/2 teaspoon nutmeg	2 tablespoons tub margarine
1/2 teaspoon cinnamon	1 tablespoon brown sugar
1/4 cup oat bran	2 to 3 tablespoons 1% milk

1. Sort, stem, and rinse fruit. Combine with sugar, water, lemon juice, nutmeg, and cinnamon in a skillet. Heat to bubbling, then reduce heat and simmer until some of the liquid has cooked away and sauce begins to thicken.

2. While the fruit is simmering, combine oat bran, flour, rolled oats, baking powder, and salt in a large mixing bowl.

3. Cream margarine and sugar together in a small bowl. Add to the flour mixture and, using a pastry blender or 2 forks, mix until the texture of coarse crumbs.

4. Add milk 1 tablespoon at a time and stir until the consistency of soft dough.

5. Drop by rounded tablespoons into the simmering fruit mixture. Cover and continue to simmer for 15 more minutes.

6. Spoon dumplings into a bowl and top with hot fruit and syrup. Serve immediately while warm.

OTHER DESSERTS

Frozen Granola Banana Pops

Here's another unique way to include granola in your diet. These frozen treats make a great substitute for sugar- and fat-loaded afterschool snacks.

YIELD: 6 servings

PREPARATION TIME: 15 minutes, plus 1 hour 20 minutes freezing time

RDOB PER SERVING: 8%

8 wooden Popsicle sticks or small skewers

1/2 cup low-fat or nonfat plain yogurt

2 tablespoons mild honey

3 firm bananas, peeled and cut in half crosswise

1 cup Maple-Walnut Granola (page 134)

1. Insert a wooden stick into the cut end of each banana half.
2. Mix yogurt and honey in a flat soup bowl.
3. Line a baking sheet with waxed paper. Dip bananas in yogurt, then lay them on the baking sheet and place in freezer for 1 hour.
4. Remove the bananas and dip in yogurt again.
5. Pour granola onto a sheet of waxed paper and roll bananas in it until they are completely coated.
6. Place bananas on the baking sheet and return to freezer for at least 20 minutes. Let stand at room temperature for about 5 minutes before serving.

This dessert soufflé has a touch of lemon plus a layer of fruits and spices in its center.

YIELD: 4 servings

PREPARATION TIME: 30 minutes

COOKING TIME: 45 minutes

RDOB PER SERVING: 19%

1 1/2 cups old-fashioned rolled oats	6 dried apricots, sliced in thin strips
3 cups skim milk	2 tablespoons honey
1/8 teaspoon salt	Juice of half a lemon
1 large apple, peeled, cored, and thinly sliced	1/4 teaspoon cinnamon
2 tablespoons raisins	2 egg whites
Grated rind of 1 lemon	

1. Combine oats, milk, and salt in a saucepan and cook for 10 minutes, stirring 2 or 3 times. Remove from heat and let cool.

2. While the oats are cooking, combine apples, raisins, lemon rind, and apricots in a small bowl.

3. Lightly oil a 1 1/2-quart soufflé dish and dust with oat bran. Preheat oven to 400°F.

4. Mix honey, lemon juice, and cinnamon into the cooled oats.

5. Beat egg whites until very stiff. Fold one third into the oats, then gently fold in the rest.

6. Carefully spoon half the oat mixture into the soufflé dish. Follow with a layer of the apple mixture. Cover with the remaining half of the oat mixture.

7. Bake for 45 minutes. Serve immediately while hot and puffed.

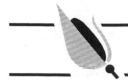

Light crepes filled with fruits, preserves, or yogurt are an elegant yet inexpensive treat. Make crepes ahead of time and fill and bake later for easier preparation on a busy day.

YIELD: 6 crepes

PREPARATION TIME: 5 minutes

COOKING TIME: 5 to 10 minutes

RDOB PER CREPE: 13%

6 Oat Crepes (page 163)

3/4 cup dessert filling (mashed bananas, honey, or maple syrup and yogurt, pure fruit preserves, chopped nuts, apples, pears, berries, or mixed fruits)

Cinnamon sugar or confectioners' sugar

1. Lightly oil a 9 × 13-inch baking pan. Preheat oven to 375°F.
2. With the second, or spotted, side of the crepe up, put about 2 heaping tablespoons of filling on one end of the crepe and roll up, keeping the attractive browned side on the outside.
3. Repeat for remaining crepes, placing side by side in the baking pan, with the overlapping edge of each crepe facing down.
4. Sprinkle with cinnamon sugar or confectioners sugar.
5. Bake for 5 to 10 minutes until heated through. Serve hot.

Granola Baked Apples

Baked apples are an easy, nutritious dessert that can be cooking while you're having dinner. By stuffing the cored apples with granola, you can give new life to an old favorite and increase your RDOB at the same time.

YIELD: 4 servings

PREPARATION/COOKING TIME: (not including granola) 40 minutes

RDOB PER SERVING: 16%

4 baking apples, cored and peeled down 1 inch from top

2 cups Raisin-Peanut-Sunflower Granola (page 135)

1. Preheat oven to 350°F.
2. Spoon 1/2 cup granola mixture into each apple.
3. Put apples in a casserole dish and add water to a depth of 1/4 inch. Cover and bake for 30 minutes.

Berry-Yogurt Crowdie

Smooth yogurt and crisp oats combine with berries for this light variation of a classic Scottish cream crowdie.

YIELD: 3 servings

PREPARATION TIME: 10 minutes

RDOB PER SERVING: 13%

3/4 cup old-fashioned rolled oats
2 1/2 cups low-fat or nonfat plain yogurt

1 tablespoon honey
1 cup blueberries or strawberries

1. Toast oats in a dry skillet for 5 minutes, stirring frequently.
2. Shortly before serving, beat yogurt with a wire whisk until smooth. Combine with honey, 3/4 cup blueberries, and all but 3 tablespoons of the oats in a mixing bowl. Spoon into 3 dessert dishes. Sprinkle remaining oats on top and garnish with remaining berries.

Make these oat bran cups ahead of time, then fill and garnish them right before serving so they'll remain crisp. Use your favorite vanilla pudding and garnish with sliced fruits in season.

YIELD: 9 cups

PREPARATION TIME: 30 minutes

COOKING TIME: 20 minutes

RDOB PER CUP: 6%

1/2 cup (4 ounces) tub margarine

1/2 cup very finely ground walnuts

1/4 cup sugar

2 tablespoons cocoa

1/2 cup oat bran

1 cup unbleached all-purpose flour

1. Preheat oven to 350°F.
2. In a mixing bowl combine margarine, walnuts, sugar, and cocoa well with a wooden spoon.
3. Add oat bran and flour and mix, first with a spoon and then with your hands, until it forms a dough.
4. Form into patties by hand or roll out with a rolling pin and press the dough in 9 unoiled muffin cups, covering the bottom and sides. Bake for 20 minutes. Let cool and unmold when ready to use. (Cups can be refrigerated or frozen until ready to fill.)

This is a creamy baked dessert that goes well with warmed applesauce as a topping.

YIELD: 8 servings

PREPARATION TIME: 25 minutes

COOKING TIME: 40 minutes

RDOB PER SERVING: 9%

1 cup milk

2 tablespoons tub margarine

3/4 cup oat bran

1/3 cup 1% cottage cheese, blended until smooth

1/4 cup brown sugar

1/2 cup raisins

1/2 cup chopped walnuts

1/2 teaspoon nutmeg

1/2 teaspoon cinnamon

2 eggs, separated, plus 2 egg whites

1. Oil a 1 1/2- or 2-quart soufflé dish. Preheat oven to 325°F.
2. Combine milk and margarine in a saucepan. Heat over low heat. Add oat bran and stir constantly for 3 to 4 minutes, until mixture has thickened. Remove from heat.
3. Add cottage cheese, sugar, raisins, walnuts, nutmeg, cinnamon, and egg yolks and mix well.
4. Beat egg whites until very stiff. Fold one third into mixture, then gently fold in the rest.
5. Carefully transfer to soufflé dish and bake for 40 minutes.
6. Remove from oven and serve while still warm.

Sweet Whole Oat "Pudding"

Similar to rice pudding, oat groats make this an excellent dessert served warm or cooled.

YIELD: 6 servings

PREPARATION TIME: 10 minutes

COOKING TIME: 35 to 40 minutes

RDOB PER SERVING: 8%

2 cups skim milk

1/2 cup water

1 cup oat groats, rinsed and drained

1 tablespoon peanut or safflower oil

1/2 teaspoon crushed cardamom seeds

1 teaspoon cinnamon

1 tablespoon brown sugar or maple syrup

1. In a heavy-bottomed 2-quart pot, heat milk and water to simmer.

2. Add groats, oil, seeds, cinnamon, and brown sugar. Cover and simmer over low heat for 35 to 40 minutes until liquid has been absorbed. Stir 2 or 3 times to prevent burning.

3. Serve warm with one of our dessert toppings (pages 50–51).

Steamed Maple Pudding

The texture of the rolled oats changes as it steams and becomes a smooth, thick, rich pudding.

YIELD: 4 servings

PREPARATION TIME: 10 minutes

COOKING TIME: 2 to 3 hours

RDOB PER SERVING: 25%

2 cups old-fashioned rolled oats	1/4 cup maple syrup
1 1/2 cups skim milk	1/4 teaspoon salt

1. Oil a 1-quart soufflé dish or 4 individual ramekins or baking dishes.
2. To a heavy-bottomed covered saucepan that is large enough to hold the dish, add water to a depth that will reach halfway up the dish. Bring to a boil.
3. While heating the water, mix all ingredients together in a medium-size bowl.
4. Pour mixture into prepared soufflé dish and cover tightly with foil.
5. Lower dish into boiling water. Reduce heat to simmer and cover saucepan.
6. Steam pudding for 2 hours for smooth consistency. (It can cook for another hour while you dine to reach its full pudding consistency.)

HOLIDAY MAPLE PUDDING   For a festive touch, add 1/4 cup water, 1/3 cup chopped prunes or other dried fruits, and 1/4 cup finely chopped black walnuts in step 3. Steam while preparing and eating your holiday meal. Serve with one of our dessert toppings (pages 50–51).

Peanut Butter Granola "Ice Cream"

Treat yourself to this when you crave a dish of ice cream similar to rocky road or praline.

YIELD: 4 servings

PREPARATION TIME: 10 minutes, plus 4 hours chilling time.

RDOB PER SERVING: 12%

1 1/2 cups evaporated skim milk
1/3 cup honey

1/4 cup unhydrogenated peanut butter
3/4 cup Basic Granola (page 129)

1. Blend milk, honey, and peanut butter in blender or food processor until smooth.
2. Pour into ice cube tray (without dividers) and freeze for 1 hour.
3. Stir in granola and return to freezer for 4 hours or until firm.

DRINKS AND SHAKES

One of the quickest and pleasantest ways to include oat bran in your diet, especially in summer, is in blended drinks and shakes. These shakes can be enjoyed all year round as breakfasts, lunches, energy boosters, snacks, and diet aids.

By starting with our recipes for high-fiber shakes, you can create your own versions incorporating your favorite ingredients. Most can be prepared in five minutes. They're best if you drink them as soon as they're blended since the oat bran will continue to thicken the liquids as they stand in most of the recipes.

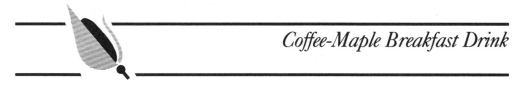

Coffee-Maple Breakfast Drink

YIELD: 1 serving

PREPARATION TIME: 5 minutes

RDOB: 13%

1/4 cup rolled oats	1 teaspoon maple syrup
1 cup skim milk	4 crushed ice cubes
1 teaspoon decaffeinated instant coffee	

1. Place oats in blender container at medium setting and process for 1 minute, stirring with a rubber spatula to mix.
2. Add remaining ingredients and blend on high setting about 1 minute or until smooth. Serve immediately.

Orange Diet Drink

YIELD: 4 servings (11
ounces each)

PREPARATION TIME: 15 minutes

RDOB PER SERVING: 13%

1 1/2 cups instant nonfat dry milk
  solids

3 cups cold water

1 can (6 ounces) frozen orange
  juice concentrate

2 egg whites

1/2 cup oat bran

2 teaspoons vanilla extract

1/4 teaspoon almond extract

1. Place 1 1/2 cups water and all the remaining ingredients in a blender container and blend on high setting for 30 seconds to mix well.
2. Pour into a 2-quart container. Add remaining 1 1/2 cups cold water, stir vigorously, and serve immediately.
3. Store remaining servings in the refrigerator. Stir before pouring.

APPLE DIET DRINK   Substitute a 6-ounce can of frozen apple juice concentrate for the orange juice, eliminate the vanilla extract, and use 1/2 teaspoon cinnamon instead of almond extract.

Banana-Orange Smoothie

YIELD: 1 serving

PREPARATION TIME: 5 minutes

RDOB: 19%

1 ripe banana, peeled, plus 2
  crushed ice cubes, or 1
  frozen peeled ripe banana

3 tablespoons oat bran

3/4 cup orange juice

1/4 teaspoon vanilla extract
  (optional)

1. Break banana into 2 or 3 pieces.
2. Place banana and remaining ingredients in blender container. Process on high setting until well combined. Serve immediately.

Fruit Shake

YIELD: 2 servings

PREPARATION TIME: 5 minutes

RDOB PER SERVING: 13%

3/4 cup assorted seasonal fruits (blueberries, strawberries, peaches, apples and pears, melon, etc.)

1 cup skim milk

5 crushed ice cubes

1/4 cup oat bran

1. Prepare larger pieces of fruit by peeling them and removing cores or pits. Cut into smaller, more easily blended chunks.
2. Place milk, ice cubes, oat bran, and fruit in blender container and blend for 1 minute on high setting until smooth. Serve immediately.

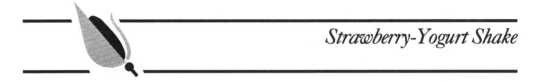

Strawberry-Yogurt Shake

YIELD: 2 servings

PREPARATION TIME: 5 minutes

RDOB PER SERVING: 9%

1 cup skim milk

1/2 cup low-fat or nonfat plain yogurt

1 egg white

3/4 cup sliced fresh or frozen strawberries

3 tablespoons oat bran

1. Put all ingredients in blender container.
2. Blend for 30 seconds on high setting or until berries are combined. Serve immediately.

Lemon-Blueberry Shake

YIELD: 2 small servings

PREPARATION TIME: 5 minutes

RDOB PER SERVING: 13%

1/2 ripe banana, preferably frozen

2/3 cup low-fat or nonfat plain yogurt

2/3 cup fresh or frozen blueberries

1 tablespoon lemon juice

4 crushed ice cubes

1/4 cup oat bran

1. Break banana into 2 or 3 pieces and put in blender container.

2. Add remaining ingredients and blend on high setting for 1 minute or until smooth. Serve immediately.

Applesauce Shake

YIELD: 2 servings

PREPARATION TIME: 5 minutes

RDOB PER SERVING: 9%

1/2 ripe banana, preferably frozen

1/2 cup unsweetened applesauce

1 cup low-fat or nonfat plain yogurt

1/8 teaspoon cinnamon

2 crushed ice cubes

3 tablespoons oat bran

1. Put all ingredients in blender container.

2. Blend for 30 seconds on high setting or until smooth. Serve immediately.

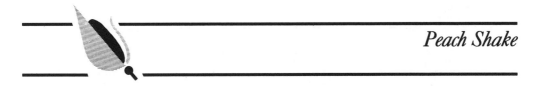

Pineapple-Berry Shake

YIELD: 2 servings

PREPARATION TIME: 5 minutes

RDOB PER SERVING: 9%

1/2 cup unsweetened crushed pineapple with juice

3/4 cup sliced fresh or frozen strawberries

1/3 cup low-fat cottage cheese

3/4 cup skim milk

3 tablespoons oat bran

1. Put all ingredients in blender container.
2. Blend for 30 seconds on high speed or until smooth. Serve immediately.

Peach Shake

YIELD: 2 servings

PREPARATION TIME: 5 minutes

RDOB PER CUP: 9%

1/2 cup skim milk

1/2 cup pineapple juice

1/2 cup low-fat or nonfat plain yogurt

1/2 cup sliced fresh peaches or canned juice-pack peaches, drained

1 egg white

3 tablespoons oat bran

1. Put all ingredients in blender container.
2. Blend on medium setting for 30 seconds or until smooth. Serve immediately.

Apricot Nectar Shake

YIELD: 1 serving

RDOB: 19%

1 cup apricot nectar   3 tablespoons oat bran

1. Put ingredients in blender container.
2. Process for 30 seconds on medium setting. Serve immediately.

Peanut Butter–Banana Shake

YIELD: 1 large serving

PREPARATION TIME: 5 minutes

RDOB: 19%

1/2 ripe banana, preferably   1 egg white
   frozen   3 tablespoons oat bran
1 cup skim milk
1 tablespoon natural peanut
   butter

1. Break banana into 2 or 3 pieces and put all ingredients in blender container.
2. Blend for 45 seconds on medium setting or until smooth. Serve immediately.

Cocoa Shake

YIELD: 2 small servings

PREPARATION TIME: 5 minutes

RDOB PER SERVING: 17%

1/3 cup oat bran
1 cup skim milk
4 crushed ice cubes

1 tablespoon unsweetened cocoa
1 teaspoon honey
1/4 teaspoon vanilla extract

1. Put oat bran, cocoa, and 1/2 cup milk in blender container and blend 15 seconds. Add remaining ingredients.
2. Blend for 1 minute on high setting. Stir and blend again if needed. Serve immediately.

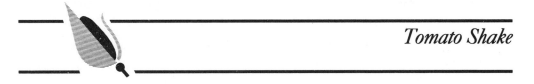

Tomato Shake

YIELD: 1 serving

RDOB: 19%

1 cup tomato juice or tomato vegetable juice

3 tablespoons oat bran

1. Put ingredients in blender container.
2. Blend on medium speed for 30 seconds or until smooth. Serve immediately.

MICROWAVE RECIPES

Your microwave oven is ideal for making oat bran and oatmeal breakfasts. We found that it also makes excellent granola and is a quick, convenient way to prepare cooked cereals and a variety of meat and poultry entrées and vegetable dishes that include oat products. Oat bran pie crust and fruit crumble desserts are part of our microwave collection as well.

The recipes that follow have been designed for full-size microwave ovens. Directions indicate heat settings as High (100%), which is "10" on some ovens; Medium High (70%), "7" on some ovens; or Medium (50%), "5" on some ovens. Since there are no industry standards for temperature dials, you may have to interpret these settings for your particular model and select the closest option. If your oven has a carousel, you can ignore the rotation directions.

Oat Bran Cereal

Oat bran is the quickest-cooking variety of oat cereal and provides the highest share of RDOB.

YIELD: 1 serving

PREPARATION/COOKING TIME: 4 minutes

RDOB: 33%

1 cup water
1/3 cup oat bran

1/8 teaspoon salt (optional)

1. Place water in 2-cup microwave-safe bowl. Sprinkle on oat bran while stirring with a fork. Add salt if desired.
2. Cook at High (100%) for 2 minutes. Stir.
3. Cook at High for 1 more minute or until cereal reaches desired consistency. Stir and serve.

Quick Rolled Oats

If you prefer to use quick oats, here are methods for making a single serving and enough for a larger group.

YIELD: 1 serving

PREPARATION/COOKING TIME: 4 minutes

RDOB: 17%

1 cup water
1/3 cup quick rolled oats

1/8 teaspoon salt (optional)

1. Place water and salt (if desired) in a 2-cup microwave-safe bowl. Stir in oats.
2. Cook at High (100%) for 1 1/2 to 2 minutes until water is almost absorbed.
3. Stir and let stand about 2 minutes.

YIELD: 4 servings

PREPARATION/COOKING TIME: 6 minutes

RDOB PER SERVING: 19%

3 cups water
1 1/2 cups quick rolled oats
1/4 teaspoon salt (optional)

Cinnamon or nutmeg
Skim milk

1. Place water and salt (if desired) in a 2-quart microwave-safe casserole dish. Stir in oats.
2. Cook at High (100%) for 2 minutes. Stir.
3. Cook at High for 2 1/2 more minutes until water is almost absorbed.
4. Stir and let stand about 2 minutes.
5. Dust with cinnamon or nutmeg, add milk, and serve.

Old-Fashioned Oatmeal

Rolled oats can also be cooked in the microwave oven with a minimum of fuss. Cook and serve in the same dish and cut your dishwashing chores in half.

YIELD: 1 serving

PREPARATION/COOKING TIME: 8 minutes

RDOB: 17%

1 cup water   1/8 teaspoon salt (optional)
1/3 cup old-fashioned rolled oats

1. Bring water to a boil at High (100%) in a 2-cup microwave-safe bowl.
2. Stir in oats and salt (if desired). Cook, uncovered, at High for 3 minutes. Stir.
3. Cook uncovered at High (100%) for 2 more minutes.
4. Stir and let stand about 2 minutes before serving.

Cinnamon-Walnut Oatmeal

This classic adapts well to the microwave.

YIELD: 2 servings

PREPARATION/COOKING TIME: 7 minutes

RDOB PER SERVING: 17%

1 1/4 cups water
2/3 cup old-fashioned rolled oats
2 tablespoons chopped walnuts

2 tablespoons raisins
1/4 teaspoon salt (optional)
1/8 teaspoon cinnamon

1. Combine water, oats, walnuts, raisins, salt (if desired), and cinnamon in a microwave-safe bowl and mix thoroughly.
2. Cook at High (100%) for 4 minutes, until thick. Stir once a minute.
3. Cover and let rest 2 to 3 minutes before serving.

Raisin-Peanut Granola

Microwave cooking produces a wonderful, crunchy granola and cuts baking time way down.

YIELD: 5 cups

PREPARATION TIME: 6 minutes

COOKING TIME: 8 to 10 minutes

RDOB FOR 1/2 CUP: 20%

2 cups old-fashioned rolled oats
1 cup oat bran
1 cup chopped peanuts or almonds

1/4 cup honey
1/4 cup tub margarine, melted
1 1/2 teaspoons cinnamon
2/3 cup raisins

1. Mix oats, oat bran, peanuts, honey, margarine, and cinnamon in a microwave-safe bowl. Spread in an 8 × 12-inch baking dish.

2. Cook at High (100%) for 8 to 10 minutes or until lightly browned. Stir every 2 minutes.

3. Remove from oven and stir in raisins.

4. Cool. Keep refrigerated in an airtight container.

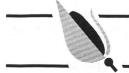

Spicy Snack Mix

This cereal mix is an easily prepared, satisfying snack. Make a large batch of it and store in the refrigerator.

YIELD: 6 cups

PREPARATION/COOKING TIME: 15 minutes

RDOB FOR 1/2 CUP: 20%

1/3 cup tub margarine
  1 teaspoon chili powder
1/2 teaspoon hot red pepper
     sauce

5 cups toasted O's cold oat
   cereal (see suppliers list on
   page 333 if not available at
   your health store)
1 cup unsalted peanuts

1. Put margarine in a large microwave-safe mixing bowl. Microwave, uncovered, at High (100%) for 1 1/2 minutes until melted.

2. Stir in chili powder and hot sauce.

3. Add toasted oat cereal and peanuts. Toss until well coated with margarine mixture.

4. Cook, uncovered, at High for 5 1/2 to 6 1/2 minutes until cereal is toasted. Stir every 2 minutes.

5. Spread out on clean surface to cool. Keep refrigerated in an airtight container.

Oat groats and vegetables combine to create the filling for the fish of your choice.

YIELD: 4 servings

PREPARATION/COOKING TIME: 15 minutes

RDOB PER SERVING: 19%

1/4 cup finely chopped onion

1/4 cup finely chopped celery

2 tablespoons tub margarine

1 1/2 cups cooked oat groats (page 49)

1/4 teaspoon dried thyme

1/8 teaspoon dried sage

1/8 teaspoon pepper

2 tablespoons lemon juice

2 fresh fish fillets, 1/2 pound each

1. Place onions, celery, and margarine in a medium-size microwave-safe bowl. Cook at High (100%) for 2 to 4 minutes until tender.

2. Remove from oven and stir in groats, thyme, sage, pepper, and lemon juice.

3. Place 1 fillet in a pan with a roasting rack. Top with stuffing and remaining fillet. Cover with microwave-safe plastic wrap.

4. Cook at High for 5 1/2 to 7 1/2 minutes until fish flakes easily. Rotate dish after 2 1/2 minutes cooking time.

5. Remove from oven. Prick and remove plastic wrap.

Salmon Loaf

You can substitute tuna or cooked leftover fish in this lemon- and onion-flavored loaf. Use a quality red salmon; the redder the salmon, the higher it is in Omega-3 oil. White albacore tuna is also higher in Omega-3.

YIELD: 4 servings

PREPARATION TIME: 15 minutes

COOKING TIME: 18 to 24 minutes

RDOB PER SERVING: 13%

1 can (16 ounces) good-quality red salmon, drained (set aside liquid) and large bones removed
Skim milk
4 egg whites
1/2 cup oat bran

1/2 cup chopped onion
1 tablespoon chopped fresh parsley
1 teaspoon grated lemon peel
1/4 teaspoon salt (optional)
1/8 teaspoon black pepper

1. In a large bowl, combine skim milk with enough salmon liquid to equal 1 cup of liquid.

2. Beat egg whites in a separate bowl. Add to milk mixture. Add salmon, oat bran, onions, parsley, lemon peel, salt (if desired) and pepper. Mix well.

3. Press into glass loaf pan. Cover with microwave-safe plastic wrap and cook at Medium (50%) for 18 to 24 minutes or until middle of loaf tests firm. Rotate pan every 6 minutes.

4. Remove from oven and prick plastic wrap. Let stand for 5 minutes to set juices before serving.

Chicken cutlets are breaded with oat bran and microwaved with a tomato-cheese sauce.

YIELD: 4 servings

PREPARATION/COOKING TIME: 30 minutes

RDOB PER SERVING: 13%

1 can (8 ounces) tomato sauce
1/2 teaspoon dried basil
1/2 teaspoon oregano
1/4 teaspoon minced garlic
1/2 cup oat bran
1 teaspoon minced fresh parsley

1/2 cup grated Parmesan cheese
2 chicken breasts, split and skin removed
2 egg whites
1/2 cup shredded reduced-fat skim mozzarella cheese

1. Combine tomato sauce, basil, oregano, and garlic in a 2-cup microwave-safe container. Cover with microwave-safe plastic wrap.
2. Cook at High (100%) for 2 minutes. Stir. Cook at Medium (50%) for 5 minutes more. Remove from oven and slit plastic wrap. Set aside.
3. Combine oat bran, parsley, and 1/4 cup Parmesan cheese in a shallow dish.
4. Beat egg whites in a second shallow dish.
5. Dip chicken pieces first in oat bran mixture, then in egg whites, then again in bran mixture.
6. Place chicken in an 8 × 12-inch microwave-safe baking dish and cover with microwave-safe plastic wrap. Cook at Medium High (70%) for 9 to 14 minutes until tender. Rearrange once after 5 minutes to promote even baking.
7. Pour the reserved sauce over chicken. Top with mozzarella cheese and the remaining Parmesan.
8. Cook at Medium High for 3 to 5 minutes until cheese melts and sauce is bubbly.
9. Remove from oven. Prick and remove plastic wrap.

Hamburgers gain a nutty flavor and softer texture from the oat bran.

YIELD: 6 hamburgers

PREPARATION TIME: 10 minutes

COOKING TIME: 6 minutes

RDOB PER HAMBURGER: 13%

2 egg whites

1 1/2 pounds very lean ground beef

3/4 cup oat bran

1/3 cup tomato sauce

1/8 teaspoon black pepper

1. Beat egg whites in a large bowl. Add beef, oat bran, tomato sauce, and pepper. Mix well.

2. Form into 6 hamburger patties.

3. Preheat microwave browning grill at High (100%) for 8 minutes.

4. Place hamburgers on grill and cook at High for 3 minutes on each side or until done to your taste.

This zucchini-tomato pie is served in our microwave Oat Bran Pie Crust. You can also use the ratatouille recipe by itself as a side dish.

YIELD: 8 servings

PREPARATION TIME: 30 minutes

COOKING TIME: 25 minutes

RDOB PER SERVING: 9%

CRUST:

  1 9″ prebaked Microwave Oat Bran Pie Crust (page 331)

1/2 cup grated Parmesan cheese

FILLING:

  1 medium eggplant

  1 medium onion, sliced

  1 green pepper, sliced

  1 clove garlic, minced

1/4 cup olive oil

  1 medium zucchini, sliced

1/4 cup oat bran

1/4 cup water

  1 teaspoon dried basil

  1 teaspoon dried marjoram

1/4 teaspoon pepper

  1 large tomato, chopped

1. Remove stem, peel, and cut eggplant into 1/2 cubes. Combine with onions, peppers, garlic, and oil in a large microwave-safe casserole dish.

2. Cook at High (100%) for 8 to 10 minutes, stirring several times.

3. Add zucchini, oat bran, water, basil, marjoram, and pepper. Cover with microwave-safe plastic wrap and cook at High (100%) for 5 to 7 minutes until eggplant is soft.

4. Remove from oven. Prick and remove plastic wrap, stir in tomato, and let stand for 5 minutes.

5. Pour into baked pie crust. Top with cheese and serve. If desired, run under the broiler of conventional oven just before serving.

Meatballs Marinara

These meatballs are a perfect accompaniment for cheese ravioli or linguine.

YIELD: 16 meatballs (4 servings)

PREPARATION TIME: 15 minutes

COOKING TIME: 16 minutes

RDOB FOR A 4-MEATBALL SERVING: 19%

1 1/2 pounds very lean ground beef

3/4 cup oat bran

1/4 cup finely chopped onion

1/4 cup finely chopped green pepper

1 1/4 cups tomato sauce

2 egg whites, beaten

1/8 teaspoon black pepper

1 can (6 ounces) tomato paste

1/2 cup water

1/2 teaspoon dried basil

1/2 teaspoon dried oregano

1. Combine beef, oat bran, onions, green pepper, 1/4 cup tomato sauce, egg whites, and pepper in a large bowl. Mix well.

2. Form into 16 meatballs. Place in an 8 × 12-inch microwave-safe baking dish and cover with microwave-safe plastic wrap.

3. Microwave at High (100%) for 6 minutes. Rotate dish after 3 minutes cooking time. Drain as needed.

4. Combine remaining 1 cup tomato sauce, tomato paste, water, basil, and oregano in a separate bowl. Pour over meatballs and cover again with plastic wrap.

5. Cook at High 3 to 10 minutes more until meatballs are done to your taste.

6. Prick and remove plastic wrap.

Lean ground beef is combined with green pepper, onions, and garlic and brushed with a piquant blend of catsup, Dijon-style mustard, and brown sugar.

YIELD: 6 servings

PREPARATION TIME: 10 minutes

COOKING TIME: 12 minutes

RDOB PER SERVING: 13%

2 egg whites	1 clove garlic, minced
1 1/2 pounds very lean ground beef	1/8 teaspoon black pepper
1/3 cup skim milk	1/3 cup catsup
3/4 cup oat bran	1 teaspoon brown sugar
1/4 cup chopped onion	1 tablespoon Dijon-style mustard
1/4 cup chopped green pepper	

1. Beat egg whites in a large bowl. Add beef, milk, oat bran, onions, peppers, garlic, and black pepper. Mix well and form into a loaf.

2. Place in a 7×11-inch microwave-safe baking dish. Cover with microwave-safe plastic wrap.

3. To make barbecue sauce, combine catsup, brown sugar, and mustard in a mixing bowl. Set aside.

4. Cook meat loaf at High (100%) for 6 minutes. Rotate one quarter turn after every 3 minutes of cooking.

5. After 6 minutes of cooking, brush with barbecue sauce.

6. Continue cooking at High (100%) for another 6 minutes, rotating after 3 minutes.

7. Remove from oven. Prick plastic wrap and let stand for 5 minutes before cutting.

Peppers Parmigiana

Beef-stuffed peppers are baked in a tomato-cheese sauce flavored with oregano.

YIELD: 6 servings

PREPARATION TIME: 15 minutes

COOKING TIME: 13 minutes

RDOB PER SERVING: 8%

3 medium green peppers	1/4 teaspoon dried oregano
1 pound very lean ground beef	1/8 teaspoon black pepper
1/2 cup oat bran	1 1/4 cups tomato sauce
2 teaspoons minced onion	1/2 cup grated Parmesan cheese

1. Cut peppers in half lengthwise and remove seeds.
2. Combine beef, oat bran, onions, oregano, black pepper, and 1/2 cup tomato sauce in a large bowl. Mix well.
3. Fill each pepper half with the meat mixture. Place peppers in an 8×12-inch baking dish. Cover with microwave-safe plastic wrap.
4. Cook at High (100%) for 10 to 12 minutes until tender. Rotate dish one half turn after 6 minutes. Prick and remove plastic.
5. Sprinkle with Parmesan cheese.
6. Cook at High (100%) for 30 seconds.
7. Heat remaining tomato sauce at High (100%) for 30 seconds. Serve with peppers.

Large cabbage leaves are stuffed with a filling of ground beef and microwaved in a spicy sauce.

YIELD: 8 cabbage rolls
(4 servings)

PREPARATION TIME: 15 minutes

COOKING TIME: 27 minutes

RDOB PER SERVING: 9%

8 large cabbage leaves

1/2 cup water

2 egg whites

1 pound very lean ground beef

3/4 cup oat bran

2 tablespoons skim milk

1/8 teaspoon black pepper

2 cups canned tomatoes, drained and crushed

2 cloves garlic, minced

1 teaspoon paprika

1. Put cabbage leaves and 1/2 cup water in a large microwave-safe bowl. Cover with microwave-safe plastic wrap and cook at High (100%) until soft.

2. Beat egg whites in a large bowl. Add beef, oat bran, milk, and pepper and mix well.

3. Place 2 tablespoons beef mixture on each cabbage leaf. Fold sides of leaves over the filling and roll, securing with toothpicks. Place, seam sides down, in an 8 × 12-inch microwave-safe baking dish.

4. Stir tomatoes, garlic, and paprika together in a small bowl and pour over the prepared cabbage leaves. Cover dish with microwave plastic wrap.

5. Cook at High (100%) for 15 to 17 minutes or until tender. Rotate dish one quarter turn after every 5 minutes of cooking.

6. Remove from oven, prick and remove plastic wrap, and remove toothpicks.

Zucchini halves, stuffed with oat groats, tomatoes, green peppers, scallions, and Italian spices create a delicious and satisfying main dish.

YIELD: 4 servings

PREPARATION TIME: 15 minutes

COOKING TIME: 10 minutes

RDOB PER SERVING: 13%

2 medium zucchini	1/4 teaspoon dried basil
1 cup cooked oat groats	1/4 teaspoon dried oregano
1/2 cup chopped scallions	1/4 teaspoon salt (optional)
1/4 cup chopped green pepper	1 tomato, chopped

1. Cut zucchini in half lengthwise and scoop out middle, leaving a shell 1/4 inch thick.

2. Chop the zucchini removed from the shells. Mix together with groats, scallions, green pepper, basil, oregano, and salt (if desired) in a medium-size bowl.

3. Put zucchini shells in an 8-inch square baking dish and fill each shell with one quarter of the groat/vegetable mixture.

4. Spoon chopped tomatoes over the groats and cover dish with microwave-safe plastic wrap.

5. Cook at High (100%) for 5 to 7 minutes until zucchini is tender. Rotate dish every 3 minutes.

6. Remove from oven. Prick plastic wrap and remove.

Here's a perfect example of using the microwave oven to prepare several elements of a multistep recipe. You can steam the broccoli in the oven while you gather the ingredients for the reduced-fat cheese sauce.

YIELD: 2 servings

PREPARATION/COOKING TIME: 15 minutes

RDOB PER SERVING: 13%

1/2 pound broccoli	1/8 teaspoon black pepper
1/4 cup chopped onion	1 cup skim milk
2 tablespoons tub margarine	1 cup grated reduced-fat
1/4 cup oat bran	cheddar cheese

1. Trim broccoli and cut off florets. Peel and slice stems. Place florets and stems in a 4-cup microwave-safe container. Cover with microwave plastic wrap.

2. Cook at High (100%) for 4 minutes. Remove from oven, prick plastic wrap, and set aside while making sauce.

3. Combine onions and margarine in medium-size bowl and cook at High (100%) for 1 minute.

4. Stir in oat bran and pepper. Add skim milk, stirring thoroughly. Cook at High (100%) for 4 minutes or until mixture is thick. Stir every 2 minutes.

5. Add cheese and stir until cheese melts. (Microwave for 15 seconds if needed.) Serve over broccoli.

Cauliflower Purée

Oat bran and pepper accent this easily prepared purée, which can be made with either fresh or frozen cauliflower.

YIELD: 4 servings

PREPARATION/COOKING TIME: 20 minutes

RDOB PER SERVING: 19%

1 medium head cauliflower, divided into bite-size florets

2 tablespoons water

3/4 cup oat bran

1/4 cup skim milk

2 tablespoons tub margarine

1/4 tablespoon white pepper

1. Place cauliflower and water in 1-quart microwave-safe casserole dish. Cover with microwave plastic wrap and cook at High (100%) for 8 1/2 to 10 1/2 minutes until tender. Stir after 5 minutes. Prick and remove plastic wrap.

2. Drain cauliflower. Mix 4 cups florets with oat bran, milk, margarine, and pepper. Purée in blender or food processor. Serve hot.

Make ahead and sprinkle on top of casseroles, soups, Italian dishes—wherever you want to add some healthful "crunch."

YIELD: 3 cups

PREPARATION TIME: 5 minutes

COOKING TIME: 9 minutes

RDOB PER 1/3 CUP: 15%

2 cups old-fashioned rolled oats   1/3 cup oat bran

1/3 cup olive or safflower oil   2 tablespoons powdered garlic

1/3 cup grated Parmesan cheese   1/3 teaspoon dried thyme

1. Mix together oats, oil, cheese, oat bran, and garlic in a medium-size bowl.
2. Spread in an 8 × 12-inch microwave-safe baking dish.
3. Cook at High (100%) for 8 to 9 minutes. Stir after each 3 minutes cooking time.
4. Add thyme and stir.
5. Cool. Keep refrigerated in an airtight container.

FRUIT DESSERTS

The microwave oven can turn out crunchy oat and fruit desserts in a flash, although they won't be quite as crisp as they are when baked in a conventional oven. However as a bonus, the oats and fruit double the water-soluble ingredients in each recipe.

Granola Baked Apples

You can have this dessert classic on the table in six minutes. The granola stuffing adds maple flavoring and a crunchy texture.

YIELD: 4 servings

PREPARATION TIME: 10 minutes

COOKING TIME: 4 to 6 minutes

RDOB PER SERVING: 8%

4 large baking apples

1 cup Maple-Walnut Granola
(page 134)

1. Core apples without cutting through bottoms. Peel apple down 1 1/2 inches from hole. Cut thin slice off bottom of each apple if needed to help it stand upright while baking.

2. Place apples in a microwave-safe baking dish. Stuff each with 1/4 cup Maple Granola.

3. Cook at High (100%) for 4 to 6 minutes until tender when poked with a knife. Rotate once while cooking to ensure even baking.

4. Serve warm, with one of our dessert toppings (pages 50–51).

Try serving this dish hot or cold as a dessert or a side dish for poultry. Apples can be substituted for the pears for variety.

YIELD: 6 servings

PREPARATION TIME: 25 minutes

COOKING TIME: 8 minutes

RDOB PER SERVING: 8%

6 cups peeled, cored, and sliced pears

2 tablespoons apple juice

1/3 cup tub margarine

3 tablespoons brown sugar

1 cup quick rolled oats

1/2 cup unbleached all-purpose flour

1 teaspoon cinnamon

1/2 teaspoon nutmeg

1. Place sliced pears in 2-quart microwave-safe casserole dish. Drizzle with apple juice.

2. Cook margarine in small microwave-safe custard bowl at High (100%) for 30 seconds. Stir in sugar, oats, flour, cinnamon, and nutmeg. Sprinkle over apples.

3. Cover casserole dish with microwave-safe plastic wrap and cook at High (100%) for 6 to 8 minutes, rotating dish once. Remove from oven when apples are tender. Prick and remove plastic wrap.

The microwaved topping on this tasty peach-walnut confection won't be quite as crunchy as a crisp baked in conventional oven, but the flavor is really excellent.

YIELD: 8 servings

PREPARATION/COOKING TIME: 15 minutes, plus 30 minutes standing time

RDOB PER SERVING: 10%

5 cups sliced fresh or unsweetened canned peaches

1/2 cup oat bran

1/4 cup tub margarine

2/3 cup quick rolled oats

1/2 cup unbleached all-purpose flour

1/4 cup brown sugar

1/2 cup chopped walnuts

1 teaspoon ground cinnamon

1 teaspoon ground nutmeg

1. Place peaches in a 9-inch round microwave-safe baking dish. Sprinkle with 2 tablespoons oat bran.

2. Cook margarine in a quart-size microwave-safe bowl at High (100%) for 30 seconds. Stir in remaining oat bran, oats, flour, sugar, walnuts, cinnamon, and nutmeg until crumbly.

3. Sprinkle oat mixture on top of peaches. Cover with a double-folded paper towel.

4. Cook, covered, at High (100%) for 10 to 12 minutes. Rotate dish every 3 minutes.

5. Remove from oven and let stand for 30 minutes before serving. Serve warm and with one of our dessert toppings (pages 50–51).

Fresh or frozen cranberries are mixed with apples, honey, and lemon and microwaved with a crumbly oat topping.

YIELD: 6 servings

PREPARATION TIME: 20 minutes

COOKING TIME: 9 minutes, plus 30 minutes standing time

RDOB PER SERVING: 17%

3 cups peeled, cored, and sliced apples	1 tablespoon lemon juice
2 cups fresh or frozen cranberries	1/3 cup brown sugar
1/3 cup honey	1 cup quick rolled oats
	1/2 cup oat bran
	1/3 cup tub margarine, cold

1. Combine apples, cranberries, honey, and lemon juice in a mixing bowl. Transfer to an 8-inch square microwave-safe baking dish.

2. Mix sugar, oats, and oat bran in a separate bowl. Using a pastry blender or 2 forks, cut margarine into oat mixture until the texture resembles coarse crumbs.

3. Place oat mixture on top of apple/cranberry mixture in baking dish. Cover with a double-folded paper towel.

4. Cook, covered, at High (100%) for 9 minutes. Rotate dish after 5 minutes. If apples are not tender, continue cooking for an additional 1 to 2 minutes.

5. Remove from oven and let stand for 30 minutes before serving. Serve warm and with one of our dessert toppings (pages 50–51).

Oat Scones

Try these rich scones for breakfast or with herbal tea or decaffeinated coffee for a snack.

YIELD: 16 wedges

PREPARATION TIME: 20 minutes

COOKING TIME: 10 to 12 minutes

RDOB PER WEDGE: 6%

1 1/2 cups unbleached all-purpose flour

2 tablespoons brown sugar

1 teaspoon baking powder

1/4 teaspoon salt

3/4 cup tub margarine

1 cup old-fashioned rolled oats

1/2 cup oat bran

1/3 cup chopped nuts

1/2 cup skim milk

1/2 cup honey

1. Lightly oil 2 baking trays.
2. Mix together all ingredients in a large bowl until well blended.
3. Divide dough in half. Place each half on a baking tray. Flatten by hand into two 9-inch circles.
4. Cut each circle into 8 wedges. Cook, one tray at a time, at High (100%) for 3 minutes. Rotate one half turn and cook for 2 to 3 minutes more at High (100%).
5. Brush with margarine and honey before serving.

While microwave cakes are not always successful, this one is definitely worth trying.

YIELD: 12 servings

PREPARATION TIME: 15 minutes

COOKING TIME: 14 minutes

RDOB PER SERVING: 8%

1 tablespoon tub margarine	1 tablespoon baking powder
3/4 cup finely ground walnuts	1 teaspoon allspice
2 tablespoons brown sugar	1 teaspoon cinnamon
1 cup peanut or safflower oil	1/4 teaspoon salt (optional)
6 egg whites	2 1/2 cups grated carrots
1/2 cup orange juice	3/4 cup raisins
1 1/2 cups unbleached all-purpose flour	
1 cup oat bran	

1. Coat a 12-cup microwave-safe fluted tube dish with margarine, then with chopped walnuts.

2. In a large bowl, combine sugar and oil with an electric mixer. Slowly add egg whites and orange juice and beat at medium speed for 3 minutes.

3. Remove mixing blades and stir in flour, oat bran, baking powder, allspice, cinnamon, and salt (if desired) by hand. Fold in carrots and raisins.

4. Pour batter into tube dish and cook at High (100%) for 13 to 14 minutes until toothpick inserted in center comes clean. Rotate one quarter turn every 5 minutes.

5. Cool in dish for 10 minutes, then remove to a wire rack to continue cooling.

This basic oat bran pie crust is excellent with hot or cold fillings for dessert pies. If you leave out the sugar, it makes a fine base for main dishes.

YIELD: one 9-inch pie crust
(8 servings)

PREPARATION TIME: 15 minutes

COOKING TIME: 7 minutes

RDOB PER SERVING: 6%

3/4 cup unbleached all-purpose flour

1/2 cup oat bran

1/2 teaspoon salt (optional)

1 tablespoon brown sugar (omit for savory dishes)

1/3 cup tub margarine, cold

3 tablespoons extremely cold water

1. Combine flour, oat bran, salt, and brown sugar in a mixing bowl. Using a pastry blender or 2 forks, cut in margarine until the mixture is the texture of coarse crumbs.

2. Add water and stir until the dough forms a ball.

3. Turn out on a floured surface and knead a few times. Shape into a well-formed ball. Roll with a rolling pin to create a circle with a diameter of 10 inches.

4. Place in a 9-inch microwave-safe pie pan and prick the bottom of the crust. Bake at High (100%) for 5 to 8 minutes. Rotate after 3 minutes cooking time.

5. Cool. Fill with a cold filling or proceed with recipe for a cooked pie.

Try it on fresh fruit, hot cereal, or ice milk.

YIELD: 4 cups

PREPARATION TIME: 12 minutes

COOKING TIME: 7 minutes

RDOB PER 1/3 CUP: 15%

1/3 cup tub margarine

1/3 cup unhydrogenated peanut butter (without sugar)

2 tablespoons brown sugar

1 1/2 cups old-fashioned rolled oats

1 cup oat bran

1. Mix together margarine, peanut butter, and sugar in a microwave-safe bowl.
2. Cook at High (100%) for 1 minute.
3. Mix together oats and oat bran in an 8 × 12-inch microwave-safe baking dish. Add the margarine mixture and mix thoroughly.
4. Cook at High (100%) for 7 to 8 minutes. Stir every 2 minutes.
5. Cool. Keep refrigerated in an airtight container.

ARROWHEAD MILLS, INC.
Post Office Box 2059
Hereford, Texas 79045

Markets oat groats, oat flakes, oat bran, steel-cut oats, Oat Bran Apple Spice Muffin Mix, Oat Bran Wheat Free Muffin Mix, and Oat Flour. The versatile muffin mixes can be used as a quick and easy base for making cookies, quick breads, and cakes as well. The baking powder used in the mixes is an all-phosphate non-aluminum type. Arrowhead will be happy to reply to individual inquiries about where products are available in your area.

THE DORSEL COMPANY FLOUR AND MEAL
P.O. Box 222
Erlanger, Kentucky 41018

Makes pinhead (steel-cut) oatmeal, which is used for hot cereal and a traditional dish called Goetta.

FEARN NATURAL FOODS
P.O. Box 09398
3015 West Vera Avenue
Milwaukee, Wisconsin 53209
(414) 352-3209

Manufactures a unique Hi-Fiber All-Purpose Whole Wheat Baking Mix that includes oat bran, stone-ground whole wheat flour, pure honey, dried buttermilk, natural soya powder, non-aluminum baking powder, and salt. This mix can become the base for such dishes as pancakes, waffles, biscuits, bread, crisps, pizza, and spinach pie. Recipes are included on the package. One package usually is sufficient for four different selections. If you cannot find this product in your area, Fearn will ship the mix to individuals in case lots.

HEALTH VALLEY FOODS
700 Union Street
Montebello, California 90640
(213) 724-2211

Concentrates on developing oat-based products. The line includes Oat Bran Flakes Cereal, Hot Oat Bran Cereal (with Apples and Cinnamon or Raisin and

Spice), and Oat Bran Fruit Jumbo Cookies, Oat Bran Graham Crackers, and Fancy Fruit Chunks Raisin Oat Bran Cookies. Fruit juice–sweetened Orangeola is a rolled oat cereal with added oat bran made with either Almonds and Dates or Bananas and Hawaiian Fruit. Real Granola, which comes in Real Hawaiian Fruit, Real Almond Crunch, or Real Raisin Nut varieties, has lysine-Amaranth grain. Healthy Crunch is a blend of oats, rye, and barley that comes in Almond Date, Apple Cinnamon, and Hawaiian Fruit flavors. Swiss Breakfast Muesli is a Swiss-style cereal available in Tropical Fruit or Raisin Nut flavors. All these products, made without sugar, salt, or artificial ingredients, are available in supermarket nutrition centers and health food stores throughout the country.

KENYON'S CORN MEAL CO. INC.
Usquepaugh, Rhode Island 02892
(401) 783-4054

Offers a full line of stone-ground meals and flours including Scotch Oat Flour in one-pound bags. Write for a free mail order catalog.

KOLLIN OAT BRAN PRODUCTS, EDWARD & SONS TRADING COMPANY
Box 3150
Union, New Jersey 07083

Offers a line of oat bran cereals including Oat Bran Crunch, Crispy Oats, and Fruit 'N Oat Bran Crunch. All products are free of salt, sugar, and wheat. Ingredients used in addition to oat bran include brown rice flour, barley malt, unsulphured dried fruits and spices.

MASON'S COUNTRY KITCHEN
P.O. Box 116
Dresher, Pennsylvania 19025
(215) 362-9272

Offers three products—High Fiber Oatmeal Cookies, High Fiber Chocolate Chip Cookies, and All Natural Concentrated Dietary Fiber—all of which are made with oat bran. The Concentrated Fiber also includes corn bran, rice bran, soy bran, peanut flour, and apple fiber powder; it can be blended smoothly into recipes for soups, stews, omelets, pancakes, juices, chili sauces, bread, and cakes. Its fine texture makes it nearly undetectable.

NEW MORNING
Leoninster, Massachusetts 01453

Supplies natural cereals that have an extremely high fiber content and contain no salt, sugar, or preservatives. Whole-grain products with added oat bran content include Oatios, toasted oat cereal with added oat bran; Honey Almond Oatios, with added oat bran; Super Raisin Bran, with added oat bran; Maple Nut Muesli with added oat bran; and Superbran, with added oat bran. All products are available in health food stores and supermarkets.

QUAKER OATS COMPANY
Chicago, Illinois 60654

Makers of the oldest and best-known oat products in America and pioneers in supplying oat bran to the consumer. Quaker Products are available in supermarkets and health food stores throughout the country. Quaker's Mother's Oat Bran has no additives, preservatives, sugar, or salt. The company also packages Quaker Old Fashioned and Quick oats and a varied line of instant oat products and granola bars.

U.S. MILLS, INC.
5 Waltham Street
Wilmington, Massachusetts 01887

Produces Erewhon products, which include Oat Bran with Toasted Wheat Germ, low-sodium Apple Cinnamon, Apple Raisin, and Maple Spice instant oatmeals, and six varieties of granola (one of which has wheat bran as an ingredient but no added salt). Contact U.S. Mills directly if you cannot find Erewhon products locally.

THE VERMONT COUNTRY STORE
P.O. Box 1108
Manchester Center, Vermont 05255
(802) 362-4667

Features a full line of stone-ground cereals and flours. Oat products include coarse-cut Scotch-Irish Oatmeal in four-pound bags and whole, hulled, and unground whole-grain oat groats in four-pound bags.

WALNUT ACRES NATURAL FOODS/ORGANIC FARMING
Penns Creek, Pennsylvania 17862
(717) 837-0601

Offers oat groats, organic oatmeal hulled from unsteamed oats, old-fashioned flaked oatmeal, steel-cut oats in coarse medium-size chunks, oat bran, a wide variety of sweetened and unsweetened granolas, oat flour, oatmeal hearth bread, and oatmeal cookies.

OAT MILLS

ILLINOIS
Elam's Inc.
2625 Gardner Road
Broadview, Ill. 60153

The Quaker Oats Co.
345 Merchandise Mart Plaza
Chicago, Ill. 60654

IOWA
National Oats Company
1515 H. Ave. N.E.
Cedar Rapids, Iowa 54202

Nor Oats Inc.
P.O. Box 399
St. Anagar, Iowa 50472

The Quaker Oats Company
400 Second Street, N.E.
Cedar Rapids, Iowa 52406

Ralston Purina Co.
433 S. Pine
Davenport, Iowa 52802

MINNESOTA
Con Agra Inc.
Fruen Milling Company
301 Thomas Avenue N.
Minneapolis, Minn. 55405

MISSOURI
The Quaker Oats Company
2811 S. 11th Street
P.O. Box 28
St. Joseph, Mo. 64502

ONTARIO, CANADA
Maple Leaf Mills Ltd.
P.O. Box 710 STA K
Toronto, Ontario, Canada
M4P 2x3

QUEBEC, CANADA
Ogilvie Mills Ltd.
Ste. 2100, No. 1 Place
Villa Marie
Montreal, Quebec, Canada
H3B 2x2

Recommended Daily Oat Bran

Appetizers, Snacks, and Crackers

Parmesan Balls 5%
Lancaster Treats 9%
Korean Zucchini Beef Rounds 13%
Chicken Nuggets S-437 25%
Cheese and Carrot Balls 19%
Peanut Crunch Spread 6%
Garlic Dip 4%
Spinach Dip 4%
Tuna Dip with Scallions and Pepper 6%
Herbed Dip 4%
Raisin Spice Flatbread 8%
Dill Flatbread 8%
Crispy Caraway Crackers 10%
Three-Grain Crackers 15%
Three-Cheese Wafers 10%
Sesame Crisp Crackers 8%
Peanut Butter Crackers 11%
Quick High-Bran Crackers 17%
Scottish Oatcakes 5%

Soups

Chicken Curry Soup 17%
Chicken Vegetable Soup 8%
Clear Chicken Vegetable Soup 8%
Toasted Oats, Tomato, and Onion Soup 9%
Tomato Minestrone 6%
Vegetable and Whole Oat Soup 6%
Turkey Soup 6%
Chicken Soup with Meat Dumplings 13%
Cream of Broccoli Soup 11%
Cream of Tomato Soup 8%
Corn Chowder 13%
Quick "Vichyssoise" 9%

Breads and Muffins

Yogurt Biscuits 8%
Baking Powder Bran Biscuits 11%
Apple-Raisin Biscuits 8%
Crisp Mini Biscuits 13%
Cheddar Biscuits 10%

Sesame Rolls 13%
Honey-Bran Rolls 8%
Buttermilk Oat Scones 4%
Dropped Oat Scones 6%
Griddle Oat Scones 5%
Dr. Anderson's Basic Oat Muffins 25%
Fruit-Nut Bran Muffins 13%
Oil-Free Raisin-Buttermilk Muffins 17%
Refrigerator Make-Ahead Muffin Mix 13%
Toasted Oat–Nut Muffins 5%
Blueberry Muffins 6%
Maple-Spice Gems 13%
Cranberry Muffins 13%
Orange-Walnut Muffins 21%
Banana-Apple Muffins 21%
Sugar-Free Cinnamon-Apple Muffins 13%
Applesauce-Walnut Muffins 8%
Pear Muffins 13%
Carrot-Orange Muffins 8%
Sweet Potato Muffins 13%
Swiss-Dill Muffins 13%
Cheddar-Mustard Muffins 13%
Zucchini Muffins 8%
Banana-Pecan Bread 8%
Maple-Walnut Bread 13%
Apricot-Peanut Bread 8%
Pineapple-Walnut Bread 11%
Double Bran Brown Bread 10%
Boston Brown Bread 16%
Gingerbread 7%
Vegetable Corn Bread 10%
Onion-Cheese Bread 8%
No-Knead Three-Grain Bread 14%
No-Knead Apple-Raisin Bread 10%
No-Knead Braided Oat Bread 11%
No-Knead Cheese Bread 10%
No-Knead Dill Bread 13%
No-Frills Oat Bran Bread 11%
Steel-Cut Oat Bread 7%

Wheat and Bran Bread 7%
Whole Wheat Vegetable Bread 6%

Cereals and Pancakes

Basic Granola 65%
Baked Oil-Free Granola 33%
Big-Batch Double-Bran Granola 25%
Seed and Almond Granola 25%
Pineapple-Raisin Granola 25%
Maple-Walnut Granola 30%
Raisin-Peanut-Sunflower Granola 38%
Nut Butter-Cinnamon-Raisin Granola 31%
Stove-Top Oil-Free Granola 17%
Traditional Familia 20%
Processed Cold Cereal Mix 27%
Basic Dry Cereal for Yogurt and Fruit 38%
Orange-Apricot Muesli 25%
Portable Hot or Cold Cereal 20%
Apple-Walnut Muesli 13%
Banana-Orange Muesli 25%
Yogurt-Berry Breakfast 8%
Basic Oat Bran Cereal 33%
Creamy Oat Bran Cereal 25%
Strawberries and "Cream" Oat Bran 25%
Apple-Maple-Raisin Oat Bran Cereal 25%
Creamy Maple Oat Bran Cereal 25%
Creamy Orange-Raisin Oat Bran 25%
Pear Porridge 25%
Pineapple-Apricot Oat Bran Cereal 25%
Crunchy Oat Bran 25%
Creamy Rolled Oat Cereal 25%
Breakfast Crunch 17%
Country Breakfast Oats 13%
Peanutty Oatmeal 17%
Allspice Oat Cereal 31%
Banana-Walnut Oatmeal 17%

Sunflower-Prune Oatmeal 17%
Sesame-Cinnamon Oatmeal 13%
Sunflower-Cinnamon Oatmeal 13%
Steel-Cut Porridge 25%
Textured Oatmeal 25%
Sautéed Oat Slices 21%
Oat Pancakes 25%
Banana Oat Pancakes 17%
Puréed Fruit Pancakes 19%
Lemon Pancakes 44%
English Breakfast "Pancake" 38%
Crunchy Breakfast "Pancake" 38%
Apple Bran Pancakes 25%
Gingerbread Pancakes 19%
Swedish Pancakes 38%
Oat Crepes 13%
Light Oat Waffles 9%

Vegetarian and Dairy Main Dishes

Vegetable Pizza 9%
Quick Pizza 6%
Mushroom Quiche 12%
Broccoli Quiche 12%
Spinach Quiche 13%
Ratatouille Flan 12%
Ratatouille Crepes 15%
Crepes with Florentine Filling 15%
Almond-Cheese Crepes 13%
Eggplant Creole 25%
Eggplant Parmigiana 19%
Vegetable-Cheese Stuffed Zucchini 13%
Zucchini, Mozzarella, and Tomato Casserole 17%
Zucchini-Vegetable Casserole 8%
Zucchini-Sunflower Bake 17%
Sunflower Seed Roast 9%
All-Oat Burgers 13%
Tofu Burgers 19%

Fish

Oat-Dill Oven-"Fried" Fish 12%

Fish Creole 12%
Bran-Cornmeal Crisp
Fish 17%
Scallops and Oat Sauté 25%
Pan-Toasted Fish
Fillets 16%
Baked Flounder
Parmigiana 19%
Fish with Whole Oat
Stuffing 13%
Spinach-Stuffed Sea
Trout 13%
Salmon or Tuna Loaf with
Tomato Sauce 13%
Salmon or Tuna Loaf with
Cucumber Sauce 13%
Dilled Salmon Cakes 17%
Crab Cakes 25%

Poultry

Chicken Salsa 13%
Chicken Dijon 13%
Chicken Creole and Whole
Oats 25%
Herb Shake-and-Coat
Chicken 13%
Garlic Shake-and-Coat
Chicken 13%
Chicken Roma 13%
Parmesan Baked
Chicken 25%
Chicken and Peppers
Marinara 19%
Beef and Peppers
Marinara 19%
Lemon Chicken 13%
Asparagus-Chicken
Quiche 13%
Chicken-Corn
Casserole 13%
Baked Chicken with Whole
Oats 28%
Chicken Empanada 19%
Dill Baked Chicken 13%

Meat

Savory Meat Loaf 9%
Whole Oat Meat Loaf 8%
Miniature Meat Loaves 13%
Gourmet Hamburgers 8%
Pork Chops with Whole
Oats 31%
Grecian Village Lamb
Stew 6%
Veal Mexicana 6%
Veal Parmigiana 17%

*Side Dishes, Stuffings, and
Salads*

Sesame-Baked
Vegetables 6%

Vegetable Medley 13%
Mexicali Tomatoes 25%
Green Bean Cheddar
Bake 10%
Harvest Casserole 13%
Potato-Oat Pancakes 13%
Home Fries 19%
Oat "Rice" 13%
Oat "Mini Rice" 13%
Oat and Cheese Soufflés 8%
Oats with Vegetables and
Herbs 25%
Mushroom Oat Pilaf 13%
Vegetable Oat Pilaf 10%
Savory Oats 8%
Oats and Toasted
Almonds 8%
Herb Dumplings 8%
Corn Fritters 25%
Oat Squash Pudding 25%
Carrot Purée 25%
Vegetable Crisp 17%
Cauliflower Purée 19%
Broccoli Purée 19%
Poultry Stuffing 8%
Iberian Stuffing 6%
Toasted Oat Stuffing 19%
Holiday Stuffing 19%
Apricot–Whole Oat
Stuffing 6%
Granola-Celery Stuffing 16%
Granola-Rice Stuffing 12%
Granola-Apple Stuffing 16%
Mixed Green Salad with
Parmesan Oats 14%
Whole Oat Tabouli 13%
Oat Sprout Salad with Lemon
Garlic Dressing 9%
Fruit Salad 13%

Cookies and Cakes

Raisin Bran Cookies 8%
Pure Fruit Cookies 10%
Energy Cookies 8%
Classic Cutout Cookies 13%
Light Oatmeal Cookies 6%
Wheat Germ Oatmeal
Cookies 19%
Apricot-Walnut Cookies 10%
Apple-Walnut Chews 5%
Chewy Almond Cookies 6%
Chewy Fruit Drops 4%
Peach-Peanut Cookies 6%
Peanut Butter Spice
Cookies 5%
Peanut Butter and Jelly Oat
Cookies 8%
Apple-Cheese Cookies 9%

Lemon Shortbread 11%
Orange-Walnut Thins 8%
Pecan Crunch Cookies 10%
Carrot Cookies 5%
Cocoa Cookies, No-Bake
Version 13%
Cocoa Cookies, Baked
Version 8%
Preserve Bars 13%
Applesauce Bars 15%
Nutty Squares 17%
Raisin Spice Cake 14%
Apple Cake 8%
Carrot-Banana-Nut
Cake 14%
Petite Oat Fruitcakes 5%
Coffee Cake 14%

Pie Crusts, Pies, and Crisps

Basic Oat Bran Pie Crust 8%
Lemon Crumb Crust 10%
Herbed Crumb Crust 17%
Yogurt Pie Crust 11%
All-American Apple Pie 22%
Blueberry Pie 18%
Strawberry Pie with Lemon
Crust 14%
Strawberry Pie with Basic
Crust 12%
Double-Crust Pear Pie 17%
Frozen Yogurt Pie 8%
Pumpkin Pie with Lemon
Crust 14%
Pumpkin Pie with Basic
Crust 12%
Fiber-Packed Prune-Apple
Crisp 6%
Pear or Apple Crisp 9%
Cranberry-Apple Crisp 5%
Rhubarb Crisp 16%
Peach Crisp 21%
Tropical Fruit Crisp 13%
Cranberry Crisp 8%
Blueberry Grunt 10%

Other Desserts

Frozen Granola Banana
Pops 8%
Peanut Butter Granola "Ice
Cream" 12%
Dessert Oat Crepes 13%
Granola Baked Apples 16%
Berry-Yogurt Crowdie 13%
Cocoa Pudding Cups 6%
Oat Bran Pudding 9%
Sweet Whole Oat
"Pudding" 8%

Steamed Maple
Pudding 25%
Oatmeal Fruit Soufflé 19%

Drinks and Shakes

Coffee-Maple Breakfast
Drink 13%
Orange Diet Drink 13%
Apple Diet Drink 13%
Banana-Orange
Smoothie 19%
Fruit Shake 13%
Strawberry-Yogurt Shake 9%
Lemon-Blueberry
Shake 13%
Applesauce Shake 9%
Pineapple-Berry Shake 9%
Peach Shake 9%
Apricot Nectar Shake 19%
Peanut Butter–Banana
Shake 19%
Cocoa Shake 17%
Tomato Shake 19%

Microwave Recipes

Oat Bran Cereal 33%
Quick Rolled Oats
(1 serving) 17-19%
Old-Fashioned Oatmeal 17%
Cinnamon-Walnut
Oatmeal 17%
Raisin-Peanut Granola 20%
Spicy Snack Mix 20%
Stuffed Fish Fillets 19%
Salmon Loaf 13%
Chicken Roma 13%
Hamburgers Deluxe 13%
Ratatouille Pie 9%
Meatballs Marinara 19%
Barbecued Meat Loaf 13%
Peppers Parmigiana 8%
Stuffed Cabbage 9%
Zucchini and Whole
Oats 13%
Broccoli au Gratin 13%
Cauliflower Purée 19%
Parmesan Crumb
Topping 15%
Granola Baked Apples 8%
Baked Pear Slices 8%
Peach Crumble 10%
Cranberry Delight 17%
Microwave Oat Scones 6%
Orange Spice Carrot
Cake 8%
Microwave Oat Bran Pie
Crust 6%
Nutty Crumb Topping 15%

BIBLIOGRAPHY

Recommendations for treatment of hyperlipidemia in adults. American Heart Association Special Report. Circulation 69:1065 A, 1984.

Anderson, James W., M.D. "Plant Fiber and Blood Pressure." *Annals of Internal Medicine*, vol. 98 (May 1983), 842–45.

———. *The High Carbohydrate High Fiber Diet Plan.* Lexington, Ky. HCF Diabetes Foundation, 1984.

———. "Hypercholesterolemic Effects of High-Fiber Diets Rich in Water-Soluble Plant Fibres." *Journal of the Canadian Dietetic Association*, vol. 45 (April 1984).

———. "High Fiber Diets for Obese Diabetic Men on Insulin Therapy: Short-Term and Long-Term Effects." *Dietary Fiber and Obesity.* Alan R. Liss, Inc., 1985, 49–68.

Anderson, James W., et al. "Hypercholesterolemic effects of oat bran for hypercholesterolemic men." *The American Journal of Clinical Nutrition*, vol. 40 (December 1984), 1146–55.

———. "Adherence to high-carbohydrate, high-fiber diets: long-term studies of non-obese diabetic men." *Journal of The American Diabetic Association*, vol. 85 (September 1985), 1105–10.

Birmingham, Frederic A. ". . . Or Perchance to Prevent a Coronary and Bypass." *Saturday Evening Post,* Jan./Feb. 1980.

Blankenhorn, David H., M.D. "Beneficial Effects of Combined Colestipol-Niacin Therapy on Coronary Atherosclerosis and Coronary Venous Bypass Grafts." *Journal of the American Medical Association*, vol. 257 (June 19, 1987), 3233–39.

Boffey, Philip M. "For the First Time, Cut in Cholesterol Is Shown to Deter Artery Clogging." *The New York Times* (June 19, 1987), A-1.

———. "U.S. Defines Cholesterol Hazards and Offers Treatment Guidelines." *The New York Times* (October 6, 1987), A-1.

Brody, Jane. "Fiber for Health." *Family Circle* (September 9, 1986), 90–94.

———. "Cholesterol Drug Hailed as Treatment Breakthrough." *The New York Times* (March 10, 1987), C-1.

DeBakey, Michael E., et al. *The Living Heart Diet.* New York: Raven Press/Simon and Schuster, 1984.

———. "Diet, Nutrition and Heart Disease." *Journal of the American Medical Association, vol. 86 (June 1986), 729–31.*

Dietary Guidelines for Americans. U.S. Department of Agriculture and U.S. Department of Health, Education and Welfare. Washington, D.C.: 1980.

Health Implications of Dietary Fiber. High Carbohydrate Fiber Diabetes Foundation. A Conference Guide prepared by the Albert Einstein College of Medicine, New York: 1986.

Kolata, Gina. "Advice about Cholesterol Is Finding an Eager Market." *The New York Times* (October 11, 1987), E-8.

Leary, Warren E. "Moderate Activity Is Said to Cut Heart Deaths." *The New York Times* (November 16, 1987), A-14.

Long, Patricia. "The Good Fat." *The Baltimore Sun* (September 9, 1987), E-1.

Mayer, Jean, and Goldberg, Jeanne. "Soluble, non-soluble fiber has health benefits." *The Baltimore Sun* (March 23, 1986), N-9.

―――. "More on Coronary Disease-Diet Link." *The Baltimore Sun* (July 26, 1987), p. N-4.

Royner, Sandy. "The Oat Bran Story." *The Washington Post* (January 15, 1986), Food Section, 1.

Specter, Michael. "Cholesterol Study Urges Strict Diets." *The Washington Post* (October 6, 1987), A-1.

Stamler, Jeremiah, M.D. "Is the Relationship between Serum Cholesterol and Risk of Premature Death from Coronary Heart Disease Continuous and Graded?" *Journal of the American Medical Association,* vol. 256 (November 28, 1986), 2824–28.

Thompson, Larry, and Squires, Sally. "Cholesterol." *The Washington Post* (October 20, 1987), 14–17.

Thorton, Harrison John. *The History of the Quaker Oats Company.* Chicago: The University of Chicago Press, 1934.

Vahouny, George V., ed. *Dietary Fiber in Health and Disease.* New York: Plenum Press, 1981.

Van Horn, Linda, et al. "Serum Lipid Response to Oat Product Intake with a Fat-Modified Diet." *Journal of the American Dietetic Association, vol. 86 (June 1986), 759–64.*

Rice
    granola stuffing, 239
    oat groats as substitute for,
        222
Rifkind, Basil, 20
Rolled oats, old-fashioned (5-
        minute). *See also* Rolled
        oats, old-fashioned,
        recipes with
    about, 30–31
    oat flour from, 48
    as thickener, 48
    toasted, 48
Rolled oats, old-fashioned (5-
        minute), recipes with
    berry-yogurt crowdie, 293
    biscuits
        apple-raisin, 83
        crisp mini, 84
    blueberry grunt, 289
    bread
        apple-raisin, no-knead,
            120
        gingerbread, 115
        maple-walnut, 110
        steel-cut oat, 126
        three-grain, no-knead,
            119
    cake
        apple, 268
        coffee, 271
        petit oat fruitcakes, 270
        raisin spice, 267
    cereal
        allspice oat cereal, 150
        breakfast crunch, 148
        cinnamon-walnut oatmeal
            (microwave recipe),
            308
        country breakfast oats,
            149
        creamy, 148
        familia, traditional, 139
        granola. *See* Granola
        honey and apple oatmeal
            (microwave recipe),
            309
        microwave recipe, 308
        muesli. *See* Muesli
        peanutty oatmeal, 149
        portable hot or cold, 140
        processed cold cereal
            mix, 138
        sesame cinnamon
            oatmeal, 152
        sunflower-prune oatmeal,
            151

Rolled oats (*cont.*)
        textured oatmeal, 153
        for yogurt and fruit, basic
            dry, 139
        yogurt-berry breakfast, 142
    chicken and peppers
        marinara, 200
    coffee-maple breakfast
        drink, 299
    cookies
        almond, chewy, 253
        apple-cheese, 258
        applesauce, 265
        apple-walnut chews, 252
        apricot-walnut, 251
        carrot, 262
        chewy fruit drops, 254
        energy, 247
        lemon shortbread, 259
        nutty squares, 266
        peach-peanut, 255
        pecan crunch, 261
        preserve bars, 264
        pure fruit, 246
        wheat germ oat, 250
    crackers
        peanut butter, 67
        quick high-bran, 68
    crisp
        cranberry, 288
        cranberry-apple, 284
        peach, 286
        pear or apple, 283
        rhubarb, 285
        tropical fruit, 287
    eggplant parmigiana, 175
    fish creole, 184
    fruit
        salad, 244
        soufflé, 291
    granola. *See* Granola
    meat loaf, savory, 207
    mixed greens with
        Parmesan oats, 241
    muffins
        blueberry, 97
        fruit-nut bran, 93
        Swiss-dill, 107
        toasted oat-nut, 96
    oat slices, sautéed, 154
    pancakes
        apple bran, 160
        lemon, 158
    peanut crunch spread, 58
    pear slices, baked
        (microwave recipe),
        326

Rolled oats (*cont.*)
    pie, yogurt, frozen, 280
    pudding
        steamed maple, 297
        oat squash, 231
    rolls, sesame, 86
    salmon loaf with tomato
        sauce, 191
    scones (microwave recipe),
        329
    sea trout, spinach-stuffed,
        190
    soup
        cream of tomato, 78
        toasted oats, tomato, and
            onion, 72
    stuffing, toasted, 237
    sunflower seed roast, 180
    topping, nutty crumb
        (microwave recipe),
        332
    tuna dip with scallions and
        peppers, 60
    tuna loaf with tomato sauce,
        192
    vegetables, sesame-baked,
        215
    zucchini-sunflower bake,
        179
Rolls
    honey-bran, 87
    sesame, 86
Romaine lettuce
    in mixed greens with
        Parmesan oats, 241

Safflower oil, 34
Salad
    fruit, 244
    mixed green salad with
        Parmesan oats, 241
    oat sprout, with lemon
        garlic dressing, 243
    tabouli, whole oat, 242
Salad dressing
    consumption guidelines for,
        35
    lemon garlic, oat sprout
        salad with, 243
Salmon
    cakes, dilled, 192
    loaf (microwave recipe), 313
    loaf with tomato sauce, 191
Salsa, chicken, 194
Sauce
    consumption guidelines for,
        35